GLORIFIED
in AMERICA

Laborers in the New World
from Saint Alexis to Elder Ephraim

The Holy Monastery of St John the Forerunner of Mesa Potamos
Translated from the Greek by Katherine Psaropoulou-Brits
Historical Context by Matthew Namee

HOLY TRINITY PUBLICATIONS
The Printshop of St Job of Pochaev
Holy Trinity Monastery, Jordanville, New York
2023

Printed with the blessing of His Grace,
Bishop Luke of Syracuse
and Abbot of Holy Trinity Monastery

Glorified in America:
Laborers in the New World from Saint Alexis to Elder Ephraim
© 2023 Holy Trinity Monastery

PRINTSHOP OF
SAINT JOB OF POCHAEV

An imprint of

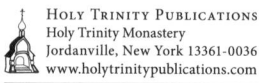

HOLY TRINITY PUBLICATIONS
Holy Trinity Monastery
Jordanville, New York 13361-0036
www.holytrinitypublications.com

ISBN: 978-0-88465-480-3 (paperback)
ISBN: 978-0-88465-503-9 (ePub)

Library of Congress Control Number 2023935214

The cover image and all internal artwork, sketches and photos;
Source: The Holy Monastery of St John the Forerunner of Mesa Potamos.
(See the Acknowledgment page for further details.)

New Testament Scripture passages taken from
the *New King James Version*, Copyright © 1982 by Thomas Nelson, Inc.
Used by permission.
Psalms taken from *A Psalter for Prayer*, trans. David James
(Jordanville, N.Y.: Holy Trinity Publications, 2019).
Used by permission.

"Praising the Lord God in His Saints,
let us honor those glorified in America
as a sign of the merciful grace of the Saviour"

Stichera to the Saints of America

Contents

Introduction to the Greek Edition

In the twentieth century, the vast North American continent has become synonymous with progress and advances in technology, science, art, and all other developments associated with wondrous improvements in every aspect of human life in its ephemeral form.

Something, however, that may not be as well-known is the miraculous growth which the important presence of the Orthodox Church in the New World brought to the eternal and spiritual dimension of its human life.

The twentieth century has seen a chorus of extraordinary laborers in the Divine vineyard of our holy church. These tireless spiritual workers sowed the seed of Christ in the North American land, a seed which truly multiplied a thousand-fold. In their missionary journeys throughout America, through their labor and their zeal to minister to the dispersed flock of the Orthodox Church, these new disciples of Christ were sanctified, and consecrated the New World with the hallowed grace of God.

Through their life and labors, these saints who lived and worked in North America proved that Christ and His Grace transcend any geographical limitation, and holiness can be achieved in any historical, sociopolitical, or geographic setting.

It would not be excessive to say that the spiritual struggles of these Saints were even more difficult than for many of their forebears, as they found themselves constantly confronted with the spirit of the world, which is so deeply antithetical to the Word of the gospel.

All the Saints who lived in the twentieth century have a special place in the life of the Church, as they managed to achieve holiness while living through the adversities and difficulty of our own, modern time. In this way, they can serve as important models for all of us who hope to reach the fullness of our calling, which was prepared by God for us before all time.

The book you now have in your hands is the fruit of many years of study, and gives the reader archival material which has not been widely published. Additionally, this book moves beyond a simple historical narrative or reiteration. It is a spiritual manual, which strives to inspire and encourage the readers in their contest for the attainment of the holy virtues that adorn the lives of the saints contained herein.

This is the reason for which our spiritual father, Metropolitan Athanasios of Limassol, asked the fathers of our monastery to study the lives of these saints and publish their biographies and services. We therefore pray that this humble effort inspires the faithful to imitate these new and luminous stars in the firmament of our Holy Church, Amen.

The Structure of This Work

The first part of the book, "Historical Context," provides the historical setting within which these saints of America lived and labored. It is far from a detailed description of the entirety of the historical period during which the events herein took place, but rather focuses on the elements which the reader needs to understand in order to fully grasp the events mentioned in the lives of the saints.

The second part presents the "Lives of the Saints." Some of these holy men lived a large portion of their lives in America, while others had a shorter ministry in the continent. However, all the saints contain herein significantly contributed to the establishment of Orthodoxy in the American continent.

The third part, "Historical Vignettes," focuses on two important figures, the first of whom is unknown to almost all Orthodox Christians, but who may very well be considered the first Greek saint of America: Archimandrite Theoklitos (Triantafyllidis). The second is the Athonite, Elder Ephraim of Arizona who in our own lifetime has contributed so much to the explosive growth of Orthodox monasticism in America.

The life and ministry of Elder Ephraim is not limited to the twentieth century, but extends far into the twenty-first. However, due to his great contribution to the history of the Orthodox Church in America, and the fact that his work began and was to a large degree completed during the twentieth century, it was deemed necessary and proper to include this important chapter in the current study.

Finally, the fourth part, "In Living Color," is an appendix of photographs of the saints contained in the book. These photographs—works of exceptional quality—were colorized specifically for the [Greek] edition, and have never before been seen in printed form. With their wonderfully natural colorization, they are able to give the entire work a new breath of life, bringing these saints of America even closer to our contemporary experience.

PART I

Historical Context

The Origins of Orthodoxy in America

When St. Sebastian Dabovich was born in San Francisco in 1863, there was no such thing as an organized Orthodox Church in what was then the United States. The first historically documented Orthodox Christian convert in the United States was Philip Ludwell III, an eighteenth-century aristocrat in colonial Virginia who converted to Orthodoxy in 1738, and whose descendants remained faithful to the Church for generations.

In 1794, the celebrated Russian mission arrived in Kodiak, Alaska: eight missionary monks from the monastery of Valaam, including the wonderworking St Herman, and St Juvenal, the first martyr of the American continent. The trip, which took 293 days and covered a distance of 7,327 miles, would be the longest missionary journey in the history of the Church. The Church of Russia considered this an internal rather than an international mission, as Alaska was, at the time, part of the Russian Empire.

When the holy monks arrived from Valaam, there was already an Orthodox presence in Alaska. Many Russian merchants and businessmen had traveled to the region during the past fifty years, and through their contact with the native populace, they had converted many indigenous Alaskans to Orthodoxy, baptizing the new believers themselves, as there were no priests. Additionally, many of these Russians had married native Alaskan women and had built Orthodox Christian families. So the fathers from Valaam and their successors began working not only for the evangelizing and catechizing of the non-Orthodox natives, but also for the spiritual nourishment of the existing Orthodox residents.

In 1799, five years after the arrival of the Alaska mission, one of the Valaam monks, Joseph (Bolotov), was elected by the Russian Synod to serve as the first bishop of the newly created auxiliary episcopal see in Kodiak. Traveling to Irktusk in Siberia where the closest Orthodox bishop was located, he was ordained. However, the perilous sojourn through the Northern Sea would claim his life before he had the chance to take office in his new episcopacy.

During the return journey, the ship was hit by a violent storm and sank near the Alaskan coast. The new bishop and the two other monks aboard did not survive, and forty years would pass until the synod would appoint a new bishop for Alaska. This hierarch was to be the great St Innocent (Veniaminov), equal to the Apostles, later metropolitan of Moscow.

St Innocent's ministry in Alaska lasted for over forty years, from 1824 to 1868. His prodigious missionary work included creating an alphabet for the indigenous peoples, and translating the Divine Liturgy and other Orthodox services, as well as spiritual books and manuals, into their language. His skills as a linguist proved priceless to the education of the native Alaskans, as he created some of the very first dictionaries, grammars, and writing systems for them. St Innocent was elevated to the episcopacy in 1840, and assigned to the diocese of Kamchatka and the Kuril and Aleutian Islands, which included Alaska. He remained in this see until 1868.

The Diocese of Kamchatka, whose diocesan seat was in Siberia, was massive, and contained vast swathes of territory; much of the diocese was located in hostile and forbidding climates which prohibited frequent travel. For this reason, an auxiliary bishop was assigned to the diocese, whose see was to be in the town of Novo-Arkhangelsk (New Archangel), today's Sitka, Alaska. Bishop Peter (Ekaterinovsky) was the first to serve as auxiliary bishop, from 1859 to 1866, and he was succeeded by Bishop Paul (Popov), who served from 1866 to 1870.

AMERICA

In the first half of the nineteenth century, Orthodox Christians trickled into the United States, mostly those connected to the import-export business in port cities like New Orleans, San Francisco, and New York. It was only on the eve of the American Civil War that some of the Orthodox in these cities had started to think of themselves as a community. It was then that a benevolent society was formed in San Francisco, and a regiment of Orthodox soldiers was established to fight on the Confederate side of the Civil War. In 1863, a Serbian immigrant couple in San Francisco welcomed a baby boy, Jovan, the future St Sebastian (Dabovich). Providentially, a few months later, Russian warships visited both of America's coasts. The chaplain of a ship visiting San Francisco baptized little Jovan.

St Innocent (Veniaminov), Enlightener of Alaska.

On the other side of the continent, merchant ships which had visited New York brought word back to Greece and Russia that there were quite a few Orthodox Christians who needed a priest.

ALASKA BECOMES AMERICAN

1867 was a watershed year. The Russian Empire sold Alaska to the United States, marking the beginning of a new era for Alaska and for American Orthodoxy as a whole. According to the terms of the sale, the Church of Russia would be allowed to retain its assets in Alaska, including its churches and schools. However, in the years to come, the American government would carve up the territory of Alaska and assign it to various Protestant denominations that mistreated the native Orthodox people and forced many children to abandon both Orthodoxy and their native languages and cultures, in favor of becoming "good Americans" and Protestants.

But that was still in the future. When the sale of Alaska was announced, some turned to St Innocent, the greatest of all the Alaska missionaries, and asked him for his opinion. At that time, the elderly St Innocent had just been elected metropolitan of Moscow, but he remained deeply attached to his beloved Alaskan people. Refuting the rumors that he had disapproved of the sale, the saintly Metropolitan wrote a remarkable letter to the Ober-Procurator (the tsar's representative to the Russian Holy Synod), stating that he considered this development a work of Divine Providence for the expansion and proliferation of the Orthodox faith to the United States, and outlining a visionary plan for America, which included the following points:

1. Do not close the American auxiliary diocese—even though the number of churches and missions there has been cut in half (i.e., to five).

2. Designate San Francisco rather than Novo-Arkhangelsk the residence of the auxiliary bishop. The climate is incomparably better there, and communications with the colonial churches are just as convenient from there, (if not more so).

3. Return the current bishop and all clergy in Novo-Arkhangelsk (except churchmen[1]) to Russia, and appoint a new bishop from among those who know the English language. Likewise, his retinue ought to be composed of those who know English.

4. Allow the bishop to augment his retinue, transfer its members, and ordain converts to Orthodoxy from among American citizens (who accept all its institutions and customs) to the priesthood for his churches.

5. Allow the auxiliary bishop and all clerics of the Orthodox Church in America to celebrate the Liturgy and other services in English, for which purpose, the service books must be translated into English.

6. To use English rather than Russian (which must sooner or later be replaced by English) in all instruction in the schools to be established in San Francisco and elsewhere to prepare people for missionary and clerical positions.

St Innocent was a singular man, perhaps the greatest missionary of modern times, and his vision and missionary zeal are displayed in this letter. He calls for an English-speaking bishop and English-language church services, books, and schools. He speaks of "converts to Orthodoxy among American citizens," and he foresees the day when "Orthodoxy will penetrate the United States."

The Russian Orthodox Church partially implemented St Innocent's proposals. The vicariate did indeed continue to exist, and was even made into a full-fledged diocese, when, on June 10, 1870, the Holy Synod separated the Diocese of Kamchatka from that of Alaska, naming the new diocese "Diocese of the Aleutian Islands and Alaska."[2] The diocesan headquarters were moved from Novo-Arkhangelsk in Alaska down to San Francisco, just as the holy metropolitan recommended. The bishop assigned to the new diocese, John (Mitropolsky), spoke English and had a missionary vision. But beyond that, things were more limited. English did not replace Slavonic as the primary language of worship and instruction, and there was no concerted effort to convert American citizens and ordain American priests.

Meanwhile, in San Francisco, the fledgling diocese and its modest cathedral were repeatedly shaken by tragedy. In June of 1882, the new bishop, Nestor (Zass), lost his life. He had only served in his position for four years, and was returning to San Francisco from a long pastoral sojourn through Alaska, when he fell overboard and drowned. Bishop Nestor was a particularly charismatic hierarch who spoke English fluently and had developed a significant missionary ministry. He fought tirelessly for the ecclesiastical rights of the Orthodox Church in Alaska, and he began the remarkable work of translating the Bible into the languages of the Eskimos. He had completed two journeys through the length and breadth of his diocese; facing a harsh climate, primitive means of transportation and communication, and a complete lack of all basic comforts, he traveled to the furthest edges of the Alaskan wilderness, seeking out souls for spiritual nourishment.

For six years after his death, the episcopal throne in America remained empty, and the diocese was administered from afar by the metropolitan of St. Petersburg. Finally, in 1887, Bishop Vladimir (Sokolovsky) was elected to the empty see. The new bishop arrived in America in March of 1888, and immediately began actively ministering to the needs of his diocese. Bishop Vladimir was a highly cultured person, particularly gifted in linguistics and music. Using these talents, he translated many Russian liturgical texts into English, and was able to produce musical settings for these texts, which were then sung by the San Francisco Cathedral choir during services. Moreover, the new bishop loved great solemnity in the celebration of liturgical services, and thus served in an extraordinarily ceremonial manner. These embellishments in liturgical life had a great impact and attracted many people to the church, which necessitated the construction of a new, larger cathedral in San Francisco.[3]

Bishop Vladimir also traveled tirelessly throughout the United States in fulfillment of his episcopal service; in his brief time in America, he crisscrossed the country several times. Despite his profoundly significant ministry in the New World, his tenure was marked by a series of scandals, some of which involved him, including the 1899 arson which resulted in the cathedral burning to the ground. Even though none of the charges were ever proven, he was recalled to Russia in 1891.

TWO HISTORICAL MILESTONES

In the last decades of the nineteenth century, Eastern Christians from the Carpathian Mountain region began to arrive in America. Upon arrival, these Uniates were met by a well-established Roman Catholic Church structure, with bishops who generally felt that these new immigrants should be absorbed into the existing Latin Catholic parishes. The Uniates, on the other hand, were not willing to submit to the religious assimilation, preferring to start their own parishes and retain their centuries-old liturgy and customs.

All this came to a head in 1889, when Fr Alexis Toth, a widowed Uniate priest, arrived in Minneapolis to serve the local Byzantine Catholic community. Following protocol, he presented his credentials to the Catholic archbishop, who greeted him with open hostility, insulting him, and referring to him as an "anti-canonical Roman Catholic priest." This event, and many which followed, led St Alexis to a momentous conclusion that would have far-reaching consequences: "I made up my mind to do something which I

Bishop Nicholas (Ziorov).

carried in my heart a long time, for which my soul longed: that is, to become Orthodox."

In March 1891, the Uniate community of Minneapolis was received into the Orthodox Church. This marked the beginning of a flood of Uniates into Orthodoxy, as tens of thousands joined the Russian Orthodox Church in America over the next several decades. The nucleus of the growing Russian Archdiocese, and the core of what we know today as the Orthodox Church in America, or OCA, consisted of these former Uniate parishes. At the time, Orthodoxy barely existed in the United States. Apart from the mission in far-off Alaska, there were just two parishes, those of San Francisco and New Orleans,[4] so the "return of the Unia" was one of the two great developments which would shape the future of American Orthodoxy.

The North American mission was entering a new era in 1891. In March—the same month that St Alexis Toth and his Uniate parish joined the Orthodox Church—the U.S. Congress passed the Immigration Act of 1891. Following this, the immigration station of Ellis Island was opened in New York Harbor, and a flood of immigrants poured into the United States. Hundreds of thousands of these new Americans were Orthodox Christians, making this the second great development which was to forever mark the history of Orthodoxy in America.

Meanwhile, in June 1891, Bishop Vladimir was recalled to Russia, and his replacement, Bishop Nicholas (Ziorov), arrived in September. A multitalented and highly educated hierarch, Archbishop Nicholas was known as a gifted orator and writer, and proved one of the most significant figures to determine the course of Orthodoxy in the New World. As hierarch of North America, he was instrumental in selecting and transferring exceptional clergy from abroad to serve in his diocese. Among those whose missionary labors have had a lasting legacy in the continent were Saints Alexander Hotovitzky and John Kochurov.[5] Bishop Nicholas ordained Saints Alexander and John to the priesthood, as well as the great Serbian priest St Sebastian (Dabovich). He set up special ministries for different ethnic groups, and imported talented non-Russian clergy, such as St Raphael (Hawaweeny) and Fr Theoklitos (Triantafilides).

The flood of Uniates into Orthodoxy began with the conversion of St Alexis Toth shortly before Bishop Nicholas arrived in America, but it was under Nicholas that the "return of the Unia" really picked up steam, and his welcoming embrace of these former Uniates assured the success of St Alexis's mission. With his spiritual and administrative talents, he was able to ensure that this new flood of conversion went smoothly, and that the new parishes entered the fold with Orthodox ethos and organizational stability, always working in harmony with the great saint and forerunner of the movement, St Alexis.

When Bishop Nicholas arrived in 1891, he found a diocese that was reeling from scandals, and had not experienced hierarchical stability since the death of Bishop Nestor in 1883. The diocese in 1891 was centered in Alaska, with only two parishes in the contiguous United States (the cathedral in San Francisco and the newly converted community in Minneapolis). Under his direction and supervision, new parishes, schools, and orphanages were established in Alaska, and new educational curricula were created to reflect its new conditions as an American territory. The bishop provided liturgical books and spiritual literature for his flock both in Church Slavonic and Russian as well as in the native languages of the Alaskan peoples. He oversaw dramatic growth in the rest of the United States, with approximately two new parishes founded every year. Having inherited an essentially nonexistent diocese, he worked with extraordinary spiritual zeal, and by the time of his departure in 1898, the Diocese of the Aleutian Islands and Alaska was not only stable and healthy, but thriving.

GREEK PARISHES IN CHICAGO AND NEW YORK

In the late 1880s and early 1890s, a failed attempt was made in Chicago to form a multiethnic Orthodox parish under Russian jurisdiction. Around the beginning of 1892, some Chicago Greeks of Spartan origin formed the Society of Lycurgus, which sent a delegation to Greece to meet with the metropolitan of Athens and ask him to send a priest to minister to their spiritual and sacramental needs. The metropolitan selected Fr Panagiotis Phiambolis, who soon arrived to form the first Greek Orthodox parish in Chicago. The church, a former storage warehouse for fruits and vegetables, was on the second floor of a small building which had been modified for liturgical use. It was named for the Dormition of the Theotokos.

A month later, a Russian church was organized in Chicago. For the first time, two Orthodox parishes answering to different ecclesiastical authorities coexisted in the same American city. Still, the ethnic divisions did not necessarily preclude inter-Orthodox cooperation. On October 7, 1894, the feast day of St Sergius, the Chicago Greek and Russian priests officiated at the Divine Liturgy at the Russian church to commemorate the hundredth anniversary of Orthodoxy in the New World. When Tsar Alexander III died the following month, a memorial service was held for him, again concelebrated by both the Greek and Russian priests at the Greek church, which was simultaneously dedicating its new building.

In 1893, Chicago hosted the World's Fair. The Russians had a big exhibit, complete with its own Orthodox chapel, and all the ethnic groups participated in the "Parade of Nations." In conjunction with the Fair, a remarkable event was held, called the "Parliament of Religions." Besides attracting representatives from every imaginable Christian denomination, there were Jews, Muslims, Hindus, Buddhists, and practically every other religion under the sun. Several Orthodox clergy participated, including the first Greek bishop to ever set foot in America, Archbishop Dionysius (Latas), from the Greek island of Zakynthos. He celebrated the Divine Liturgy at the church of the Dormition, becoming the very first Greek Orthodox archbishop to liturgize in America.

NEW YORK

While all this was going on in Chicago, the growing Greek community in New York City began to organize itself. The Society of Athena was formed, composed primarily of Greeks from Athens. In 1891 the New York Greeks wrote to Archbishop Methodius of Syra, and Archbishop Methodios of Andros, asking for a priest. Archimandrite Paisius (Ferentinos), appointed by the archbishop of Athens, arrived in January 1892. Thus began Holy Trinity parish.

In January 1894, Archimandrite Kallinikos (Delveis) arrived in New York, and a second Greek parish, Annunciation, was born. This was the result of a direct appeal from a group of New York Greeks to the patriarch of Constantinople himself. Delveis, an "accredited representative" of the patriarch, brought with him sacramental Holy Chrism which had been consecrated by the patriarch. Given all this, it is apparent that the Annunciation community was founded as a parish directly under the jurisdiction of the Ecumenical Patriarchate.

From 1900 to 1917, more than 340,000 Greeks, nearly 19,000 per year, arrived in the United States. These immigrants built Orthodox parishes throughout the length and breadth of the continent, some of which were under the jurisdiction of the Church of Greece, and some which were directly under the Patriarchate of Constantinople. Given the transcontinental distance, however, and the difficulty and delays of transatlantic communication, close supervision and oversight of these new parishes were next to impossible. As there was not a single Greek bishop in America, the individual parish councils often became the ultimate governing authorities in many of these communities, not only in administrative, but also in religious matters. This was a deleterious and dangerous precedent, and one which would later become difficult to root out, once canonical ecclesiastical authority was established in America. Bishop George Papaioannou writes that "administratively there was complete chaos."[6] There was virtually no episcopal oversight of the Greek parishes. Fr John Erickson notes, "In practice [the Greek] parishes were independent of any authority beyond the local community."[7]

The Greek parishes in the United States did not, at any period, officially place themselves under the jurisdiction of the extant diocese of the Aleutians and North America. This is verified by the records of the Russian diocese, which does not note any Greek parishes in its lists.[8] Very few natively Greek priests acknowledged the Russian diocese as their canonical head, though one of the clerics who did was Archimandrite Theoklitos (Triantafilides), a great twentieth-century spiritual figure whose contributions to the Orthodox Church in America are incalculable.

SAINT TIKHON'S VISION FOR THE REORGANIZATION OF THE RUSSIAN DIOCESE

St. Tikhon, later patriarch of Moscow, succeeded Bishop Nicholas in America in 1898. His ministry across the continent sealed the pages of the history of Orthodoxy in America. The quintessence of his work as bishop of the Aleutian Islands and North America was in the realization of his vision for the future creation of an autocephalous American church.

Considering the polymorphic ethnic makeup of the American Orthodox flock, he believed that a successful Orthodox ministry in America could be more easily achieved if every ethnic group had its own bishop, from its own country, who spoke its own language. In his opinion, which was based on the reality of the time during which he lived and served in the New World, this process should initially begin under the aegis of the Church of Russia, which at that time was the most organized in the continent. In the near future, autocephaly should be given to the church in America, as, in his view, that was the only way the church could function in a robust and healthy manner, and adequately serve the unique cultural and ecclesiastical requirements of the vast American continent.

As he began his program for the reorganization of the Diocese of America, St Tikhon received approval from the Holy Synod of the Church of Russia to ordain the Syrian St Raphael to the rank of auxiliary bishop. As opposed to the Greek parishes in America, the majority of the Syrian and Serbian parishes recognized the Russian diocese as their ecclesiastical head. When the Syrian St Raphael arrived in America in 1895 to assume his pastoral ministry over the Syrian immigrants in New York, he came as a priest of the Church of Russia, to which he had been transferred during the 1890s, after requesting and receiving release from the Patriarchate of Antioch. He worked closely with both Bishop Nicholas and St Tikhon, both of whom regarded him with deep friendship and mutual respect.

Along with the ordination of St Raphael to the episcopacy, St Tikhon established the Syro-Arab Diocese of Brooklyn in 1904. This was to serve as an auxiliary diocese to the Russian diocese of the Aleutian Islands and North America. In every service and Divine Liturgy in every Syro-Arab parish across America, Bishop Raphael of Brooklyn was to be commemorated alongside St Tikhon.

Although Meletios, patriarch of Antioch, supported the election of St Raphael under the jurisdiction of the Church of Russia, the way in which the Patriarchate of Antioch viewed the Syro-Arab Diocese of America had always been vague. During his life, St Raphael was able to navigate the political morass and retain a diplomatic balance, but after his repose in 1915, problems began emerging in relation to the true nature of the Diocese of Brooklyn, and the relationship between the Church of Russia and the Patriarchate of Antioch in America.

SERBIANS

The situation with the Church of Serbia was similar, though not identical. St Sebastian (Dabovich) served as the head of the Serbian Orthodox Mission in America, which was founded and administered by the Russian diocese in America. In the case of the Serbs, however, the complications and disputes regarding their relation to the Diocese of Russia had begun much, much earlier.

When the Serbian immigrants first came to America, they were not sufficiently organized, and did not have the necessary stability and structure, so for them the Russian Orthodox parishes were the only choice, and, truth be told, an unspeakable blessing. The ability to participate in the sacraments of their church in a new and strange land, so far from their homes, was dampened only by the element of ethnic distinction. With the passage of time, however, more and more Serbs crossed the Atlantic and began to make new lives in America, and a multitude of Serbian parishes were formed throughout the continent, under the supervision and pastoral care of St Sebastian. These ever-expanding Serbian communities then began to ask to leave the guardianship of Russia and come under the administrative aegis of their own country and their own patriarchate.

THE FINAL EVOLUTION

The year 1907 was a formative year for the Orthodox Church in America. It was the year in which the Russian diocese of the Aleutian Islands and North America completed its first Pan-American Clergy-Laity Congress, for which St Tikhon had worked for so tirelessly. In that same year, the sainted archbishop was elected metropolitan of Yaroslavl and learned he would have to depart for Russia immediately. His successor in America would be Archbishop Platon. It was also in 1907 that St John Kochurov left America for his homeland. He had been one of the foremost figures of the Russian diocese in the United States, and one of its most active priests and effective ministers.

Two years later, St Alexis Toth, one of the most significant missionaries in the history of the New World, reposed in the Lord. The foundational shifts in the North American Orthodox stage became even more pronounced during the period of the Balkan wars and of World War I. In 1914, after two decades of service in America, St Alexander Hotovitzky, unquestionably the most important cleric in the Russian diocese at the time, departed for Russia. One year later, in 1915, St Raphael of Brooklyn fell asleep in the Lord at age fifty-four. St Sebastian (Dabovich) traveled to Serbia as a chaplain during World War I and ultimately moved there permanently. Although America lost, in a short interval, so many consequential spiritual figures, these great men set the stage for the future of Orthodoxy, both in America and globally, in the century that followed.

In 1913 the Serbian clergy in America came together and made the official decision to separate from the American Russian diocese, but it was not until

1921 that the Patriarchate of Serbia established its own episcopal see in the country, the first bishop of which was St Mardarije (Uskoković).

The Greek parishes of America also followed roughly the same path. In 1908, Patriarch Joachim III of Constantinople published a patriarchal tome transferring all the Greek parishes of the diaspora, including those in America, to the Church of Greece, which would now have to send a bishop to America. Despite his best efforts, however, this did not happen, and the events of World War I set the Greek Orthodox of America in a new trajectory.

During those years, Greece was divided between Royalists and supporters of Prime Minister Eleftherios Venizelos, who were called "Venizelikoi."⁹ This bitter and acrimonious conflict reached across the Atlantic to America, influencing the Greek immigrants in the country. In 1918, then metropolitan of Athens, Meletios (Metaxakis) visited America along with Bishop Alexander of Rodostolos. The purpose of this visit was to organize the Greek Orthodox parishes of America, and Metropolitan Meletios worked with the bishop to establish a Greek archdiocese in the United States. However, it so happened that both of these hierarchs were supporters and proponents of Venizelos, and in 1920, after the fall of the prime minister, the new government restored former metropolitan of Athens Theoklitos I, and deposed Metaxakis.

Despite his deposition, Metropolitan Metaxakis returned to America in 1921, and, on his own initiative, took over the organization and administration of the Greek parishes throughout the continent. That same year he assembled the first Greek Orthodox Clergy-Laity Congress, and officially established the Greek Orthodox Archdiocese of North and South America, which the Church of Greece did not recognize.

On November 25, 1921, Metropolitan Meletios was elected ecumenical patriarch of Constantinople by the Holy Synod of the Patriarchate. Soon after his elevation, he issued the Patriarchal and Synodal Decree of March 1/14, 1922, which rescinded the Patriarchal Tome of 1908 and brought the Greek diaspora directly under the jurisdiction of the Ecumenical Patriarchate. After two years of opposition and resistance to this measure, the Church of Greece finally accepted the Patriarchal decree and circulated the official decision throughout all the Greek parishes in Europe and the Americas.

That same year the Patriarchate of Antioch also established its own official diocese in the United States. The year 1924 also saw the creation of an autonomous Russian diocese, which was established as a result of the impossibility of communication between America and the Patriarchate of

Moscow due to the fierce persecutions in Russia which were being carried out against the Church by the new Communist regime. Most of the parishes of the pre-revolutionary Russian jurisdiction in America became, after 1924, part of the functionally independent Russian Metropolia, which later evolved into the Orthodox Church in America (OCA).

In hindsight, 1924 served as the final year of America's astonishing Orthodox founding. In a surprising coincidence, this was sealed by a final conclusive measure, when the Congress of the United States passed the 1924 Immigration Law, setting strict immigration measures, and effectively stopping the previously free and sustained flow of Orthodox immigrants into the country.

PART II

Lives of the Saints

Saint Alexis Toth of Wilkes-Barre

THE DEFENDER OF ORTHODOXY IN AMERICA

His memory is commemorated on May 7

SEVERED ROOTS

Saint Alexis was born on March 18, 1854, near the city of Prešov in present-day Slovakia, at the time a part of the Austro-Hungarian Empire. His parents, George and Cecilia Toth, were of Carpatho-Russian descent, and, as most Carpatho-Russians in the empire, were Eastern Rite Catholics. Indeed, his Byzantine Catholic pedigree was quite formidable, as both his father and brother were priests in the Uniate Church, his uncle was a bishop, and his wife was the daughter of a Uniate cleric.

Carpatho-Russians descended from the historically vibrant area of Central Europe surrounding the Carpathian Mountains; that area is today divided amongst the countries of Ukraine, Poland, Slovakia, Hungary, and Moldova. Geographically and historically, they were and continue to be known by many names, including "Carpatho-Russians," "Rusyns," "Ruthenians," "Galicians," and so forth. Just like their name, their culture is both varied and difficult to define with any exactness. Carpatho-Russians were originally Orthodox Christians, but in the sixteenth and seventeenth centuries, the new Roman Catholic authorities subjected them to harsh persecutions, torture, and even death, with the result that vast swathes of the populace were Latinized and agreed to join the Roman Catholic Church in a series of "unions."[1] Though these unions subjected them to the authority of the Pope, in return, it allowed them to retain most of the outward forms of Orthodox worship and practice, including a married priesthood. This schism continues to exist today, and the Uniates, also known as the Eastern Catholic Church, or Byzantine Catholics, continue to maintain a strong presence, especially in Ukraine.

The geographic area that comprised the homeland of the Carpatho-Russians was in the center of the frequent border shifts that characterized nineteenth-century Europe. Before World War I, the area was almost wholly part of the Austro-Hungarian Empire. In the interim between the wars, it was passed to Czechoslovakia, and during World War II it belonged to the Kingdom of Hungary. Finally, after the war, it was given to the Soviet Union and became a part of Soviet Ukraine. To this day, a significant number of ethnic Carpatho-Russians reject the national title "Ukrainian," retaining, as far as possible, their prewar designations.

The young Alexis received an excellent education, and spoke several languages. He was fluent in Rusyn (the language of Carpatho-Russians), Hungarian, Russian, German, and Latin, and could read and write in Greek. While still in his early twenties, he married Rosalie Mihalich, and shortly afterwards, on April 18, 1878, he was ordained to the priesthood in the Uniate Church.

A tragedy, however, soon upended his life and future trajectory. His beloved wife and their only child suddenly died within months of each other. This would have brought any man to his knees, but Fr Alexis handled the loss with prayerful, persevering fortitude, and an unshaken faith in the love and providence of God.

IN THE NEW WORLD

On May 5, 1879, Fr Alexis was appointed secretary to the bishop of Prešov and given the responsibility of administrator of the diocese. Two years later, he was also elected professor of Church History and Canon Law at Prešov seminary, and made director of the area's orphanage. This would have been an honorable tenure for any priest, but the Lord had a much different, far greater future planned for him. In October 1889 he was appointed to serve at a Uniate parish in Minneapolis, Minnesota.

Over 5000 miles away, across an ocean, and on a new continent, Fr Alexis would be like a new Abraham, following in obedience, though not knowing the mission for which the Holy Spirit was preparing him. "Leave your country; leave your family and your father's house, and go to the land that I will show you … I will bless you and make your name great, and you shall be a blessing".[2]

America had no Eastern Catholic bishops at the time, so upon his arrival, Fr Alexis presented himself to the local Roman Catholic archbishop, John Ireland. Archbishop Ireland belonged to a group of American Catholics who favored the "Americanization" of Catholicism in the United States.

Their vision for the future focused on uniting all American Catholics of all ethnicities, customs, and languages into one English-speaking flock, which followed American observances and traditions. As Ireland supported the use of English for everything except liturgical services, ethnic parishes, practices, and languages did not fit his vision. Thus, when Fr Alexis came to present his credentials, the archbishop greeted him with open hostility, refusing to recognize him as a legitimate Catholic priest, and denying him permission to serve in his diocese.

Later, Fr Toth would write a detailed account of all that happened in his meeting with Archbishop Ireland.

> I came to America as a Uniate. As a former professor of Church Law, I knew that here in America, as a Uniate priest, I must respectfully obey that Latin Bishop in whose diocese it shall be my pleasure to serve—this is demanded by the Unia, Papal Briefs and Decrees, because there is no Uniate Bishop here and never was. This was written in my resolution and certificate of assignment. The place of my assignment was Minneapolis, Minnesota, diocese of Archbishop Ireland. As a loyal Uniate, by order of my former bishop John Valyi, I personally appeared before Archbishop Ireland, December 19, 1889, as customary kissed his hand (but did not kneel and bow down—and this was my biggest mistake as I found out later) and presented my credentials. I well remember, scarcely had he read that I was a "greco-katholic" his hands began to tremble! It took him nearly fifteen minutes to complete the reading. He then sharply asked me: (the conversation was in Latin).
>
> "Do you have a wife?"
>
> "No!" I answered.
>
> "But did you have?"
>
> "I am a widower … "
>
> When he heard my answer, he threw the papers on the table and loudly exclaimed:
>
> "I already sent a protest to Rome, not to send me such priests … "
>
> "What kind do you mean?"
>
> "Such as you … "
>
> "But I am a Catholic priest of Greek rite! I am a Uniate! I was ordained by a lawful Catholic Bishop!"

"I do not consider you or that Bishop a Catholic; furthermore, I have no need for Greek Catholic priests, it is sufficient that in Minneapolis there is a Polish priest, he can be priest for the Greek Catholics."

"But he is of the Latin rite; our people cannot understand him; they will not go to him for service-it is for that reason that they built themselves a separate church … "

"I gave them no permission to build, and give you no jurisdiction to act in any capacity here."

Extremely distressed with such remarks and action of this high church dignitary, I answered, sharply: "In that case I need not your jurisdiction, nor your permission. I know the rules of my church, and I know under what conditions the Unia was established, therefore I shall act accordingly."

The Archbishop flew into a rage … It went so far that it is not worth-while to repeat the conversation.[3]

As an historian and professor of Canon Law, Fr Alexis knew the rights which Eastern Catholic clergy held under the terms of the Unia, and would not accept Archbishop Ireland's uncanonical decree. He decided to stay and fight, and in October of 1890 he arranged for a meeting of all the Uniate priests in the United States. At the time there were only ten in total, and eight of them assembled at Wilkes-Barre, Pennsylvania.

By this time a significant number of American Catholic bishops had written petitions to Rome, demanding that all Uniate priests in America be returned to Europe. As the Unia was primarily an Eastern European phenomenon, and Uniate priests and congregations were heavily ethnic, they feared that these parishes would hinder the assimilation of Catholic immigrants into American culture. The overarching problem was only exacerbated by the Uniate bishops in Europe, who refused to listen to their own priests' pleas for help. These bishops had long held feelings of inferiority to their Latin counterparts, and these feelings of subservience caused them to fear upsetting the more "legitimate" Roman Catholic authorities.

Fr Alexis sent letter after letter to his Uniate bishop in Europe, asking for his assistance, but to no avail. When the belated response finally came, it was of little help, " … for God's sake, be patient; and if the Archbishop doubts that you are a faithful Catholic, let him know that you are willing to take your oath on it!"[4]

A NEW BIBLICAL EXODUS

In 1890, while Archbishop Ireland continued his offensive against the Uniate priests in his diocese, Fr Alexis traveled across America, raising awareness for the plight of his fellow priests, and his own uncanonical treatment. However, the situation was worse than he expected. The Catholic bishops had been largely successful in their endeavors, with the result that most Eastern Catholic parishes and communities in the United States did not have a priest. Those who had built churches had been forced to lock the doors in despair. Fr Alexis further realized that while the number of Carpathian immigrants to the North American continent had been staggering, sometimes leaving some villages in the Carpathian regions almost depopulated, the people who flocked to America were, by and large, illiterate. Contemporary estimates put the number of Carpatho-Russians in America who were able to read and write at little over 30 percent. It was for these reasons that Uniate bishops in Europe were so eager to send priests to the new continent; the populace needed not only spiritual and religious, but also academic, civil, and cultural education.

Additionally, these men and women, who had suffered for so long under persecution, were now overwhelmed, finding themselves with freedoms they had never imagined possible. After the Hungarian revolution of 1848, life for the Carpatho-Russian population in Europe had become almost unbearable. The long-standing pressures that they had been subjected to by Western Catholic clergy had now been replaced by equally formidable intimidations from the civil sector. The newly formed independent Hungarian government added new complications to their already difficult lives. Those who were able to escape and find themselves in America, amongst them many of Fr Alexis's congregation, were almost inebriated by the complete freedom, and like unsupervised children, used their newfound independence unwisely. St. Alexis wrote about this phenomenon:

> Our people who came to America, oppressed in their home in Hungary, got here full liberty, which they understood poorly, and they explained to themselves that they, as free people, do not have any responsibilities even toward God! ... And they started to look on their priest as only on their servant ... They were not paying me, and so I had to suffer need, but always I have been calling God's name, and I didn't lose heart and didn't fall into

despair ... I prayed, and God and especially the most Holy Virgin Mary, didn't abandon me.[5]

All these elements, which had been brewing for years, finally boiled over, and led to one of the greatest events in the history of Orthodoxy in America. St Alexis wrote:

> I made up my mind to do something which I carried in my heart a long time, for which my soul longed: that is, to become Orthodox. But how was it to be done? I had to be very cautious. The unfortunate Union, the source of our decline and all our ills, had been part of our people too long. We had already borne that yoke on our shoulders for 250 years. I fervently prayed God to grant me the power to make all this clear to my unenlightened parishioners, and the Lord answered my prayers.[6]

His initial efforts to educate his congregation about the history and fallacies of the Unia met with surprise and even shock. Most Eastern Catholics in America were not at all aware that they were Catholic; they considered themselves fully Orthodox. Fr Alexis patiently instructed them, explaining that in centuries past they had, indeed, been Orthodox, but political, financial, and social pressures, accompanied by widespread physical intimidation and violence, had led their ancestors to sign the series of religious oaths that led to the Eastern Catholic Church.

His efforts soon paid off, and the entire congregation of his parish, the Dormition of the Theotokos in Minneapolis, agreed that it was time to throw off the yoke of Catholicism and submit themselves to their mother church, Orthodoxy.

> Though they wanted to join their fellow Slavs in the Russian Orthodox Church, they were not sure where in America they could find a Russian bishop. At the time, enquiries of the sort were not quick, and they were not easy. St Alexis wrote about this challenge:
>
> I knew absolutely nothing. I only knew that in San Francisco there lived a Russian Consul. Therefore, under the name of Andrew Potochnak, I sent the following inquiry to the Russian Consulate: "Is it true that a Russian Orthodox bishop lives in San Francisco? If so, what is his name and where does he live?"[7]

St Alexis Toth.

Ten days later, on December 18, 1890, he received a reply, informing him that the Russian Orthodox leader in America was His Grace Bishop Vladimir (Sokolovsky), who lived in San Francisco. The next step was to send one of the members of the community to meet him in person and find out whether he was a canonical Orthodox bishop, or a schismatic or old-believer.[8]

John Mlinar, the representative who was selected to make the trip to California, faced his own challenges once he arrived. The bishop and his clergy spoke a pure form of Russian and he spoke only the "lower" more "vulgar" Carpatho-Russian dialect. As best he could, he informed the bishop about the situation in Minneapolis, but he was unable to communicate successfully. Bishop Vladimir decided to write a letter for him to take back to Fr Alexis, seeing it as the best way to ascertain the facts; the letter asked if they were Uniate or Orthodox, and if Uniate, whether they desired to be reunited to the Orthodox Church. After the representative's departure, the bishop realized that a simple letter may not be sufficient, and sent a second letter, asking Fr Alexis to come visit him in person and explain the situation in detail.

After receiving the second letter, Fr Alexis immediately prepared to depart, and on February 11, 1891, he began the 2000-mile journey to San Francisco. The meeting was momentous, and historically pivotal. Fr Alexis described the condition of the Uniate priests and congregations in America, and more specifically his own parish and struggles. He expressed his desire, and that of his flock, to join the Orthodox Church.

A month later, Bishop Vladimir traveled to Minneapolis to see the situation for himself, and finding that the congregation was, indeed, both prepared and eager to convert, he received Fr Alexis and his 361 parishioners into the Church on March 25, 1891. The day fell on the feast of the Sunday of Orthodoxy, a highly symbolic day, and the saint later wrote: "We returned there, from where our forefathers were separated by lie, by flattery, by force and by malice ... Glory to the Lord for His grace to us!"[9]

An eyewitness of this event, the parish choir director Paul Zaichenko remembered:

> In the Russian Orthodox Cathedral of San Francisco, Bishop Vladimir is serving the Divine Liturgy. The choir, under my direction, is singing splendidly. In the center of the church stands a stranger. He is clean shaven, with a short military haircut. He wears a cassock, fastened with a row of buttons, and

around his waist is tied a wide purple sash ... All eyes are on him, but no one knows who the stranger is. Bishop Vladimir, in all his vestments, comes forward from the altar, holding the Bible and the cross. According to the Church ritual, the stranger is accepted into the Orthodox faith. In a loud voice, he renounces papism and enters the fold of the Holy Orthodox Church. At that moment his face lights up with an internal light. This new convert was Father Alexis Toth, young, handsome, and energetic ... [10]

On July 14, 1892, over a year later, the Holy Synod of the Church of Russia, having thoroughly reviewed the situation, sent the Minneapolis parish an official letter of acceptance.

> The ruling All-Russian Holy Synod, being informed of the conversion and re-uniting with the holy Orthodox Church of the pastor and his faithful parishioners who emigrated from the Carpathian Mountains into America, namely 361 Russian Uniates and their pastor, Father Alexy G. Toth, joyfully raising their prayers in thanks to the Lord God upon the blessed occasion impart Orthodox pastoral benediction upon the Reverend Father Toth and his parishioners, henceforth Orthodox faithful. Dated July 14, 1892. [11]

IN THE FURNACE OF PERSECUTION

While the mass conversion was greeted with joy from friends, it caused anger, and even vitriol, from those opposed to Orthodoxy. This phenomenon would be repeated over and over during the next two decades, when thousands of Uniates found their way back to the faith of their ancestors.

This development was something the American Catholic bishops neither foresaw nor expected. While they had disliked the Uniate clerics before, now they viewed them with outright hostility, and nursing their wounded egos, they began a smear campaign against the conversion, and against its initiator, Fr Alexis. A few weeks after that celebratory Sunday, the saint wrote:

> The Archbishop of Presov Diocese ordered me to return home at once. I did not obey, refusing because I was now Orthodox ... From Presov I received requests to leave Minneapolis and temporary [sic] accept pastorship in some other parish in America, then return and everything would be forgotten and the action taken would not reflect upon the future of my priestly carrier [sic]. [12]

> The Papists will not let it pass in silence. And immediately there started to thunder condemnations in the kostels[13]—especially in the Polish … The archbishop again condemned (me) by damnation. There was no such means which was not used against me: it was said that I sold the Christian faith to the "Muscovites" for 30,000 rubles, that I am a cheater, that I am a thief who stole the orphans' money in Hungary and ran to America … In other words, the entire arsenal of Papal cunning and malice was used against me. The dressed-in-civil Jesuit ksendzes[14] started to visit secretly my people and excite them. Some of the people began to have doubts, and to my unhappiness the Holy Synod at that time recalled Bishop Vladimir to Russia; I stayed here without protection.[15]

One of the main accusations leveled against Fr Alexis after his conversion was that he was motivated by greed, and it was financial considerations that made him go under the aegis of the Russian Church. Nothing could be further from the truth. The community in Minneapolis was poor, and many times they lacked the basic necessities, even for themselves and their families. They were not able to support their priest, not even in part, and he received no financial assistance from the diocese, as he had not yet received an official blessing from Russia. Indeed, it took nearly a year and a half for the Synod to officially approve his position, and in that time, he lived entirely without salary. Despite that, he faithfully fulfilled his pastoral and liturgical duties, and supported himself by taking a job at a nearby bakery. Even though his funds were meager, he did not neglect to give alms to the poor and needy. He shared his money with other clergy worse off than himself, and contributed to the building of churches and to the education of seminarians in Minneapolis.

> I received no salary … I was terribly in need … I lived through very difficult days. But regardless of the difficult situation and privations, I did not rescind from my temporary thorny road. The Lord gave me strength to overcome the difficulties of being scorned and disdained as a slave of my past connections. All this trouble with its many uncalled-for offenses against me, I was able with the help of God to overcome. "Glory be to God for His great mercy."[16]

WILKES-BARRE

Saint Alexis has become known to the Orthodox world as "Saint Alexis of Wilkes-Barre," and this is the reason: Wilkes-Barre, a town in Pennsylvania, had one of the largest, most organized, and most religiously fanatical Uniate communities in North America. Fr Alexis had heard of them, and did not believe that there would be any interest in Orthodoxy in a place where the national identity had for so long been inextricably entwined with the Eastern Catholic Church. Yet he was willing to go wherever Christ led, and his own writings describe the events which followed.

"In the last days of November, 1892, I received a letter in Minneapolis, Minnesota from the curators [wardens or trustees] of the church (in Wilkes-Barre), in which they called on me to accept the leadership of the parish in Wilkes-Barre, and I have to admit that this surprised me very much! What is Wilkes-Barre? The future cathedra of the future Uniate bishop? ... I thought, that this was either a joke, or some kind of misunderstanding; because of that I wrote a long letter (on 11 double pages!) to the curators: what is the Orthodox faith, what is the Uniate, asking them if they know, what they are doing? What is the reason for such action on their part? To this I received a reply by telegraph: "We know all of that, but come as soon as you can".

What could I do? ... In spite of the terrible distance (very far) 1,200 miles, I went there and arrived on December 3rd new style[17] in Wilkes-Barre, but I did not go to the parish house but to the Hotel Wyoming. As soon as one curator Michael Jevcsak learned about that, he came there, and involuntarily I had to leave the hotel and move to the parish house! Even though this was Saturday, the parish house was filled with people, and I clearly made explanations about everything: what it means to unite with the Orthodox Church; they were all satisfied, and namely they like, that finally they will have a bishop.

The next day the 4th of December during the service after the Gospel, I, to considerably many gathered people, explained clearly in their native language, what is Unia, when and where it started, what kind of harm and what disaster it brought, for the Galician and Russian people in Hungary, how the Russian people were persecuted, how they were tortured, how the jerk and villain 'Hieromartyr' Josaphat Kuntzevich set fire to the churches and killed people and for this the Papacy made him 'a saint;' then, what is Orthodoxy? What does it teach? That only the Orthodox-Russian Church and faith can call itself

31

redeeming, since it was preached and spread with Christ, by His Apostles and the Holy Councils, and by the Holy Fathers.

I showed that, the supremacy of the Pope, his infallibility is a human invention; that he spoiled the symbol of the Creed, that the Roman teaching of 'immaculate conception of the Holy Virgin' all this opposed the teaching of Christ and the Church, that "indulgences" are foolishness and have been invented, to fill the Pope's pockets, and so on; only the sermon continued for more than an hour and a half! After that I called them, if they give up and are ready to renounce all this Uniate foolishness, and to believe in that which the Orthodox Church and Faith teaches, then I will accept the church from them. And to let them have enough time to think about this and to talk it over, I am giving them a full three days, and only then, that is on the 6th of December in the evening, I would like to hear their decision. After the service all curators came to the parish house. It was told to them, that they would go to all places where there are living people belonging to the church and would ask them the following:

1) Do you want to unite with the Orthodox Church and Faith? ...

2) Are you agreed, that the church, the parish house and the cemetery would be given over to the Russian Orthodox Bishop, who lives in San Francisco, Cal.?

3) Do you renounce the tie to the Uniate-Papist faith?

If all these points will be answered clearly, with determination, then let each sign his name, or put the sign of the cross on his name on the paper which was given to every curator, and which is confirmed by the church seal; it is severely prohibited under oath to talk people into it or to say anything else; it was also instructed not to ask for signatures from Roman Catholics and Protestants, since the church is only a Uniate one, and the Catholics are not considered to be its parishioners! ... On the same evening there was again a crowd of people in the parish house, and all were talking happily, that "finally there is going to be order" ... and they asked first one, then another about Unia, about Orthodoxy and even more than one of them admitted, that they already from their own pastors, that "that faith, which we have now (Unia), is not the right faith: it is only forced upon us" ...

Until late night I led the discussion with them, and in the morning about 7 o'clock I went to Hazleton, and from there to Shenandoah and I returned only on Tuesday afternoon. In the evening about 7 o'clock the parish house started to fill with people; the entire house, the yard and the basement of the church were full of people, there were present all the curators and the lawyer McAniff. To all people gathered once more I explained shortly about Unia, and about Orthodoxy, and finally I asked them, do they wish to unite and to save themselves in the Orthodox Faith, do they wish to give all the church property to the Orthodox Bishop in San Francisco to subordinate themselves under his spiritual rule? … all unanimously answered: 'We wish!' …

Then the petition to the Orthodox Bishop in San Francisco was read, to the Most Reverend Nicholas, in the Little-Russian language, which Michael Jevcsak explained in the Slovak language …

To my question 'Did everyone understand everything?' they loudly answered: 'We understood!'

'Do you give the church, and everything else to the Orthodox Bishop of your own will, freely without force?'

The answer was 'We give!'

Then I took out a watch and word for word said, 'Now it is 8 o'clock. I give you 15 minutes more, and if only one person be found who will protest giving up the church, then I will agree and will depart from you, without demanding anything for my expenses, which are more than $80,[18] and the matter will remain as if we never talked!' … And there was silence: it can be said—not one word was heard … I went to another room … After 15 or 20 minutes passed, I returned, and again I asked, 'Do you want to give the church? Are you uniting with the Orthodox Faith? Are you going to subordinate to the Orthodox Bishop … Did you think it over well?'

'We thought and we wish it so' … was the unanimous answer.

'Then sign the petition and the statement about this' I told them, and all curators, as the representatives of the church, two presidents of the fraternities—namely: Saint Peter and Paul, and John the Baptist, signed it, and then put the church and fraternity seals on these documents: and the key of the church, as the sign of the surrender, was given into my hands by the head curator Andrei Pivowarnick with the words: 'I give to you our church and its property freely, by my own will and with the agreement of the entire parish'! …

The signed petition, and the statement with all the signatures, collected by the curators, which on that evening were 400, and by the next Sunday there were more than 600, were sent by me to San Francisco, and on the 12th of December I left for Minneapolis, Minnesota.

By the request of the people of Wilkes-Barre, by the blessing of the Bishop I remained in Wilkes-Barre during the holidays of the Nativity of Christ, Epiphany, and, seeing that, the church had neither iconostasis and had not been built right: its altar was to the west, and there was no Oblation Table on it, and instead of the Oblation Table there was a washstand, after long conferences with the curators, decided to rebuild the church, so that it would as much as possible look like a Russian Church; I showed the plans of the church and nobody said a word against it, there has been agreement and peace among the people, and the blessing of the church was done on the 29th of June, 1893 by the Most Reverend Bishop Nicholas in the best order.

The Russian seamen, who at that time arrived from New York, were met by the parishioners, received, and treated with zeal ... and this didn't give any peace to the enemies of Orthodoxy—to the stubborn Uniate ksendzes, especially because at the same time as the people in Wilkes-Barre, the Uniates in Pittsburgh, Allegheny, and Osceola started to move for unity with Orthodoxy: this frightened the ksendzes and they started to counsel among themselves, but they couldn't find a reason to seize upon! ... they ran around Washington, around Baltimore, by the Papal delegate, along the Cardinal and along the bishops' entrance halls, and assured them that the 'schism' threatens to swallow 'Unia!' ... But what can be done? According to reliable reports it was decided first, that they will make a report to our Federal Government, that the 'schismatics'—horrible to say! in their churches are praying for the Russian Czar! ... and they forget, that they are not in Austria but that they live on free American soil, and that here with such fears there cannot be put 'fear to the Liakhs'[19] and that nobody can be proven committing 'hochverrat.'[20] Nothing can be proven and they would only make themselves look silly." [21]

There was an extended period during which Fr Alexis was forced to travel back and forth from his parish in Minneapolis to Wilkes-Barre, a distance of over 1,000 miles, an arduous and sometimes even dangerous journey. Considering the spiritual welfare of his flock, Fr Alexis wrote to Bishop Nicholas (Ziorov), asking him to send a temporary replacement to take over the Minneapolis parish until he was able to fulfill his duties to his Pennsylvania flock. Indeed, the bishop sent Fr Sebastian Dabovic, later St Sebastian of Jackson, who cared for the flock of the Holy Dormition for almost a year.

Finally, on March 3, 1893, St Alexis was permanently transferred to Wilkes-Barre, a place where he was to live until the end of his life.

The evil one, however, who fights against all salvific measures, intervened here as well. Despite his success in converting most of the Wilkes-Barre Uniates to Orthodoxy, there remained a staunch and determined minority who refused to accept his teaching or leadership. Despite their lesser numbers, they demanded he cease use of the church for Orthodox services, as it was their, Eastern Catholic, church. The saint refused, pointing out the documents which the parish leaders had signed, but to no avail; they hired an attorney and took the case to civil court.

On April 26, 1894, the saint was called to appear and defend himself against the charge that he and his followers commandeered the Wilkes-Barre church illegally. The case lasted six years, and on April 24, 1900, the judge ruled against him and his flock, citing precedents from Catholic and Protestant Churches, as there was no precedent such as this. The saint was forced to abandon the church, and begin the arduous struggle of fundraising for the construction of a new church building for his growing community.

COMPLETION OF THE WORK

Despite all these challenges, St Alexis, who was a passionate and effective preacher and defender of Orthodoxy, continued teaching and writing against the Unia, becoming one of the greatest American apologists for the Orthodox Christian faith. Having accomplished great successes in his 1890 journey, building strong and intimate relationships with the Ruthenian Uniate immigrants, he decided to undertake another such journey, this time with the aim to bring his own compatriots back to the faith.

Indeed, both the immediate and the long-term results of his missionary efforts are incalculable. By the grace of God, he was able to bring seventeen Eastern Catholic parishes back to the fold. He almost single-handedly organized, united, strengthened, and established these parishes in the Orthodox world. By 1909, the time of his blessed repose, over 20,000 Carpatho-Russian and Galician Uniates had returned to Orthodoxy. Over the years, over 300 more parishes would return to the Orthodox fold due to his example, teachings, and effort. This was a major event in the history of the North American mission, which would continue to shape the future of Orthodoxy in the United States for many generations to come.

St Alexis undertook the writing of a series of articles and pamphlets for the enlightenment and support of the neophytes, as well as the edification of others, who "were not yet of the fold." These documents related the history of the creation of the Unia, explained where the two faiths diverged, elucidated the practical and doctrinal differences between the two, described orthopraxy in a simple and accessible manner, and offered practical advice for those who had recently joined the church. Despite his extensive academic knowledge, he wrote for his audience. His work was not ostentatious or abstract; it was composed in the language of the commoners, and was simple, though not simplistic, and straightforward. Indeed, his bishops Vladimir, Nicholas, Tikhon, and Platon recognized his special gifts, often sent him out to preach and teach wherever there were people of Slavic background.

Recognizing his authorial talent, the Synod of the Diocese of the Aleutian Islands and Alaska appointed him a member of the three-person panel of the newly formed Editorial Organization (the other two members being St Raphael of Brooklyn and St John Kochurov), which oversaw the publication and dissemination of Orthodox books and pamphlets in America. On April 1, 1897, he accepted the post.

In December of 1899, a Uniate priest sent Fr Alexis a letter, attempting to discredit Orthodoxy in the guise of "honest questioning." Full of zealous love for the faith, but also paternal love for God's children ensnared in the confusion of the Unia, the saint wrote: "You ask me, what is Orthodoxy and what does it mean to be Orthodox? As I understand it, according to the teaching of the Ecumenical Orthodox Church, an Orthodox Christian is a person who follows the faith and teaching of our Lord Jesus Christ, preserves and confesses it as the Lord Himself has ordered, and as His Holy Apostles, the Holy Fathers, the Holy Seven Ecumenical and the Ten Local Councils were teaching, were missionizing and as they have ordered us to follow.

To please God and to save the soul, this Holy Faith was given to us in its pureness without any additions and human inventions and it must be preserved as such until our death! He who indeed does that and confesses rightly the Faith, is correctly following God's commandment, he glorifies God correctly, and that is consequently the reason why such a person is called an Orthodox Christian, consequently also the faith and the church of such a person, which has this teaching is the Orthodox Faith and the Orthodox Church! In Greek and in Latin it is called Orthodoxa (orthos is right, doxia to glorify) Fides, Orthodoxa Ecclesia!

The Orthodox Church, preserving the Orthodox Faith, is Holy, since its Founder is the Holy God-Man Jesus Christ, and its way is also Holy, that is the Sacraments, Prayers, Services, etc. (there is One God, One Baptism,

One Faith): the Ecumenical (catholic), since everyone everywhere was called to this Church. Wherever it is there is the same teaching, the same Holy Sacraments and it is and it was from the beginning in common matters administered by the Councils ('soborno') Apostolic, since it was spread by the Apostles and their successors, the bishops! 'The Church is also called Orthodox Greek catholic, since it began in the East, where the Greek language was' dominant, and where all the Gospels (with the exception of St. Matthew), the Holy Books, the Epistles of the Holy Apostles, for example Sts. Peter, Paul, Jacob (James), the Holy Liturgy, the Canons, the Dogmas and the Resolutions of the Holy Councils were all written in Greek. But even though the teaching of the Faith was the same everywhere, it is divided by nation: there is the Orthodox Russian Church, the Greek, the Serbian, the Syrian, the Romanian and others."[22]

Father Alexis's efforts did not go unrecognized. In 1896, Tsar Nicholas II honored him with the Cross of the Order of St. Anna, 3rd class, for distinguished service and devotion to God and country, and in 1900, elevated him to 2nd class.[23] In 1903, he was honored with the Cross of the Order of St. Vladimir, 4th class, and in 1906, was elevated to 3rd class.[24] He received a jeweled mitre from the Holy Synod, and was considered as a candidate for the episcopal office. He declined this honor, however, humbly pointing out that this responsibility should be given to a younger, healthier man.

It is difficult to comprehend the amount of work that the saint managed to do in only seventeen short years, especially when remembering that the entire time he worked for Christ and his church, he was relentlessly persecuted by Catholic and Uniate authorities with accusations and slanders. It is for this reason that he was given the title "Defender of Orthodoxy in America." His fellow Slavs also sealed his honorary career by giving him the title Batko (батько), meaning father. Indeed, like a father he selflessly sacrificed himself for his people, giving his all, and in the end, even his health, which began to decline in the last months of 1908.

He wished to continue ministering, but was unable. His body, which for so long had obeyed the demands of his soul, gave up. For two months he was unable to even get out of bed, and finally, on May 7, 1909, he gave his soul to the Saviour he had so faithfully served. He was fifty-five years old.

In his last will and testament he commended his soul to God's mercy, asking forgiveness from everyone and forgiving everybody.

His relics are preserved in the monastery of St Tikhon, in South Canaan, Pennsylvania.

First Workers in Newly Constructed Church
1 9 0 0

Prof. Michael Perhach, Choirmaster,   Very Rev. Archpriest Alexis G. Toth, Pastor,   John Repa — President of Church Committee

186   Амэриканскій Православный Вѣстникъ

рукъ смерти.

Долго боролась натура покойного съ разрушительнею жизни; по временамъ болящій впадалъ въ безсознательное состояніе. Но приходя въ себя, интересовался событіями дня и съ особенною любовью останавливалъ свой взоръ на помѣщенномъ напротивъ его кровати на стѣнѣ

слѣдними словами о. Товта были: „Вотъ мой отецъ. Мать. Иду ко Отцу моему Небесному".

Кончина о. протоіерея Алексія была тихая и мирная.

Рука безжалостной смерти не рѣшилась обезобразить всегда доброе, милое и симпатичное лицо усопшаго протоіерея Але-

О. прот. Товтъ въ 1900 году.

портретѣ Владыки Платона и теплыми словами вспоминалъ своего Архипастыря.

Нѣсколько разъ о. Товтъ, предчувствуя близкую кончину, прощался съ близкими людьми. И къ переходу въ вѣчность приготовился чрезъ таинства исповѣди, причащеніе и елеосвященія. По-

сіи. А, наоборотъ, наложила на него печать какой то неземной красоты и святости. Быть можетъ, можетъ, затуманеннымъ слезами взглядомъ показалось, а можетъ быть и дѣйствительно лицо о. Товта просвѣтлѣло отъ радости, что наконецъ душа его сего труженика и борца нашла для себя упокоеніе въ обителяхъ Отца Небеснаго.

38

Pages from the "Russian American Orthodox Messenger."

Saint Tikhon

PATRIARCH OF MOSCOW AND ALL RUSSIA

His memory is commemorated on April 7

HIS FIRST YEARS

Our father among the saints, Tikhon of Moscow, was born Vasily Ivanovich to John and Anna Bellavin on January 19, 1865. His father was a priest in the rural Toropetz district of the Pskov diocese,[1] so Vasily's childhood and adolescence were spent in a small village surrounded by the Russian peasant life of poverty, hard work, and the daily struggle for a meager existence. From his earliest years, the young boy showed a distinct love for the Church, and a character of rare meekness and humility.

One night, when Vasily was still a child, he was sleeping in the hayloft with his father and brothers. Suddenly, his father woke up and roused the three boys. He told them that his mother, their grandmother, who had passed away a number of years prior, had appeared to him in a dream and told him what would happen to her three grandsons. The first, she said, would be unfortunate throughout his whole life, the second would die young, and the third, Vasily, would grow up to be a great man. This prophetic vision proved entirely accurate, and the brothers' lives went exactly as foretold.

Vasily graduated from primary school in 1878, and for the next five years he studied at the Theological Seminary in Pskov. After graduating, he was accepted into the prestigious Saint Petersburg Theological Academy, where he remained for the next five years. The young Vasily was tall and fair-haired, and his pleasant personality, excellent sense of humor, and warm, considerate nature made him a favorite amongst his fellow students, who also respected him for his piety, intelligence, academic drive, and readiness to help anyone who needed assistance with the classes or material. In his later years at seminary, his classmates even began to affectionately call him "your eminence," and "patriarch."

THE BEGINNING OF THE JOURNEY

In 1888, at the age of twenty-three, Vasily graduated from the Theological Academy and returned to his hometown. He was still a layman when the seminary at Pskov hired him to teach Ethics, Dogmatic Theology, and French. He led a simple life, living in the annex of an older, wooden house, and his simplicity and character endeared him to both his students and the entire town of Pskov. In 1891, after turning twenty-six, he decided that it was time to fulfill his long-held desire of complete devotion to God, and on December 14, he took his monastic vows in the chapel of Pskov seminary. Nearly the whole town gathered for the tonsure, which was led by the then bishop of Pskov, Hermogenes. The chapel was so full that the roof had to be reinforced, in case the multitudes caused an accident. Vasily Ivanovich was now Tikhon, in honor of the great Russian hierarch, Saint Tikhon of Zadonsk.

The day after his tonsure, the young monk was ordained a deacon, and on the 22nd of the same month, he was elevated to the priesthood. In March of the next year, 1892, he was transferred from Pskov to the Kholm Theological Seminary and raised to the rank of archimandrite. His activity during this time was extremely important in preparing him for his later life. The city of Kholm[2] had been under Polish occupation for decades, and so the vast majority of the residents were Roman Catholic or Uniate, descendants of Orthodox families which had been Latinized through the years. With his kindly demeanor and caring personality, Archimandrite Tikhon was able to bring many of these former Orthodox back into the fold of the One, Holy, Catholic, and Apostolic Church. His successes in Kholm led to his being widely known and admired, which in turn led to his first honorary distinction, given to him by Tsar Nicholas II of Russia. On May 6, 1895, he was awarded the Cross of the Imperial Order of Saint Anna, 2nd Class.[3]

Seeing his zealousness and love for the Church, the archbishop of Kholm, Flavian, suggested to the Holy Synod of the Church of Russia that Fr Tikhon be consecrated a bishop. Despite his being six months short of the canonically decreed age of thirty-three, the synod agreed, and on October 19, 1897, he was ordained assistant to the archbishop of Kholm and Warsaw, and bishop of the diocese of Lublin. His ordination took place in St. Petersburg, at the church of the Holy Trinity in the Lavra of St Alexander Nevsky. During the homily he gave at his elevation, he spoke the following words: "'When I was a child, I spoke as a child, I understood as a child, I thought as a child; but when I became a man, I put away childish things.'[4] Now I understand that the honor of the episcopacy is not one of power, reputation, and authority; quite the opposite, it is primarily one of hard work, struggle, and ascesis."

His astonishing success at bringing the Uniates in his diocese back to the fold of the Church was only matched by his organizational and administrative skills. Seeing his array of pastoral and managerial gifts in action, the Synod of Russia decided that he was the ideal candidate for one of the most important positions in the Orthodox diaspora: the Diocese of the Aleutian Islands and Alaska, the single Russian diocese in the North American Continent. Since 1891, largely due to the efforts of St Alexis Toth, the number of Orthodox Christians in America had grown exponentially, and each new year brought thousands more to the Church. Led by the scores of former Eastern Catholics who had converted, and continued to convert, immigrants in America were coming back to the faith and to the Church, and this new movement required a charismatic, gifted, and holy bishop to lead them through the ever-changing times. This diocese of the Russian Church, more than any other, needed Bishop Tikhon.

Though he was only thirty-three years old, and had been a bishop for barely a year, the young cleric had shown that he was capable of great things, and on September 14, 1898, the Russian Synod assigned him to North America. When news of his transfer arrived, it was met with unspeakable grief and sorrow from the local populace in Kholm. Even Archbishop Ieronymos, the successor of Archbishop Flavian, publicly wept when he heard about his episcopal assistant's transfer. Multitudes of men, women, and children flocked to hear his last words and be present at his last services. Even the local Jewish population went to the deacon of the church and inquired as to why they were removing such an excellent bishop from their town.

Bishop Tikhon's last liturgy in Kholm, on October 11, 1898, was an event that was sealed into the hearts and memories of all who were there. After the completion of the service and his farewell sermon, the humble hierarch made a full prostration to the assembled flock, asking for their forgiveness for anything he may have done to offend them. The entire church was shaken with weeping and cries.

In a desperate, last-ditch effort to stop the inevitable, dozens of men from every social class in Kholm gathered at the train station from where the saint's train was to depart and lay down on the tracks directly in front of the train to prevent its leaving. This extreme measure showed their unspeakable love for the saint, and the whole city's grief at his departing from them. It was only

43

through the saint's repeated and humble intercessions that the men finally agreed to get off the tracks and allow the train to move.

After arriving in St. Petersburg, Bishop Tikhon immediately began to prepare himself for his future task, asking to meet with anyone who had any information about the New World, and the Orthodox Church's presence and history there. He interviewed everyone he could, finding out about the number, location, and state of churches in his diocese, the problems, issues, and triumphs that they had faced, and the priests under his omophorion.[5] It was through these discussions that he discovered that the man he was succeeding was a notable and beloved hierarch, who had managed to turn what had been a hopeless case into a series of successes. Bishop Nicholas (Ziorov), who was returning to Russia, was formidable, and his position would not be easy to fill.

ARRIVAL IN THE NEW WORLD

On November 17, 1898, St Tikhon and his younger brother Michael, whom he had employed as his personal secretary, ascended the train which would take them from St. Petersburg to Le Havre, a port in the Normandy region of Northern France. The train, which stopped at Berlin and Paris, would transfer them to the steamship which was to leave three days later, on November 20.

The Atlantic crossing would take ten days, and when they landed in New York on November 30, the Ambassador General of Russia along with St Raphael of Brooklyn and a number of representatives from various Russian organizations were there to greet him. Several newspapers, including the *Kansas City Star*, were present to record the event:

> New York, Dec 13. Among the passengers arriving on the French line steamship Champagne was Bishop Tikhon, newly appointed head of the Russian church in America, although nominally he is bishop of the Aleutian Islands and Alaska. He was met at the pier by the Russian consul general and members of the Russian colony in this city, and escorted at once to the Russian church where, in accordance with the custom of his church, he conducted a service of thanksgiving for his safe arrival.[6]

St Tikhon was led to the Russian parish in New York, where he was greeted by Father Alexander Hotovitzky (later saint), the parish priest. Greeting him on behalf of all the Russians in his new diocese, Fr Alexander said:

You have now put your episcopal hand on the rudder … O Master! There are many wild branches in the vineyard which the Lord has made your lot: childish whims and the stubbornness of human hearts, and the whims of children who lack their father's kindness … Faithlessness preys on the people's hearts here; our brothers, segregated by the heterodox milieu and oppressed by need, have fallen here, members of the holy Church. The Uniat hosts are blinded; they scorn truth and veracity; for them, Orthodoxy is hateful! … And in Alaska, there are the fervent tears of the unfairly-treated Orthodox sons of our Church! … A difficult and sorrowful path — but is it not through this struggle that you will achieve your purpose? The Lord, who cares for all will not leave your zeal, love, care in vain, but will allow us to see the moment when your flock will, in return, for the care you show it, call your name blessed. Then the Lord who cares for all will accept their prayers, and, in return for the moments and spiritual difficulties and physical ills, will crown you with a heavenly reward …. Where the labours are great, the crown is great too! May the Lord give you strength in this new apostolic labour![7]

In his response, Bishop Tikhon answered that the prayer by which he began his new ministry would be "May Thy Kingdom Come," as the whole missionary endeavor of Orthodoxy was simply that, to prepare the world for the coming of the Kingdom of God.

Fr Raphael (Hawaweeny) was also present at the service, and spoke the following words, welcoming the new Russian prelate on behalf of all the Syro-Arabic Orthodox Christians in America:

Blessed is he that comes in the name of the Lord!

All twenty thousand members of the Syro-Arab colony living in New York and elsewhere in North America together with me greet Your Grace, our new spiritual Father and Archpastor, on the occasion of your safe arrival. We are so bold as to ask Your Grace for one thing only, that you will continue to give to us, the Orthodox Syro-Arabs living within the boundaries of your diocese, the same maternal love, the same paternal care, the same archpastoral attention, that was given to us by your most gracious predecessor. And we, on our part, remembering the words of the Apostle, "obey your leaders and submit to them, for they are keeping watch over your souls",[8] not only promise to the Holy Synod and to Your Grace our full obedience and our filial submission to all your paternal commands and arch-pastoral directions, but we also fully deliver ourselves over to your archpastoral care and blessings.

May our Lord Jesus Christ, through the prayers of the holy Nicholas of Myra in Lycia and Tikhon of Zadonsk, help Your Grace in this your new archpastoral ministry for the benefit of the Orthodox Church and the flowering of the Orthodox Faith in this New World. Amen.[9]

In answering this gracious welcome, Bishop Tikhon responded:

I promise you that I am and will be equally well-disposed to all Orthodox of whatever nationality, for Orthodoxy is catholic; if in Russia we do not experience that catholicity, so to speak, it is because all Orthodox there are Russians. But here, outside of Russia, where under the roof of an Orthodox Church the Russian, the Greek, the Arab, etc., are all striving equally, the concept of catholicity is fully clear for us.[10]

Another New York newspaper, which was there for the ceremony, wrote a detailed account of both the service and the bishop, and included a sketched illustration of St Tikhon:

Bishop Tikhon won the hearts of all present, not only by his words, but also by his beautiful simplicity and cordiality of manner. He is tall, slender, with long light brown hair and the reddish golden beard which is distinctively Russian. Bishop Tikhon's secular name is Vasily Bellavin. He … has attained his prominent position at an early age for a Russian ecclesiastic. He has graduated from the Saint Petersburg theological Academy in 1888 and immediately entered upon pedagogic work at which he continued almost to the time of his election to his present ecclesiastical rank.[11]

At the end of this first day, and after all the customary greetings and introductions, there was an all-night vigil at the Russian church of St. Nicholas, and in the morning, Divine Liturgy, after which St Tikhon was immediately ushered into his first ordination as a bishop, that of a young deacon. Later that same day, St Alexis Toth arrived, and the two great pillars of the American church were introduced to one another.

Two weeks later, on December 15, St Tikhon celebrated the Divine Liturgy at the Syro-Arabic church of St. Nicholas, of which St Raphael of Brooklyn was dean. After the service, which was partly in Russian and partly in Arabic, his eminence ordained another deacon. After the services were completed, Fr Raphael presented his homily, saying: "He has been sent here to care for the flock of Christ. The Russians, Syro-Arabs, and Greeks, who are dispersed throughout the entire North American continent."[12]

Despite New York being his introduction to his new diocese, the saint's final destination was San Francisco, where the See of the diocese lay. Beginning the cross-country journey on December 16, Bishop Tikhon made sure to stop in several places, including Chicago, where he met the future hieromartyr John Kochurov, whose parents he had met before his departure from Russia. St Alexander Hotovitzky accompanied him on this intercontinental journey. Though both Fr Alexander and the entirety of the American flock had been hesitant about the new metropolitan, as they had so deeply loved and respected his predecessor, they found that their fears about a subpar replacement had been unfounded, as the new metropolitan was just as dedicated and selfless as Bishop Nicholas (Ziorov). Bishop Tikhon did not seek status, luxury, or aggrandizement, and did not support petty politics and ethnic divisions, but rather was a servant and a father to all, seeking only what would be best for his new diocese.

Finally, on December 23, nearly two weeks after his initial disembarkation in America, St Tikhon arrived in San Francisco, where he was met by the dean of the Cathedral, St Sebastian, the saintly archimandrite from Texas, Theoklitos of Galveston[13], and a plethora of representatives from the different ethnic groups within the diocese, Russians, Serbs, Greeks, and Arabs.

Fr Theoklitos met the bishop at the church entrance, holding a cross, while another cleric sprinkled holy water on him. When St Tikhon entered the church, his predecessor, Bishop Nicholas, came out of the altar through the royal doors and greeted him, handing him the episcopal staff of St Innocent of Alaska, the Enlightener of the Aleuts. In the greetings which followed, St Tikhon invited all the priests of the diocese to serve as his advisors, and encouraged all the laymen and women of the church to fully utilize their talents and gifts as members of the body of Christ.

The immediate reactions to St Tikhon's presence and personality were overwhelmingly positive. He had none of the characteristics of the typical Russian hierarch. He was not at all pompous, quite the opposite, in fact;

he was exceedingly humble. He had a pleasant disposition, a simple way of speaking, and an ingenious sense of humor. Even when he had to scold someone, or correct certain behaviors, he did so in a delicate way which did not cause adverse reactions. He showed great interest in the needs of his flock, paying attention to the smallest details and the most minute concerns of their lives. What was even more striking was the fact that he did not simply listen, he also dedicated himself to solving problems in the most effective and timely fashion possible. He had an incredible gift of perceiving the root causes of issues, and finding solutions for not only the symptoms, but the underlying cause. This made his entire flock deeply love him, and almost immediately they wholly devoted themselves to his spiritual and pastoral guidance.

APOSTOLIC ACTIVITY

The first few weeks after St Tikhon's arrival in America made clear what the three most important fields of his episcopal duties would be. These three would require his full pastoral care, strength, and energy. The first issue he faced was the sheer size of his diocese, which contained the entirety of the United States, Canada, and Alaska. Given the relatively slow speed of communication at the time, this required that the archbishop travel almost constantly, as that would be the only way he could remain in contact with the developments and needs of the distant Orthodox communities in a timely manner.

The second problem he faced was that his vast diocese was comprised of multiple ethnicities: Russians, Serbs, Slavs from multiple other Baltic countries, Greeks, Arabs, creoles, Native Americans, Aleutians, and Eskimos. Part of this flock had emigrated from Orthodox countries, like Russia, Greece, and Serbia, while others came from the Ottoman and Austro-Hungarian Empires. There was also a large number of former Uniates, and Americans, who had recently converted to Orthodoxy through the efforts of older missionary fathers who had worked in Alaska and the Aleutian Islands. St Tikhon clearly saw that in order to guide such a diverse flock, and successfully lead a multiethnic, multinational diocese, he would have to have the gifts of spiritual flexibility and creativity.

The third obstacle he faced, which would be perhaps the most difficult, was the construction of canonical Orthodox churches. In his first few months in America, he had visited three of the largest and most populous cities in the country: New York, Chicago, and San Francisco. What he found was disheartening. None of these cities, which contained the largest and most active Orthodox communities, had a single church sufficient to their sacramental needs. Most of the faithful celebrated the Divine Liturgy and other services in private homes, which had been modified to satisfy the most basic functions necessary for a Eucharistic service.

This last problem, most evident in the large cities, with the most numerous Orthodox flock, was the first which the saint decided to tackle. Returning to the East Coast in May and June of 1899, he met with local Orthodox organizations regarding this issue, and proceeded to inspect and approve two locations selected to build new churches.

St Tikhon's long and arduous pastoral journeys through America became a constant reality. He crisscrossed the North American continent from end to end, spending countless hours in trains, coaches, and on horseback. The official periodical of the Russian diocese of North America, the *Russian-American Orthodox Messenger*, contains detailed, month-by-month descriptions of his travels. These visits, which contained travel through some of the most inhospitable and difficult terrain in America, Canada, Alaska, and the Aleutian Islands, were not simply perfunctory. In every community he visited, he took up a series of tasks, overseeing the activity of the parish councils, inspecting the building works, observing the children in Sunday school, and sitting in for all clergy, community, and organization meetings of the church. All this while keeping in constant contact with the central offices of the archdiocese, as he had them forward all letters, communiques, and notes to wherever he was. He maintained control over, and continued to respond to and resolve, all the issues of his 10 million square mile diocese, a superhuman feat.

The diocese was, for all intents and purposes, in its infancy, and while the number of Orthodox Christians, both immigrant and American, continued to grow, the ecclesiastical structure to nurture and support them spiritually, sacramentally, and pastorally was both small and distant. In many cases Orthodox communities did not even have space which could serve as a church. Most parishes did not have the financial means to support a permanent priest, and different ethnic organizations and brotherhoods often meddled in parish matters which did not concern them, and sought privileges which they thought rightfully belonged to them due to the financial support they offered the churches.

Additionally, the lack of priests and the fact that the Orthodox Christians of North America often lived hundreds of miles from the nearest church, at a time where most rural areas were still far from the nearest railway station, meant that they were forced to baptize their infants and bury their dead without a priest. Weddings suffered the same fate, and many Orthodox couples were only able to obtain a civil marriage. It was common for Orthodox men and women who deeply desired a sacramental wedding to resort to clerics of other denominations, such as the Uniates, the Roman Catholics, and the Episcopalians, depending on who had a church in their locale.

The new bishop had to fight along multiple fronts. He had to cultivate an Orthodox ecclesiastical conscience amongst a vastly dispersed flock, correct a multitude of mistaken impressions that had developed over years of isolation, and establish correct liturgical and governing habits in the diocese.

At the end of June 1899 St Tikhon visited his Alaskan flock for the first time, covering a distance of nearly 10,000 miles through terrain that even modern transportation considers difficult. Upon arriving at the cathedral church of the Archangel Michael in Sitka, he felt intensely the presence of his great predecessor, St Innocent, Enlightener of Alaska. He venerated the Holy Cross on the altar, which St Innocent had held, and celebrated the Divine Liturgy on the very same antimension that bore the great Enlightener's signature. During this first visit, St Tikhon remained in Alaska until September. Upon returning to California, he visited the church of St Savva of Serbia in Jackson. This church had been the very first Serbian Orthodox church not only in America, but in the entirety of the Western Hemisphere, and none other than St Sebastian of Jackson had been responsible for its construction, which had been completed in 1894. Upon meeting, St Sebastian greeted the archbishop with the following words: "May you and this little-cultivated field enjoy forever that blessing of the Apostles, the success of the great Hellenic hierarchs, the power of the Syrian martyrs, the prayers of the Russian monks, and with them, the Serbian miracle-worker, Bishop Savva.[14] Amen."[15]

Starting in 1900, St Tikhon began organizing his pastoral program more methodically. He spent one year visiting the parishes in Alaska, and one year visiting the rest of the parishes throughout the North American continent. The only break he took from travel was for the periods of Holy Week and Pascha. That same year, 1900, he once again journeyed to Alaska, where he remained for seventy-eight days. During that time, he visited places deep in the interior of the country, which had not been visited by a bishop for nearly fifty-five years. One of the older Alaskan natives who accompanied him on this trip, wrote: "The inconveniences of travel in this region often oppress even the local people who are used to them. How much more difficult must our travels have been for the bishop, a novice. But not only did the bishop never express fatigue or inconvenience, he even inspired cheerfulness in us by his good-natured attitude toward the various inconveniences."[16] In order to reach some of the more remote Orthodox communities, the intrepid hierarch had to travel via kayak, suffering the stings of swarms of unknown insects, and sleeping for days in forests and on the ground. The Alaskan natives immediately embraced him as a father, as he truly considered them and treated them as his children. He ate what they ate, he slept where they slept, and suffered the same inclemencies they suffered. He carried presents for them, brought medicine and cared for the ill, and celebrated beautiful services, which many of them remembered until the end of their lives.

However, the problems in these areas were not limited to harsh conditions and a difficult life. In writing to the holy Synod, this saint mentioned: "During my visitation of the parishes in Alaska, I noticed that several priests were engaging in trade. This is why I issued an encyclical to the Alaska clergy, urging the pastors to set an example for the parishioners by enriching themselves not with treasures that perish, but with treasures of the spirit, with faith and love, and to acquire furs and pelts from their parishioners at market prices and by no means to engage in the sale of furs."[17]

In this same letter, Saint Tikhon mentioned many instances of pagan superstitions and a lukewarm faith, which were being taken advantage of by heterodox missionaries, such as Jesuits, Presbyterians, and Methodists "who attract our people not so much by doctrine as by affection and gifts ... The heterodox missionaries entice our orphaned children, or children born of mixed marriages, to their orphanages, and rear them there in the spirit of their own doctrine."[18]

Bishop Tikhon decided that the only way to battle these influences was by "equal weaponry," i.e., the opening of a greater number of orphanages. He wrote: "In view of this, at the end of last year I proposed that the Alaska Deanery deliberate the question of opening an orphanage for girls, and I hope that such will be opened in the near future."[19]

St Tikhon in 1901, when he was bishop of the Aleutian Islands and Alaska.

St Tikhon in 1903, when he was bishop of the Aleutian Islands and North America.

In 1901, St Tikhon received the honorary distinction of the Cross of the Order of Saint Vladimir, 3rd class.[20] This was also the first year in which he journeyed through Canada, traveling from Vancouver in British Columbia through Calgary, Alberta, and Edmonton. This was the same exact journey the very first missionaries to Canada had taken, only three years before, when they began organizing the different Orthodox communities and parishes in the region. St Tikhon did not limit himself to the large cities, but traveled to rural villages, in order to meet with all the sheep of his flock. Unfortunately, during the end of this journey, he was seriously wounded in the legs in a carriage accident. After his journey through Canada, he sent to Russia for icons, holy relics, and liturgical objects to send to the rural communities he had visited.

BUILDING THE NEW WORLD

Soon, St Tikhon's efforts paid off, and on May 10/23, 1901, he lay the cornerstone for the Russian Church of Saint Nicholas in New York. The Russian Tsar himself had donated 5,000 rubles[21] toward its construction, and St Tikhon gratefully praised him as the "most important donor, the zealous protector of the Orthodox faith, the emperor." [22] The next day, May 10, the *New York Times* wrote that the service of the laying of the cornerstone was the first of its kind in the history of New York.[23] Early the next year, on March 31, 1902, the saint blessed the foundation for the Church of the Holy Trinity in Chicago, whose priest, John Kochurov, would later be martyred during the Russian Revolution. On October 27 of the same year, he celebrated the consecration of the new church of the Syro-Arabic community in Brooklyn, the Cathedral church dedicated to Saint Nicholas. Speaking at that joyous occasion, he told the assembled flock:

> We rejoice because we are your brothers in Faith. We have with you one Lord, one Faith, one system of sacraments, and, here in America, one hierarchical principle. We rejoice also because, just as in your homeland of Syria, the Russian people co-operate with you in preserving your Faith and nationality, so too, here, we have helped in building your church. Here is a donation from our most pious Emperor, and a mite from the spiritual authorities and local Russian people. Therefore your church is near and dear to us as well. Let today's celebration of consecration bring us even closer together and bind us with the unbreakable bonds of faith and love

53

for Christ Jesus, to the greater glory of the Orthodox Church and to our common good.[24]

Finally on November 11/24, 1902, St Tikhon celebrated the consecration of the Russian Orthodox Church in New York, dedicated to St Nicholas. From the very beginning, this church held a special significance for him, and he considered it a trace of mother Russia in the New World. The *New York Times* covered the ceremony:

> With all the pomp of its rites, the magnificence of the vestments of its clergy, in the presence of the members of the Russian Embassy, and before a crowd of worshipers that occupied nearly every inch of standing room, the new Russian Orthodox Church of St Nicholas was consecrated yesterday morning. The edifice at 15 East Ninety-seventh Street was decorated at the entrance with the red, white, and blue of the American flag and the white, blue, and red of Russia.
>
> Delegations of Russian societies marched into the church carrying their national flag, the colors of their adopted country, and a religious banner bearing pictures of the Saviour, the Virgin Mary, and Saints ... There were lavish decorations of palms and chrysanthemums. On either side or the doors ... are pictures of the Madonna and the Saviour ... Two golden crosses and insignia yesterday for the first time flashed in the sunlight, which came pouring In through the stained glass windows of blue and yellow. Hundreds of candles about the altar added their light and many of the congregation carried other candles, which they burned during the service, which lasted for three hours and fifteen minutes.
>
> The services began at 10:00 o'clock yesterday morning. The church was crowded. There were seats for the visitors, but the congregation stood, as the manner of the Eastern churches. It was noticeable however, that the members of the Russian embassy were seated, as being the representatives of the Tsar, and as a matter of etiquette, that the visitors might not be embarrassed in their seats.
>
> Next to the Russian ambassador was mayor Seth Low, to whom Count Cassini explained the significance of the ritual. The clergy performed the rite of blessing the water. They then greeted Bishop Tikhon at the entrance of the church while the chorus sang the hymn "from the rising of the sun into the going down of the same, the Lord's name be praised."

The Bishop prayed before the sanctuary, having blessed the people while holding in each hand a silver holder with three candles, their lighted ends coming together in one flame to represent the Trinity. He then proceeded to the dais in the center of the church where he was clothed in the gorgeous vestments of his office. Over these a white tunic was placed. The clergy then put on their tunics in preparation to dress the altar. Preceded by the Bishop, all the clergy entered the sanctuary while prayers and psalms were sung. The table of the altar was fastened in place, the resounding strokes of the hammer ringing out above the singing. It was then sprinkled with holy water, with rose water, and with wine, anointed with holy chrism, and the first covering was put up on the table. This was bound fast with a cord. The second covering was arranged upon which the antimension, the Tabernacle, the book of the gospels, and the cross, all brilliant with gold and jewels, were placed.

Led by the deacon, carrying a lighted taper, the bishops censed the altar in the church, accompanied by the priests, one of whom sprinkled the four walls with holy water and anointed them. Returning to the sanctuary, the bishop lit from the censer a taper from which the other tapers were lighted. He then removed his mitre of gold and jewels and placed upon his head the antimension with the holy relics.

Preceded by the stars and stripes, the standard of Russia, the church banner, and the clergy, the bishop went out into the street. Returning to the main door, he exclaimed from the outside:

"Lift up your gates, and the King of Glory shall come in."

The choir sang "Who is this King of Glory?"

"The Lord of Hosts, He is the King of Glory!"

Entering the church again, he laid the holy antimension on the altar … Assembling in the center of the church with all the clergy, the bishop blessed it with a cross, turning to the four sides that all might be blessed … the deacon intoned a brief litany containing petitions for all present. The bishop delivered an address in Russian and the rector preached in English … The consecration ceremonies being at an end, the regular service of the church, the liturgy of Saint John Chrysostom followed in the usual order. The communion was given to several little children, to the congregation, and then after the members had kissed the cross held in the hand of the bishop, they left … The new church was begun about two years ago and cost $150,000 of which the czar is said to have contributed 50,000.[25]

The above churches, important as they were, not the only ones erected during St Tikhon's time in America. A number of other Orthodox churches in the North American continent owe their existence to his support and active engagement. Some of these were built from scratch, and others were created from extant structures, which were modified to serve their new ecclesiastical purpose. Additionally, during his visits to different communities and parishes, the holy bishop almost always tonsured readers, ordained subdeacons, deacons, and priests, consecrated new churches, and celebrated a plethora of other sacraments. There were many times when he would even become the godfather for children who did not have a sponsor.

His constant contact with his flock soon brought St Tikhon up to speed with the most pressing problems facing the administrative and pastoral services of his diocese. Aiming to overcome these difficulties, and create a foundation for a stable and healthy development of Orthodoxy in America, St Tikhon knew that he would have to spearhead a complete and wholesale reorganization of his diocese. Starting on November 16, 1899, he petitioned the Holy Synod of Russia to rename the diocese from "Diocese of the Aleutian Islands and Alaska" to "Diocese of the Aleutian Islands and North America."[26] The Holy Synod approved of the new name, and sent it to Tsar Nicholas II for his signature.

St Tikhon would soon be given the opportunity to personally present the issues facing his diocese to the Holy Synod of Russia, though it came about through a tragic and unforeseen circumstance. On December 16, 1902, while he was in New York, his brother Michael, who had followed him to America from Russia, and had been by his side throughout his mission, serving as secretary of the Diocesan See in San Francisco, had suddenly died. As soon as he received the news, St Tikhon returned to San Francisco and sent a message to the Russian Synod requesting a leave of absence in order to accompany his brother's body to Russia for burial, and comfort their elderly and grieving mother in Toropetz. According to his official request, the saint also wanted to participate in the celebrations for the canonization of Saint Seraphim of Sarov, which were to take place during the same time.

On February 24, 1903, St Tikhon received the synod's permission, and he immediately began preparing for his journey. On March 16, while traveling from San Francisco to New York, from where he would depart for Russia, St Tikhon had the opportunity to consecrate the Church of the Holy Trinity in

Chicago. Construction on this church had begun in April of 1902, and had just finished only days prior to St Tikhon's arrival. During that same journey, the hierarch had the joy of restoring the formerly Uniate community of Mayfield, Pennsylvania back to the fold of Orthodoxy. This community would soon prove of vital importance for Orthodoxy in America.

Finally, on May 13, St Tikhon boarded the steamship which would take him back to Russia for the first time since his transfer to America five years earlier. As he was departing, leaving behind a sorrowful and heartbroken flock, a priest observing his leave-taking wrote: "In him we had a Guardian Angel, protecting and encouraging us in the darkest moments when the ignorance of the people whom we were called upon to save, and the continuous intrigues of the enemies of Orthodoxy contrived to dash our brightest hopes and to frustrate our efforts—it was such a comfort to know that in difficult moments, our leader was with us."[27]

REORGANIZATION OF THE AMERICAN DIOCESE

During St Tikhon's absence, rumors began circulating that he was not going to return. In July of 1903, it had been announced that the bishop of America had been elected to be a member of the Holy Synod of the Church of Russia, which meant he would have to remain in Saint Petersburg at least until the end of 1903, as important conferences and councils were taking place at the time. While rejoicing that this honor had been bestowed on their bishop, and glad that his hard work and dedication to the Faith had been recognized, his spiritual children in America began to be worried, concerned, and anxious about the continued absence of their beloved father. A steadily growing stream of telegrams began crossing the Atlantic and flooding the offices of the Synod in Saint Petersburg, all with the same content: a request to allow the bishop to return to America.

Whilst awaiting the council's decision regarding whether or not he would return to America, St Tikhon continued to work with zeal for his diocese. His visit to Saint Petersburg gave him the opportunity to discuss at length the pressing issues in America with individual members of the Holy Synod. Additionally, he also used the time to develop and mature his plans for the reorganization of the Russian Orthodox Church in America.

The editors of the *Russian-American Orthodox Messenger* wrote that the saint was working hard to get approval from the Holy Synod for a number of important measures, including the creation of a second episcopal position in

57

America, the transfer of the diocesan see from San Francisco to New York, the creation of a theological school, and the transfer of able priests to serve the needs of the American flock. However, the editors noted that they could not confirm if the bishop would return to America, or if he would be succeeded by someone else.

St Tikhon's efforts paid off, and the Holy Synod agreed to ordain an adjutant bishop in America and on November 29, 1903, the holy Tsar Nicholas confirmed the decision and officially established the Diocese of Alaska. A few weeks later, on December 12, the Synod elected Archimandrite Innocent (Pustynsky)[28] as the first bishop of Alaska, and his elevation took place two days later at the cathedral church of Kazan in Saint Petersburg. St Tikhon concelebrated, and as the head of the Diocese of North America, he handed the new bishop of Alaska the episcopal staff, and gave the official sermon at the end of the service. Bishop Innocent had already served in North America between 1893 and 1895 under Bishop Nicholas (Ziorov), who had tonsured him a monk and ordained him a deacon and presbyter at the cathedral Church of San Francisco in October of 1894.

On Monday, January 12, 1904, the *San Francisco Call* newspaper wrote:

BISHOP TIKHON RETURNS.
New York, January 24.

Right Reverend Tikhon, Russian Orthodox Bishop of North America, is among the passengers on the Auguste Victoria which was reported off Nantucket this morning and will reach her dock early tomorrow. The bishop is returning from an extended visit in Russia, where he went in the interests of the Russian church in America. Simultaneously with his arrival the announcement is made that the Synod has decided to create a new episcopal see in Alaska with a bishop coadjutor, and that Right Reverend Innocent has been appointed to the position.

The creation of the new see was demanded by the growth of the Russian church in this country. During the past five years the number of its parishes and its congregations have been doubled, and the enormous territory which the Russian American mission covers made it impossible for Bishop Tikhon to care for it alone. His diocese includes all North America and the Aleutian Islands, and the necessity for a Bishop coadjutor has been made more pressing by the general movement on the part of the Austrian and Hungarian Slavs of the Roman Uniate confession who have been immigrating to America in large numbers to return to the Eastern Orthodox confession, from which they were separated in the 17th and 18th centuries. This religious movement had its origin largely in the eastern part of Bishop Tikhon's vast diocese, and as it demanded his personal attention and care he represented to the holy Synod the necessity of a coadjutor in Alaska. His representations were successful, and Bishop innocent will have his residence in Sitka, which until 1872 was the cathedral challenge of the Russian Orthodox mission.

The see of the governing bishop will remain for the present in San Francisco, but it is proposed in the near future to transfer it to New York, which possesses in the cathedral of Saint Nicholas on E 97th St, the finest Russian church in America.

Bishop Innocent is a young man, being now in his 36th year, and as a hieromonk has done much missionary work in this country. He is an English scholar and is thoroughly familiar with American conditions. At the time of his selection as Bishop coadjutor of Alaska he was abbot of the monastery of the Miracle at Moscow. Bishop Innocent is expected to arrive here early in February and will proceed immediately to Alaska.[29]

The joy of the Orthodox in North America, who had been earlier informed about the return of their bishop, was indescribable. On the first Sunday after his return, he spoke the following words to them: "I have placed myself and my path in life in God's care, and I rejoice that in the New Year I shall have to cross the old field of my ministry, that I am amongst you again after an eight-month separation. But while I was away physically, in spirit I remained always with you, and my link with my flock never broke. Even in Russia, I occupied myself with your concerns; I was an advocate for your needs, and prayed constantly for you whenever I served—for you, the flock which God has given me. I have gratifying witnesses that you, too, did not forget me in my absence."[30]

The very first assistant bishop of America was expected within a few weeks, but within that time, another joyous event took place. In a document dated February 4, 1904, the Holy Synod informed St Tikhon that his proposal to elevate the Syrian archimandrite Raphael to auxiliary bishop had been approved. St Tikhon had made this request while still in Russia, and it was a great comfort and relief to know that the holy archimandrite would now be the second assistant bishop in North America. On February 29, 1904, Fr

Raphael of Brooklyn was elevated to the episcopal see by Bishops Tikhon and Innocent, at the cathedral Church of Saint Nicholas in Brooklyn. The event had immense historical significance, as it was the first Orthodox episcopal ordination that had ever taken place in the North American continent. Understanding its importance, Orthodox Christians from all over New York, the East Coast, and the continent flocked to the Church of Saint Nicholas, to be witnesses to the event.

The ordination of the second auxiliary bishop of North America was part of the saintly hierarch's wider plan for the complete reorganization of the Russian Orthodox Church in America. St Tikhon's vision encompassed not only the present, but the future, and he imagined a united American Orthodoxy, which would retain the beauty of the different Orthodox traditions while being able to serve the special pastoral needs of the different ethnic groups. Putting his plan to paper, St Tikhon sent an official attaché to the Synod in 1905, in which he analytically presented his plan for the wholesale reorganization of the diocese. He wrote: "As to the see of North America it ought to be made into an exarchate of the Russian church. The fact is that this see is composed not only of different nationalities, but also of different Orthodox churches, which, though one in faith, each have their peculiarities in the canonical order, the office ritual and the parish life. These peculiarities are dear to them and altogether tolerable from the general Orthodox point of view. This is why we do not consider we have the right to interfere with the national character of the churches in this country and, on the contrary, try to preserve it, giving each a chance to be governed directly by chiefs of the same nationality.

Thus, the Orthodox Syrian church in this country was given its own bishop (the Right Reverend Raphael of Brooklyn), who nominally is the second vicar of the Archbishop of the Aleutian see, but who in his own field of Activity is almost independent. The bishop of Alaska is similarly situated. The Serbian parishes are directly subject to a separate chief, who at present is an archimandrite, but may be consecrated a bishop in the near future. The Greeks of this country also wish to have their own bishop and have entered into communication with the Synod of Athens on this subject. In short, it is possible that there will be formed in America an entire exarchate of national Orthodox churches with their own bishops, whose exarch is to be the Russian archbishop."[31]

In 1904 the Tsar of Russia, Nicholas II, honored St Tikhon with the Medal of the Order of Saint Anna, 1st class, an honor which was normally reserved only for hereditary nobility. That same year, St Tikhon made another pastoral visit to Canada, where he consecrated several new churches in the cities and in the countryside.

When the holy bishop traveled, and especially during his visits to the rural communities, he made it a habit to stay at the houses of the faithful, rather than more comfortable lodging accommodations. Indeed, there were many cases in which the parents had to go and work the fields in the morning, and the saint would remain in the house and care for the young children.

In 1905, work was finally completed on the Church of Saint Nicholas in New York. At the same time, there were letters from the Holy Synod and the Tsar confirming the diocesan see's transfer from San Francisco to New York. After celebrating Pascha in San Francisco, the holy bishop bade farewell to the faithful of the cathedral Church of the Holy Trinity, and left for New York. A few hours after his departure, a telegram arrived from Saint Petersburg announcing his promotion to archbishop, and recognition of his position as a metropolitan of a diocese with two bishops under him. Two days later the official letter arrived from Tsar Nicholas II, mentioning, among other things, that this promotion was given to the saint for his "his extraordinary zealous service and special labours."[32]

Continuing his journey east, St Tikhon stopped in Chicago, where he elevated St Sebastian to the rank of archimandrite and placed him in charge of the Orthodox Serbian Mission. Giving him his pastoral staff, he called him to be firm, but at the same time kind, toward his flock. As he wrote in his proposal to the Russian Synod a few months later, he had hoped that St Sebastian would one day be ordained a bishop and take over the pastoral service of the Serbian Orthodox of America. However, St Sebastian's journey proved to be far different, full of sorrows, trials, and crucifixional sacrifices, which did not allow for his further elevation within the clerical ranks.

Finally, on September 20, St Tikhon reached his destination. St Raphael of Brooklyn, joined by an entourage of diplomats, clerics, and members of the parish council, greeted him at the train station in New York. Later, at the cathedral, St Raphael gave the official welcoming sermon, and in responding St Tikhon mentioned that transferring the Episcopal see was designed to better serve the entire diocese.

According to the official correspondence of St Tikhon, and his predecessor Bishop Nicholas, the transfer of the diocesan see was judged necessary for two primary reasons. First, only two or three parishes of the American Diocese of the Church of Russia were close to San Francisco, as opposed to the 15 or 20 which were nearer New York. The second reason was that the majority of the Uniate parishes which showed interest in returning to the Orthodox Church were also located in the eastern states. As St Tikhon himself wrote, "the Uniates are returning to Orthodoxy in the dozens, and at times in the hundreds."

BYZANTINE CATHOLICS RETURN
TO THE ORTHODOX CHURCH

The mass conversions which took place in North America at the time comprised an important phenomenon, which unquestionably contributed to strengthening the Orthodox presence in America more than any other factor. The new metropolitan's experience in encouraging Uniates to return to the church of their ancestors had been tried during his time in Kholm, and was one of the primary reasons he was chosen as bishop of America. Truly the tireless hierarch once again proved his great spiritual and practical gifts, and especially that of discernment, in the way he handled this issue. In a letter to the holy Synod in Russia, he wrote: "We ought to treat the chants and customs of those who have returned to our church, such as are not contrary to Orthodoxy, with wise care and condescension. Over the three-hundred-year period of the existence of the Unia, of course, certain customs and deviations from the Orthodox way have manifested themselves; but if they are not dogmatic in nature, contrary to Orthodoxy (as was the case among the Polish Uniates but which, fortunately, is not the case with many American Uniates), and if these customs are beloved by the people, and they value them, this must of necessity be taken into account, even though 'it is not done that way in Russia.' One cannot in a matter of years do away with what was formed over a period of centuries. And as they become accustomed, they will not only do away with other things, but introduce [good customs] themselves ..."[33]

As an example, Bishop Tikhon cited a case when, in one of the reunified parishes, he found a service (vespers and matins): "far closer to the typicon than in our parishes, and the parishioners were very pleased when they saw that with their coming over to Orthodoxy they were permitted to keep their beloved chants and customs, and that I did not disturb anything or throw

St Tikhon during his tenure as Bishop, and later
Archbishop, of North America.

anything out; furthermore, our enemies often frighten those who want to unite with us by saying that we will do away with their customs and chants ...[34] Most of the attention and care of our mission on the North American mainland is directed toward the Uniates, to their return to the path of historical truth."[35.]

The overarching problem of the lack of priests in America did not only affect the Orthodox communities, but it also affected the ability to bring the Uniates who were thirsting to return to the fold and back into the arms of the church. "The need for priests is not only felt in Canada, but also in the States. Because of the lack of priests the work of spreading Orthodoxy among the Uniates is suffering. The search for a priest for a new community takes several months, and sometimes as much as a year. During that time Uniate priests come to the community, sow discord and try to lure the flock back into Uniatism, while the people become disappointed because of the lack of attention paid to them."[36]

THE FIRST ORTHODOX MONASTERY IN AMERICA

As archbishop of a missionary metropolis, and one which contained an entire continent, and a multiethnic flock, St Tikhon had to establish ecclesiastical foundations which would be able to help the church in America become religiously self-sufficient. St Tikhon considered monasteries and ecclesiastical schools the two most important establishments for this purpose. Neither, of course, existed in America, and in his 1905 report to the Synod in Russia, we read the following:

> During a visitation of the Diocese, I repeatedly happened to meet Orthodox and even Uniates seeking the monastic life. True, in America the soil is, as it were, not very favorable for this: business, work and practical benefit stand in the forefront for Americans; but all the same, here too idealistic impulses and strivings toward the contemplative life have not completely dried up: we see that not only among the Latins, but even among the Episcopalians in America there is an ample number of persons living in monasteries. There are reasons to think that our monasteries also will not remain empty, and that Russian people will readily go to them. The monastery could render a service also to the monks struggling here in the missionary field (there are now nineteen such men). They all live in parishes in the "world" amidst the tumult and vanity of life, and, of course, each of them at times

experiences a pull towards their previous, accustomed monastic life. And so our monk-missionaries could at times live in monasteries in order to refresh themselves from the bustle of parish affairs, in order to fortify themselves and to gather courage and strength for further missionary ministry; and others, when they grow old, can entirely remain in them, being "elders" both of the monastic life and of missionary activity.

A monastery can also be a good school for preparing psalm-readers. A great need for them is felt with the constant dividing of parishes in the States. To send for them from Russia is very costly.

A monastery can in general also perform an educational service for the Orthodox mission. For this, it is necessary to open it where many Orthodox and Uniates live nearby. "Pilgrimages there will replace the various American 'excursions' (pleasure outings), which local Russians take in imitation of Americans."

Finally, the tasks and significance of a monastery in America are not exhausted only by its educational ministry—it can also perform charitable service: as it can be an orphanage, the opening of which the Orthodox Mutual Aid Society of local brotherhoods is thinking about. It is easier for an orphanage to exist under a monastery's ready management, and under the protection of a holy monastery they will grow up better and succeed in religious life.[37]

In May of 1905, while journeying from his old diocesan see in San Francisco to New York, St Tikhon visited Mayfield, Pennsylvania, to inspect some parcels of land, which the owners were willing to offer at a low price for the construction of the first Orthodox monastery in America. The parcels were large enough to also erect an orphanage, and indeed, in one of the parcels some faithful Ruthenian farmers had already built a small chapel, which they had dedicated to the Nativity of the Theotokos. This community was the one the saintly bishop had brought back into the fold of Orthodoxy two years earlier, in March of 1903, while traveling to New York with his brother's remains.

Inspecting the area, St Tikhon sanctioned the site, and performed a small Supplication service there. However, his soul was not at peace, and he decided to scrutinize the location further. Going around the larger area in which the parcels were located, he realized that the location was far removed from any emergency services, including fire departments and hospitals. Investigating further, he recognized that the plots were not fertile enough to support the needs of a large monastic community. With delicacy and paternal kindness, he thanked the farmers for offering the land, and told them he would also be surveying another plot, which another Ruthenian community had offered, to see which would be best for the new monastery. This other plot would be close to them, so even if he chose it, they would remain within a day's distance from the monastery.

The second parcel, located in South Canaan, Pennsylvania, a small community near the town of Carbondale, was larger, more fertile, in a better location, and much closer to basic emergency services. It also had the possibility of easy expansion, as the neighboring plot of land was also for sale. Recognizing that God's providence had selected this area for the first monastic community of the New World, the saint turned to the East, and thanked God, praying that His grace would bless the works.

His eminence assigned the responsibility of final negotiations to Fr Arseny Chagovstov, later Bishop Arseny of Winnipeg, who would also serve as the monastery's first abbot. Returning to Mayfield in the horse-drawn carriage, the two monastics made frequent stops to admire the beautiful landscape of Pennsylvania, and joyfully discussed the future of the monastery.

Fr Arseny was able to finalize the sale within a few weeks, and on June 26, 1905, the plot, with all the accompanying buildings, flocks, and equipment had been purchased. Work began immediately to modify the existing structures into monastic residences and a church. St Tikhon wrote: "In Mayfield, a farm (eighty-two acres of land) with a house, farm buildings and a garden has been purchased. An orphanage for twelve children has been opened; a building for monks is being constructed (in the beginning it is planned to settle two monks and seven novices therein). A blessing has been received from the Holy Synod for the founding of a men's monastery 'with such a number of brethren as the monastery itself will be in a position to maintain.'" [38]

On December 5, six months after the purchase, St Tikhon traveled to Pennsylvania again to bless the laying of the cornerstone of the church, as well as its cross and dome. Both the church and the monastery would be dedicated to St Tikhon of Zandonsk. As the carriage with the archbishop approached, Fr Arseny, in full monastic dress, came out to greet him along with the monastery's first two novices, Sister Maria, the matron of the new orphanage, and the first two orphaned children who had moved into the monastery. They made a full-length prostration, and the children offered the saint bread and salt, a Russian tradition. A service followed at the small, makeshift church.

Inspecting the building which had been altered to serve the needs of an orphanage, St Tikhon found it far superior to many of the extant orphanages in Russia. The changes which had been made to the structure were impressive, and on the second floor of the building, above the children's living quarters, there was a room prepared for him to stay when he visited.

The saint examined the monks' living quarters, noting every detail, down to the books which they were reading. He stopped and prayed in the locations where the church and the cemetery were to be built, and after sharing a meal with the children, he retreated to his cell. Fr Arseny celebrated Vespers and Compline at 6:30 p.m., after which those present began repeating the Jesus Prayer in silence. Morning Prayers and Matins began at 4:30 a.m., followed by the Divine Liturgy, which was attended by some of the local farmers. St Tikhon spent the rest of the morning trout-fishing, and at noon dined with the monks as the Lives of the Saints (*Synaxarion*) were being read. In the evening, the archbishop discussed building plans with Fr Arseny. The next day, following the morning services, St Tikhon chanted the Akathist to his patron saint, Tikhon of Zadonsk, and prayed for the new institution. After lunch and prayers, he departed.

In May 1906, Archbishop Tikhon returned to the monastery, along with Bishop Raphael, in order to consecrated the newly completed church. Before the commencement of the Divine Liturgy, St Tikhon gave Fr Arseny the Abbatial Staff, and clothed the two new novices with the monastic novitiate cassocks. According to the *Wayne Independent* newspaper:

> The services continued throughout the whole day ... the monastery building was architecturally beautiful, and ... it had 30 rooms. The Temple was large enough to accommodate 250 persons ... more than 20 Russians had left the mines to live on land near the monastery ... there are already more than 20 orphans being cared for at the orphanage, and that there were plans to erect a home for the aged besides.[39]

North America's first Orthodox monastery was ideally located, in a place both beautiful and tranquil. There, the monks could live in peace, focus on God, grow in love for Him, and praise and worship Him as He commanded human beings to do. They could love the land they tilled, and the orphans for whom they cared. St Tikhon himself found the monastery to be the spiritual refuge his soul desired, the place where he could break away, even momentarily, from his difficult and all-consuming pastoral duties, and devote his entire self to communion with God. From the very first summer after the monastery opened, St Tikhon spent several days there, helping the monks chop wood in the forest, tilling the ground, gathering crops, picking vegetables, working on the beehives, and helping with construction, carrying planks of wood and nails from one place to another on his own shoulders. He followed the monastic program with simplicity, and would not allow the monks to show him any preferential treatment. He participated in the daily services, and read the *Unseen Warfare* by Saint Nikodemus the Hagiorite. On August 13, after vespers, he tonsured the monastery's first monk, and the next day, following Divine Liturgy he tonsured the second monk. In this way, St Tikhon proved to be the founder and establisher of Orthodox coenobitic monasticism in America.

THE FIRST ORTHODOX SEMINARY IN AMERICA

From the time of his visit to Russia in 1903, St Tikhon had begun preparing a blueprint for the establishment of a seminary in America. The urgent need for an ecclesiastical school was clearly evident, as the conditions under which pastoral activity had to operate in America were vastly different from those of Russia. Until now, the vast majority of the clergy operating in North America had been sent for from Russia, and only a few native-born Americans, having completed their education in seminaries in Russia, had returned to serve in America. The practice of sending for clergy had severe shortcomings. Many could not accept "the completely different mold of American life, which for the Russian man is not always attractive,"[40] and had therefore asked to go home. Additionally, parishes preferred clergy from their own ethnic background, who were better acquainted with their language and culture, the latter being especially important for the parishes that have joined from Uniatism. American candidates for the priesthood were better acquainted "with the conditions of local life and the state of church affairs,"[41] and the best candidates amongst them had been sent to Russia to receive their theological education, but this too had its shortcomings. American seminarians, many of whom did not speak fluent Russian, were often unable to master the courses of the Russian seminaries; additionally, they were forced to "study such subjects in Russia that are not needed here."[42] Some of them forgot the

English language altogether, and while in Russia fell in love with the Russian Orthodox way of life, so when they completed their studies, they were reluctant to return to America "to do that work for which precisely they were sent to Russia."[43]

In a report to the Russian Synod, the saint wrote:

> I proposed to make use of the two-class missionary school that we have in Minneapolis, in order to transform it gradually into a seminary. And since it is difficult to enter a seminary—having finished only a simple regular parish school—a preparatory school ("a bursa" as the Ruthenians love to call it) with a dormitory has been established by us in Cleveland. The pupils of the latter, on the one hand, are obliged to attend American public schools, where they study general education subjects (through this they are not torn away from the American environment and language and, in case of not entering the seminary, they can easily find a place for themselves in the various branches of American "business"); on the other hand, at home they study church subjects (catechism, the Typicon, biblical history and church singing) and secular subjects—Russian literature, history and geography (these latter in moral-patriotic forms).[44]

On August 10, 1905, the holy Synod approved St Tikhon's proposal, and the first Orthodox seminary in America was established in Minneapolis, Minnesota. The fall of 1905 saw the first classes at the new seminary.

THERE IS AN INTEREST AMONG AMERICANS IN THE ORTHODOX FAITH

St Tikhon strove to maintain good relations with all the Christian denominations in America, but he was particularly close to the Anglicans/Episcopalians, and maintained a close friendship with the eminent Anglican Bishop Grafton. During that time, there arose a notion amongst the Orthodox that the return of the Episcopalians to the true church was imminent, however, this idealistic aspiration was far from reality. It is true that there was a genuine and intense interest in Orthodoxy in Episcopalian circles, and indeed, in some of its most notable clerical adherents, but unfortunately those circles were few and far between, and while many prominent personalities and eminent persons in the Anglican Church considered a move, there was never a wholesale desire for mass conversion amongst the common majority of the

Episcopal congregations. St Tikhon understood this, and despite his close and brotherly friendships with many Episcopalians, and his ardent desire to bring souls to the fold of the church, he knew where to draw the line, both dogmatically and personally.

His caution proved judicious and astute after an incident in 1905, which, while causing him great sorrow, also illustrated the overall sentiment which prevailed in the Episcopal hierarchy toward the Orthodox. That year, he had ordained a former Episcopal priest, Fr Ingram Irvine into the priesthood in the Orthodox Church. This caused a massive scandal amongst the Episcopalians, who reacted badly to the ordination. Among those who responded to the event with hostility were some Anglican clerics who had previously held deeply cordial relations, and even friendships with the saint. Despite his deep disappointment at their hypocrisy and vitriol, St Tikhon continued to advocate for the spread of the true faith throughout America. In a 1903 letter, he wrote:

> There is, however, an interest among Americans in the Orthodox Faith, and it is growing all the time: in our churches here, and especially in New York, one often sees Americans, who very much like our rites and singing and who want to become acquainted with the doctrine of our Church, in attendance at services. The Episcopalians are quite sympathetic to our Church, and seek rapprochement with us. That this interest may not weaken and may in fact bear noticeable fruit, we must work further on it, so that Americans may come to know and understand us. The main thing here is the language, without which it is difficult for us to move ahead.[45]

Saint Tikhon wholeheartedly strove to encourage the use of the English language for the wider dissemination of the Orthodox faith throughout the North American continent. Several years earlier, during the period of the episcopacy of Nicholas (Ziorov), an exceptional author and translator, Isabel Florence Hapgood, had taken on the challenge of collecting and translating all the services of the Orthodox Church from Russian to English. Hapgood, a devout Episcopalian, was already widely known for her translations of the works of Tolstoy, Gogol, and Victor Hugo. In fact, during her first visit in Russia, which lasted two full years, she had been a guest at the farm of Leo Tolstoy. Staying with him for several weeks, she had closely worked with the Russian author on her translations of his works.

Hapgood was a pious Christian, and despite her lifelong commitment to the Anglican confession, she played a pivotal role in the spread of Orthodoxy in America. She had been deeply impressed by the sacramental tradition of the Orthodox Church, and even without being Orthodox, had desired to translate all the Orthodox services, including the Divine Liturgy, into English. The work took eleven years, and was completed only after St Tikhon had already been elected archbishop. The Russian bishop and the American translator developed a close friendship, and Hapgood even helped with organizing the Orthodox choir for the celebration of the consecration of the new cathedral church in New York in 1902.

Despite the completion of the translation, the publication of the book originally seemed almost impossible, due to the lack of the necessary funds. The work was 655 pages long, and printing it would incur a substantial cost. St Tikhon managed to obtain $1,000[46] from the holy Synod of Russia, but this amount was not sufficient to cover the costs of printing, let alone the numbers required to provide a copy for every parish in the diocese. Providence, however, was to step in yet again, this time in the form of a visit from Count Sergei Witte, who had recently arrived in America as the representative of the holy Tsar Nicholas II. The count had come to the United States to participate in the negotiations surrounding the end of the Russo-Japanese war, but during his visit, St Tikhon was also able to secure an imperial donation of $2,000, an amount which finally allowed for the publication of the liturgical manual, which was printed and distributed in 1906, with the title *Service Book of the Holy Orthodox Catholic Apostolic (Greco-Russian) Church*. Hapgood's book remains in use to this day.

Copies of the new English service book were sent to the imperial family in Russia, who responded, expressing their warmest feelings of joy and gratitude. Consequently, during her last visit to Russia, Hapgood was personally invited by Empress Alexandra to visit her, in order that the Tsarina could thank her in person. On November 29, 1916, the two women met, and the Empress gave Hapgood a gift of a photo album from the consecration of the Cathedral Church of Feoderovski, in Tsarkoye Selo (today's Pushkin).

One of the primary reasons behind Hapgood's last visit to Russia was to meet with St Tikhon, to discuss his plans for the republication of the service book. Tragically, the 1917 Revolution put those plans on hold. Hapgood suddenly found herself trapped in Russia, and only managed to escape, albeit narrowly, with the help of the American ambassador. She was one of the first to publish in the American press about the murders of the Romanov family.

SOMETHING EVEN GREATER MUST BE BEING PREPARED FOR HIM BY DIVINE PROVIDENCE

During 1906, St Tikhon continued his usual pastoral journeys to the different parts of his vast archdiocese. Fr Theophan Buketovof, a priest who was serving under him, preserved some characteristic descriptions from the saint's life: "In order to spare the mission the cost of automobile travel, he always took the train. At every station, his 'patriarchal figure' in a warm blue cassock and hat from which flowed long hair, attracted attention. People stood up. Many approached him, shook his hand, and asked advice. Many of the places he visited were so isolated that trains stopped only once a day, so he spent the night in rectories, and, in many places lacking permanent clergy, in private homes. He lives like a true Apostle, without complaint, bearing with joy all the difficulties and inconveniences while proclaiming the Good News about Christ. He has truly taken the form of a servant,[47] being afforded none of the royal treatment taken for granted by hierarchs in the Old World ... something even greater, more responsible must be being prepared for him by Divine Providence."[48]

From the very beginning of his ministry in America, St Tikhon took every opportunity to bring his priests together to discuss the different issues and problems in the archdiocese and to make decisions for their resolution. These conferences were far from perfunctory; they were opportunities where the bishop could personally meet with his priests, be apprised of their needs, and provide guidance and solutions. This active hierarchal care can be seen in the minutes of the Clergy conference of June 2, 1905, which took place in Cleveland, Ohio. During that conference, St Tikhon told the assembled priests that they had to come together to explore the possibility of the active participation of lay members of the church in the work of the rejuvenation of the ecclesiastical life in America, not only at the parish level, but also at the community, city, and even state levels. His speech was greeted with enthusiasm, and a decision was made to meet again in Pennsylvania on August 2 of that same year in order to organize the very first Clergy Laity Congress of America, and to set up the agenda for the meeting.

However, when the time came for this historic Clergy Laity Congress, which owed its existence to the holy archbishop, St Tikhon would be preparing for a completely new arena in his service to the church.

On January 13, 1907, the *Russian-American Orthodox Messenger* led with the news that "trusted, though not official," sources had confirmed that Archbishop Tikhon had been elected to the Episcopal see of the historic city of Yaroslavl, in Russia. The editors of the *Messenger* congratulated their beloved archbishop for his promotion, but noted with deep sorrow that "the American Mission cannot conceal the feeling of deepest sorrow in parting with their kind, fatherly, solicitous, and wise Archpastor."[49]

The official announcement arrived on February 15/28, in a letter dated January 26, which bore the seal and signature of Tsar Nicholas II. At the end of February, the very first Orthodox Pan-American Clergy Laity Congress, which had been St Tikhon's brainchild, met in Mayfield Pennsylvania. Officially, the saint was no longer archbishop of America, as Archbishop Platon (Rozhdestvensky) had already been appointed. However, as the new archbishop had not yet arrived in the continent, St Tikhon was called upon to oversee, if not officially preside over, the Sobor (council). This historic meeting established the foundations for many future aspects of the missionary work in America. It was also decided to draft an official statute outlining the administrative structure of the diocese. On the last day of the congress, between meetings, the holy father invited all the priests of the archdiocese to a meal, at the end of which he stood and spoke the following words, wishing in this way to leave his legacy and show his coworkers in Christ the necessary elements for the successful maintenance and continuance of the work of the church in America.

> Fathers and Brothers:
>
> This is our farewell meal, but the sorrow of my parting with my flock is tempered by the fact that I have the possibility today of seeing almost all of my colleagues in the States. And so, I take the opportunity of this gathering to express to you my thanks for our work together. We laboured and toiled together. In some matters, I took the initiative for you, inspired you, and you did the work, realising my ideas. Conversely, in other cases, you gave me ideas, and I am not ashamed to admit it. Then I sought the means and possibility to realise your idea practically. I appealed to you to work together from the very beginning, in my first speech in the San Francisco

Cathedral, and my words were not in vain. If anything has been done here, it has not been by me alone, but together with you. (It is evident that the Lord God helped us.)

More than once have I told you that the more I study the history of the Orthodox Church in this country, the more I am convinced that our work here is God's work, that God Himself is helping us; that when it seems as though everything we do is ready to fail, the work of Russian Orthodoxy, on the contrary, it not only does not die, but it grows in new strength and brilliance.

I recall how strongly I was disturbed by the news of my appointment to America. I was not saddened so much by leaving the flock in Chełm whom I had gotten used to and where (it seemed) I was of some use. I was sorrowful not so much at the thought of having to go to a country distant and of leaving my very old, ailing mother at home, as I was depressed when I realised that I was little suited for this work for which I was being sent, and little acquainted with it. And what happened?

"Who else but God?"

He helped me spend over eight years here in service which not only gained praise from people, but was somewhat useful for our work here itself. And now, I am inclined to think that even my appointment to America occurred not so much by human judgment as by God's design, that it was well-timed for the flock here ...

From the very beginning I gave my colleagues wide room for initiative. As long as the work got done, it was not important to me whether it began with me or others. And the consequences of this were not slow in being told: parishes began to multiply, new churches were built, the number of parishioners grew, new institutions were established. On the other side, they cannot reproach me for lack of firmness or patience. On the contrary, when others thought it necessary, for example, to abandon some project or take some stringent measures to suspend someone, I always took my leave humbly and patiently, preferring to wait it out, fearing that I might extinguish smoking flax and shatter a broken reed. And who knows how many people and projects have thus been preserved ....

But I should not boast; better I turn to my weaknesses.

You know that there is no full perfection in the world, that very often our virtues and perfections border on faults and weaknesses. It is not in vain that they say that genius and insanity are related. So, too, with me.

That which was worthy, that which brought good to the diocese, especially in the beginning, little-by-little changed, and in the final account, could be accompanied by harm. As we said, I gave my colleagues wide initiative and independent work. But tell me, are sensible and true voices not sometimes heard to say, in effect, "We are allowed too much". That 'Something needs to be suppressed' (which is sometimes done, but after the fact). Or, for example, does my patience not sometimes pass over into connivance? Or, for example, I sometimes boast that I have string instead of nerves, it is hard to draw me out, that I bear the most unexpected misfortunes with relative composure, that I do not lose my presence of mind over them, that it is hard to perturb me by them. But this is close to apathy, to complete indifference, to stony insensitivity, which are not only not virtues or merits, but, on the contrary, can be evil and sin, from which we pray that God will deliver us.

And so, I think that those things in which I was useful here for a while, for which I was perhaps even sent here, have now passed and are no longer needed; that you need something different, a different worker with a different approach and character. It is in this thought that I find the chief motive and justification for the transfer of hierarchs from one diocese to another, and not at all in a desire for greater comforts, peace, honour, and other earthly blessings, the desire for which is ascribed (not always rightly) to hierarchs when they are transferred.

Let me depart, Fathers and Brothers, with peace to a place where the qualities I manifested here will, perhaps, still be of value. And allow me to wish you further successes in your tasks, and to remain here happily.[50]

Tears flowed freely and plentifully amongst the clergy present. In an unspeakably humble manner, the holy archbishop had opened his heart and revealed how he himself had experienced his service in America. In a modest way, he had shown the godly fruits of the path he had forged, giving all the credit for his successes to God, and keeping for himself only the responsibility for whatever negative elements there had been during this journey. Finally, before the end of the conference, St Tikhon gave one last address to the clerics of his archdiocese, noting the following: "You know, of course, that I am departing from you, and perhaps shall not see many of you again. Under these circumstances, the touching prayer of Christ our High Priest to His Heavenly Father comes to my mind, the prayer for the Apostles and believers.[51] Preparing to part with His disciples, the Saviour beseeched God to keep the flock together as Christ Himself had kept them, to preserve them from enmity so that none would be lost, to sanctify them in mutual love. Following the image of our Supreme Shepherd, Jesus Christ, I too, preparing to part with you, pray first of all for my former flock … And my present prayer to the Heavenly Father before parting is that He would preserve you in the True Faith and defend you against the malevolence of enemies.

Our Saviour, parting from this world, feared for the fate of his not-numerous disciples who were facing many enemies. 'Simon, Simon, behold, Satan has desired to have you, that he may sift you as wheat.'[52] How can we help fearing for our small flock? How easily the candle can be extinguished by the wind coming through the open window. How easily can an oarsman in a frail boat be overturned by the sea waves. Here, we cannot boast of great numbers, neither of renown, nor of wealth, nor of learning, all that is valued in this world. We are strong here only in one thing: in possessing the True Orthodox Faith, but even 'that not of yourself, it is the gift of God,' and we should ask the Lord for the increase of this gift.[53]

Let them stand fast in Your Holy Church, in the Orthodox Faith. And you, brethren, when departing from here and going to those who delegated you, strengthen your brethren in the Faith and the love of Orthodoxy. Moreover, I will endeavour that you may be able after my decease to have these things always in remembrance." [54, 55]

On March 11/24, the Sunday of Orthodoxy, St Tikhon celebrated his last Divine Liturgy in North America. Taking this opportunity, he expressed his thoughts about what it was to be Orthodox in the New World: "It is not enough, brethren, to celebrate the 'Triumph of Orthodoxy'. We have to concur in this triumph. And for this, we have to guard sacredly the Orthodox Faith, to stand firm in it, disregarding the fact that we live in a non-Orthodox country, not giving heed to opinions one hears, such as: 'This is not the Old Country, here. This is a free land. Therefore, supposedly, we may not have to observe everything that the Church requires', as if the Word of God is suitable only for the Old Country and not for the whole world; as if the Church of Christ is not catholic! as if the Orthodox Faith is not the one that 'sustains the universe!'

But guarding the Orthodox Faith sacredly and loving it is not enough. Christ the Saviour said that lighting the candle, one does not put it 'under a bushel, but on a candlestick,'[56] and the light of Orthodoxy is lighted not for a small circle of people. No, the Orthodox Church is catholic, she remembers

St Tikhon leaving America.

the will of her Founder: 'Go into all the world and preach the Gospel to every creature, teach all the nations.'[57] We ought to share our spiritual wealth, truth, and light with others ... Thus, each of us should consider this task of propagating the Faith as his own task, dear to his heart.

I have spoken of this many times to my flock, and now, departing from here, I leave it to you as my last will to cherish and to fulfill. And first of all, you, brethren of this holy Temple ... testify to your beliefs as Russian people in your cultural traditions .... May God strengthen you always in devotion to the Orthodox Faith! ...

Farewell to you, America. For some you are a fatherland, for others you were a haven and gave them shelter, work, and prosperity. Still others in this free land obtained the right to profess the sound, true Faith. In antiquity, God spoke through the prophets: 'And seek the peace of the city to which I have caused you to be carried ... and pray the Lord for it: for in its welfare you shall find your welfare.'[58] And we pray likewise 'for the abundance of the fruits of the earth, for healthful seasons ... in all our services. So let the blessing of God be with this country and this city and this Temple, and may the blessing of God be with all of you, now and always and unto the ages of ages.[59]

On March 13, 1907, St Tikhon bade a final farewell to America, and departed for Europe on the Steamboat SS Kronprinz Wilhelm. The manifold

77

fruits of his pastoral service in America proved more abundant than anyone could have possibly imagined, and far more than the Russian Synod could have hoped when they first ordained him. St Tikhon sealed the history of Orthodoxy in America with his saintly presence, wise guidance, and multifaceted and truly miraculous achievements."

RETURN TO THE MOTHERLAND: YAROSLAVL AND VILNIUS

On February 7, 1907, St Tikhon was elected to the Episcopal see of the historic city of Yaroslavl, approximately 160 miles northeast of Moscow, and one of the most significant dioceses in the empire. During the first year of his episcopacy there, St Tikhon took the opportunity to visit the much-beloved Russian saint, John of Kronstadt. During the visit they discussed a variety of spiritual issues, but at one point, St John unexpectedly got up from his seat, and turning to the archbishop, he said "now, your eminence, you sit in my seat. I am going to go rest." St Tikhon perceived that the words of the great saint had some prophetic meaning, but in his humility, he could not possibly imagine how he could ever take the great saint's seat, or even approach his position as intercessor for all of Russia. He remembered this event years later, in the historic hours before his election as patriarch of Moscow and all Russia, and it was only then that he finally understood St John's prophetic foretelling.

He served in Yaroslavl until the end of 1913, when, on December 22, he was elected to take over the episcopal seat of the large city of Vilna at the western borders of the empire. Vilna, modern-day Vilnius, in Lithuania, was named after the Vilnia River, which flowed through the region, and was, at the time, part of Imperial Russia. Though nominally Russian, it was comprised of a non-Orthodox majority of Jews, Catholics, and Uniates, and it was precisely for this reason that the charismatic and diplomatic archbishop was chosen for this position. His vast experience operating successfully in countries where Russians and Orthodox Christians formed only a small minority had made him one of the few ecclesiastics in the empire who could be counted upon for the difficulties and challenges the demographic layout entailed. Shortly before his transfer, he was awarded the honorary distinction of the order of Saint Alexander Nevsky.[60]

In Vilna, just much like his first diocese in Kholm, Orthodox Christians comprised only a minority, living amongst a majority of Roman Catholics and Jews, so the saint once again began the work of restoring cordial relations between Orthodox and heterodox. However, the very first year of his tenure in Vilna was marked by the tragic beginning of World War I, and it was not long because before the city was completely overrun by the Germans, who forced the saint to leave his see and flee to Moscow. Before his departure, the holy bishop made sure to secure the relics of the three martyrs of Vilna, Anthony, John, and Efstathios (+April 14, 1347).

Despite the threat to his life, the saint took the first opportunity to return to the only part of his Episcopal diocese which had not been occupied by the German troops, and from there he worked tirelessly to support his flock. All his powers, body and soul, wholly turned to dealing with the tragic consequences of this worldwide crisis. Refugees, homeless, orphans, and every destitute sufferer, regardless of religion or nationality, found in the saint a warm protector and a caring father. The bishop would often visit the trenches and the front lines, where he would provide spiritual and emotional support for the soldiers, and celebrate the divine services for them, frequently during intense firefights and German bombardments.

AT THE RUDDER OF THE CHURCH DURING THE CATACLYSM

Tragically, the human cost and destruction of the Great War, and the hardships to which the saint was exposed during this period would soon be completely overshadowed by the unspeakable horrors which were about to deluge his beloved country in blood. The beginning of the end came on February 7, 1917, with the coup d'état, the forcible abdication of the tsar, and the formation of the provisional government.

The Holy Synod of the Church of Russia had long been planning an All-Russian Local Council,[61] but the alarming social and political developments expedited the organizational process. On July 4, 1917, St Tikhon was elected archbishop of Moscow, and immediately assumed the responsibilities of organizing the Council. This historical gathering would discuss the serious ecclesiastical issues which had been created by the recent political developments, but would also address the long-standing issue of the restoration and reestablishment of the Russian Patriarchate.[62] A few weeks after his election to the see of Moscow, on August 15, the saint was elevated to the rank of metropolitan.[63]

The All-Russian Local Council of 1917–1918 was the zenith of the reformative movement that the Church of Russia had embarked upon at the end of the nineteenth century. Tsar Nicholas II had shown a special

St Tikhon, bishop of Yaroslavl.

interest in these reforms, and had cooperated with the church in their efforts; however, the serious internal upheavals which had already begun in 1905, and the turmoil following the World War I did not allow him to continue with his previous active engagement. Finally, after the 1917 coup, the church was forced to move forward without him, and call for an All-Russian Local Council. The Council began its meetings on August 15/28, the feast of the Dormition of the Theotokos, at the Cathedral church of Christ the Saviour in Moscow after the festal Archierarchal Divine Liturgy at the Kremlin's Dormition cathedral.

St Tikhon was unanimously elected chairman of the council. A total of 564 representatives from all across Russia, of which 265 were clergy, and 299 were laymen, participated in the Council. The topics which were to be discussed primarily had to do with ecclesiastical governance, education, ecclesiastical financial management, ecclesiastical publications, and a series of important theological matters. The issue of the restoration of the patriarchate soon came up, and intense debates broke out immediately. However, historical political developments soon overtook the country, and the conciliar disagreements were overshadowed by the October Revolution[64] and the Bolshevik Coup.[65] On November 13, the historic decision was made to elect a new patriarch of Russia. The council decided to hold a secret ballot, and to choose amongst the three candidates with the highest number of votes by drawing lots. The three candidates were Metropolitan Antony (Khrapovitsky) of Kharkov, Metropolitan Arsenius (Stadnitsky) of Novgorod, and Metropolitan Tikhon of Moscow.

On November 5/18, following the Divine Liturgy, the vote took place, and immediately after, lots were drawn. On that day, St Tikhon Belavin was elected the first patriarch of Moscow and all Russia in 217 years. He was fifty-two years old. Learning of the results, St Tikhon responded with the following prophetic words. "Your news of my election to the patriarchate is for me that scroll on which was written, lamentations, and mourning, and woe, which the prophet Ezekiel had to eat (Ezek. 2:10-3:1). How many tears must I swallow and how much must I groan in my impending patriarchal ministry, and especially in these present difficult times! ... From now on, the care of all the churches of Russia is laid upon me, and dying for them all my days awaits me. And who even among those stronger than I can have the strength for it? But may God's will be done!"[66]

His enthronement took place on November 21/December 4, 1917, at the Kremlin cathedral. The chanting could not drown out the sounds of cannons and gunfire from the deadly street battles which were taking place in the roads and alleys of Moscow. "As he received the pastoral staff, Patriarch Tikhon said: 'The patriarchate is being restored in Rus' at a terrible time, in the midst of shooting of weapons of death-dealing fire. Perhaps it will itself be forced to resort more than once to anathemas in order to bring the disobedient to their senses, and to restore Church order. However, as in ancient times, the Lord appeared to the Prophet Elias not in the storm nor in the earthquake but in the coolness and the breath of a quiet breeze,[67] so now to our pusillanimous reproaches "Lord, the sons of Russia have abandoned Your covenant, they have destroyed your Altars, they have fired at the holy things of the Temples and the Kremlin, they have slaughtered your priests,"[68] the quiet breath of Your words is heard: "there are still seven thousand who have not bowed the knee to the contemporary Baal, and have not betrayed the true God." The Lord, as it were, says to me: "Go and search for those for whose sake the Russian Land still stands and is maintained, but do not abandon the lost sheep who are doomed to destruction and slaughter, sheep who are truly pitiful. Shepherd them, and for this, take this, the staff of goodwill. With it, search out the lost sheep, return the oppressed, bind up the wounds of the wounded, strengthen the sick, destroy those who have grown fat and obstreperous; and shepherd them with justice.'" [69]

After the end of the service, the saint led a procession around the Kremlin with the cross, blessing the walls with holy water.

St Tikhon's patriarchal tenure was one of martyrdom and sacrifice from the very first day, as the Bolshevik regime began promulgating one anti-ecclesial law after the next. At the same time, news would arrive from every corner of Russia, informing the patriarch of the mass murders and assassinations of clergy and faithful alike. Shocked at the bloodthirsty politics and violence against the church, St Tikhon took a bold step, and on January 19, 1918, he anathematized the perpetrators. In this encyclical, dated February 1, 1918, the saint showed a different aspect of his personality, proving that true and fatherly love does not manifest only through tenderness. Many times, true, Godly love can only be shown through ultimate firmness, and strictness may be the only appropriate love which can lead to the salvation of imperiled souls.

World War I.
St Tikhon in the trenches of the front lines in Vilna (Vilnius),
during the period in which he was archbishop there.

THE HUMBLE TIKHON, by the Grace of God Patriarch of Moscow and of All Russia,

To all God's beloved, prelates, priests, and all faithful children of the Orthodox Russian Church.

"That He might deliver us from this present evil world."[70]

The Holy Orthodox Christian Church is passing through a period of stress. The open and concealed enemies of the truth of Christ have started to persecute that truth and are aiming a mortal blow at the cause of Christ. In place of Christian love, they are sowing seeds of malice, envy, and fratricidal war.

Christ's precept to love our neighbor is forgotten and trampled tinder foot. Every day we learn that innocent people, not excluding those lying sick in bed, are being frightfully and brutally murdered for the sole offense that they have honestly discharged their duty to the country and have devoted all their energies to serve the welfare of the people. These crimes are committed ... in broad daylight with unprecedented effrontery and outrageous brutality ... in almost every city of our native land ...

These crimes fill our heart with deep sorrow and compel us to denounce sharply these monsters of the human race ... in accordance with the precept of the Holy Apostle: "Them that sin reprove in the sight of all, that the rest also may be in fear."[71]

Think what you are doing, you madmen! Stop your bloody reprisals. Your acts are not merely cruel, they are the works of Satan for which you will burn in Hell fire in the life hereafter and be cursed by future generations in this life.

By the authority given me by God, I forbid you to partake of the Christian Mysteries. I anathematize you if you still bear a Christian name and belong by birth to the Orthodox Church.

And you, faithful children of the Orthodox Christian Church, I beseech you to have nothing to do with this scourge of the human race: "Put away the wicked man from among yourselves."[72]

Violent outrages are being committed against the Orthodox Christian Church. The blessed mysteries, which sanctify the birth of man or the union of husband and wife in a Christian family, are openly declared unnecessary and superfluous. Holy Churches are being destroyed by gunfire (churches of the Moscow Kremlin) or looted and desecrated (the chapel of Our Saviour in Petrograd); monasteries most revered by the

Above: From the opening ceremony of the council.
Below: One of the meetings of the council.

faithful, such as Aleksandro-Nevskaia and Pochaevskaia Lavras, have been seized by the godless rulers of darkness under the pretext that they are the people's property. Schools maintained by the Orthodox Church for the training of ministers and religious teachers have been declared useless and turned either into schools of atheism or into nurseries of immorality.

Church and monastery properties are being confiscated under the pretext that they are the property of the people, but the legitimate will of the people is never taken into consideration. And, finally, the government which promised to give Russia justice and truth and safeguard freedom and order acts everywhere and toward everyone, including the Holy Orthodox Church, with unrestrained arbitrariness and violence ...

Is there no limit to this insolence? Is there no way of stopping the aggressiveness of the enemies of the Christian Church?

I summon you, faithful and loyal children of the Church. Come to the defense of your outraged and oppressed Holy Mother! ... I summon you, beloved children of the Church, even if you should have to suffer for the cause of Christ ... for the Apostle has said: "Who shall separate us from the love of Christ? Shall tribulation, or anguish, or persecution, or famine, or nakedness, or peril, or sword?"[73]

And you, fellow prelates and priests, sound the call ... for the defense of ... the Orthodox Church, without an hour's delay. Organize unions of crusaders of the spirit ... who can resist external force with the zeal of the faithful, and I firmly believe that the enemies of the Church ... will be vanquished by the Cross of Christ, because the edifice of the Divine Crusader cannot be demolished ... "I will build My Church; and the gates of Hell shall not prevail against it."[74]

TIKHON
The Patriarch of Moscow and of All Russia[75]

This was not the only daring declaration the patriarch made against the cruelties and viciousness of the godless regime. In March of the same year, the Treaty of Brest-Litovsk was signed.[76] This treaty proved the ultimate humiliation for Russia, which lost Finland, Poland, the Baltic states of Estonia, Lithuania, and Latvia, Ukraine, the Crimea, and the majority of the Caucasus. This massive loss, which cost Russia over 155,000 square miles, in which over fifty-six million people (more than 1/3 of the population of the former Russian Empire) lived, was condemned in the harshest terms by the Russian patriarch, who wrote:

"Those who live by the sword shall die by the sword".[77]

We address this prophecy of the Saviour to you, the current makers of our Fatherland's fate, who call yourself "the people's" commissars. For an entire year, you have been gripping the power of the government in your hands, and you are already preparing to celebrate the anniversary of the October revolution, but the rivers of the blood of our brothers, pitilessly murdered at your rallying, cry out to heaven and force us to tell you the bitter truth.

Having seized power and called the people to entrust themselves to you, what promises have you given them, and how have you kept these promises?

Truly you have given them a stone instead of bread, and a serpent instead of a fish.[78] To a people worn out by a bloody war you promised to give peace 'without annexation or contribution'.

What victory could you have turned down, you who have led Russia to a shameful truce, with humiliating conditions that even you did not resolve to make fully public? Instead of 'annexations and contributions' the great Motherland is conquered, diminished, dismembered; and as pay for the tribute placed on it you secretly transport to Germany gold that you yourself did not amass.

You have taken away from the soldiers everything for which they had valorously fought. You have taught them, only recently brave and invincible, to leave off protecting the Motherland and to run from the field of battle. You have extinguished in their hearts the inspiring consciousness that there is no greater love than should one lay down his life for his friends.[79] You have traded the Fatherland for soulless internationalism, although you yourselves know perfectly well that when it comes to defending the Fatherland, the proletarians of all countries are those countries' faithful sons, and not their betrayers.

And although you have refused to protect the Motherland from external enemies, you are ceaselessly gathering armies.

Against whom will you lead them?

You have divided the entire nation into warring camps and cast it into a fratricide unprecedented for its cruelty. You have openly exchanged love of Christ for hatred, and instead of peace you have artificially fomented enmity between the classes. And there is no end in sight to the war you've

87

generated, since you aim to deliver triumph to the phantom of world revolution with the hands of Russian worker and peasants.

It was not Russia who needed the disgraceful peace with its external enemy but you yourselves, who have plotted to irreparably destroy Russia's internal peace. No one feels safe; everyone lives in constant fear of searches, robbery, eviction, arrest, and execution. Hundreds of defenseless people are seized, then languish for whole months in prisons, are often executed without investigation or trial, even without going to the court you have simplified. Not only those who are somehow guilty before you, but even those who are in no way guilty, but were taken only as "captives"; these unfortunate people are killed to answer for crimes committed by persons who not only are not of one mind with them, but very often your own followers or those with convictions similar to yours. Bishops, priests, monks and nuns who are guilty of nothing are executed simply because of some wild accusations of vague and indeterminate "counterrevolution". This inhuman execution is made even more onerous for the Orthodox because they are deprived of the final consolation before their deaths, the Sacraments, and the bodies of the slain are not given to their families for a Christian burial. Isn't this the height of aimless cruelty on the part of those who pretend to be the benefactors of mankind and who themselves supposedly suffered from cruel rulers?

But it's not enough for you that you have reddened the hands of the Russian people with their brother's blood. Hiding behind various names, contributions, requisitions, and nationalization, you have pushed them into the most barefaced and wanton thievery. At your hinting were plundered or seized lands, mansions, factories, houses, farm animals, money, personal things, furniture, clothing. First the wealthy, whom you've called "bourgeois", were robbed; then under the epithet of "kulaks"[80] were the more well-off and industrious peasants also plundered, thus increasing the number of paupers, although you cannot but recognize that with the impoverishment of a great multitude of individual citizens the wealth of the nation as a whole is lost, and the country is impoverished.

Tempting uneducated and ignorant people with the opportunity for easy and unpunished gain, you have fogged their consciences and muffled in them the awareness of sin; but no matter what names you hide this evil-doing behind, murder, violence, and robbery will ever remain serious sins and crimes that cry out to heaven.

You promised freedom.

Freedom is a great good, if it is properly understood, like freedom from evil, not oppressing others, not turning into lawlessness and willfulness. But you have not given that freedom; the freedom you have given consists in all manner of indulgence to the lowest crowd instincts, in murder and theft with impunity. All manifestations of both truly the civilian and higher spiritual freedom of mankind have you mercilessly crushed. Is it freedom when no one can bring home food or rent an apartment without special permission, when families, and sometimes all the inhabitants of whole buildings are evicted and their possessions are thrown into the street, and when citizens are artificially divided into ranks, certain of which are consigned to hunger and being plundered? Is it freedom when no one can speak his opinion openly without fear of being accused of counterrevolution? Where is freedom of speech and press, where is freedom for preaching in church? Many bold preachers have already paid with their martyrs' blood; the voice of social and governmental discussion and criticism is being stifled; all press, other than the narrow Bolshevik press, has been completely strangled.

Especially painful and cruel is the violation of freedom in matters of faith. Not a day goes by when the most monstrous slanders against Christ's Church and her servants are not published in the agencies of your press, along with malicious blasphemy and mockery. You deride the servants of the altar, force bishops to dig trenches, and send priests to do dirty work. You have raised your hand against the Church's inheritance gathered through many generations of the faithful, and have given no thought to violating their posthumous will. You have closed a large number of monasteries and churches without any excuse or reason. You have blocked access to the Moscow Kremlin, that sacred inheritance of the faithful people. You are destroying the ancient form of church community, the parish; you destroy brotherhoods and other charitable and educational Church institutions, close and rout diocesan meetings, and interfere with the Orthodox Church's internal government. By banishing sacred images from schools and forbidding the teaching of faith to children there, you deprive them of the spiritual food necessary for an Orthodox upbringing.

What else can I say? The time fails me[81] to describe all the catastrophes that have stricken our Motherland. I will not speak of the collapse of a once great and mighty Russia, of the total fracturing of our railroad, of unprecedented agricultural devastation, of hunger and cold that threatens death in the cities, and of the lack of everything needed for maintaining a household in the villages. This everyone can see. Yes, we are experiencing terrible times in our reign, and it will not be erased from the peoples' soul for a long time, having darkened the image of God in it and stamping in it the image of the beast. The words of the prophet have been fulfilled: *Their feet run to evil, and they make haste to shed innocent blood: their thoughts are thoughts of iniquity; wasting and destruction are in their paths.*[82]

We know that our rebukes will evoke only anger and indignation in you and that you will look for an excuse in them for accusing us of opposition to the authorities, but the higher your "column of wrath" rises, the more proven will be the testimony to the truth of our rebukes.

It is not our business to judge earthly authorities; all authority, allowed by God, would attract our blessing if it were truly "God's servant" for the good of its subjects, and not a terror to good works, but to the evil.[83] Now to you, who are using your authority to persecute your neighbors and decimate the innocent, we extend our word of instruction: celebrate the anniversary of your coming to power by freeing the prisoners, putting a stop to the bloodshed, violence, devastation, and persecution of faith; turn not to destruction but to the establishment of law and order, give the people their desired and deserved rest from civil war. Otherwise all the righteous blood you have spilled will be required of you,[84] and you who took sword in hand will yourselves die of the sword.[85, 86]

When this letter was read in a meeting of the Holy Synod, many members attempted to convince the patriarch to refrain from publishing it, fearing that it would place him in grave and immediate danger. The patriarch carefully listened to the concerns expressed for his person, but his decision remained firm. His flock needed to know that their leader stood with them. His divine fearlessness was exemplary. In July of the same year, when he publicly condemned the cold-blooded murder of the tsar and his family, many of his closest advisors pleaded with him to leave the country, as they feared that he would soon suffer the same fate as the tsar. The saint answered, "The flight of the Patriarch would be too convenient for the enemies of the Church; they would use this for their own ends. Let them do what they will."[87]

FAITHFUL TO THE END

His advisors' fears proved well-founded, and on November 24, 1918, Bolshevik soldiers showed up at the door of the patriarchate, demanding to conduct a search, as the saint had been accused of "counter-revolutionary activities." Not finding anything, they immediately placed him under house arrest, and began a series of interrogations which would be repeated with the same hostility over the course of the next few years. Not wanting a "second Hermogenes,"[88] Lenin strictly forbade that the patriarch be physically assaulted, but his house imprisonment was not lifted until nearly eight months later, on Pascha of 1919, and the confinement was often repeated throughout 1920.

During the period of the Civil War, which broke out in November 1917, St Tikhon maintained a strict neutrality, refraining from siding with either political faction, and asking his clergy to do the same. He repeatedly reminded them that as shepherds of the church their duty was to the spiritual support of their flock, and that their ministry should be devoid of any worldly ideology.

However, things rapidly deteriorated, and the situation became progressively worse. In 1921, a great famine broke out, and a new challenge faced the saint and the church, as millions of people began dying of starvation. The patriarch immediately took action, mobilizing churches and monasteries for the relief of the hungry, and asking for help from his contacts outside of Russia.

Seeing the church's efficacious generosity, the regime proved its inherent callousness and lack of care for the Russian people. Focusing on sustaining their atheist agenda at all costs, they knew they could not afford to allow the church's philanthropic work to be showcased, and so proceeded to launch a concerted effort to suppress all news of his activity. Articles began appearing in newspapers slandering the supposed greed of the church, and demanding that all ecclesiastical assets be given to the state, allegedly for the relief of the hungry. The state's ulterior motives, namely, the destruction of organized religion and the funding of the continued Civil War, were an open secret, and indeed, one that was never well kept. Lenin himself, obsessed with the idea that it could be possible to plunder several billions of rubles from the Church, wrote to the Politburo[89] on March 19, 1922: "Right now and only now, when people are eaten by hunger everywhere ... we can (and therefore must) seize Church valuables with the most frantic and merciless energy and not stop suppressing any resistance .... The more representatives of the reactionary clergy and reactionary bourgeoisie we are able to shoot on this occasion, the better."[90]

Violent fights broke out throughout the country over the looting of churches, with church officials and laymen on the one side, and governmental agents, or sometimes mobs of disgruntled peasants or criminals, on the other. Thousands were murdered, arrested, interrogated, exiled, or executed during this period, and any attempt to put a stop to sacrilege was seen as a treasonous measure.

St Tikhon saw the writing on the wall, and attempting to avoid further bloodshed, published a declaration instructing every priest and parish to hand over any decorative ecclesiastical object which was not used for sacramental purposes to the State, with the condition that it be handed over willingly, and not taken by force. Despite this, in February of 1922 the All-Russian Central Executive Committee of the Soviet Union published a decree demanding that all ecclesiastical objects, sacramental or not, be immediately handed over to the government for the purpose of famine relief. The results of this decree were swift and brutal. Bloody conflicts between the faithful and the authorities began once more, as relics, Eucharistic items, and icons were seized, stolen, desecrated, and destroyed. Over 10,000 Christians were martyred and killed during the confiscations. There followed arrests and trials of over 2,000 church members, from priests to simple Orthodox laymen, with a charge of obstructing the law. Priests who had simply attempted to stop sacrileges and looting in the church were accused of hoarding ecclesiastical objects. In one such trial, the saint appeared as a defense witness, and when asked by the president of the court if he considered the laws of the regime binding, he answered, "yes, I acknowledge the authority of the law, to the degree that it does not contradict the laws of piety."

On May 6, 1922, the saint was placed under house arrest yet again, this time with the charge of obstruction of justice, and two weeks later, on May 19, he was moved to the monastery of the Theotokos in Donskoy where he was put under careful observation, and kept in complete isolation. At the same time, he was frequently transferred to the jails of Lubyanka, where he was subjected to endless interrogations.

The removal of its patriarch and head signaled the beginning of a great ecclesiastical tragedy for the Orthodox Church in Russia. A faction of modernist clerics, who called themselves "ecclesiastical reformists," found the chance to push their novel canonical innovations. The Living Church,

93

as its founders named the movement, expressed full support for the Soviet government, even going to the lengths of declaring capitalism a mortal sin. The government, in turn, saw the new faction as a useful tool for their stated goal of the complete disintegration of Russian Orthodoxy, and therefore backed their measures and granted them official status. The Soviet authorities began to arrest and exile all the priests and bishops who remained faithful to the patriarch, while at the same time the Living Church took over all extant ecclesiastical administration, persecuting the canonical bishops, removing them from their sees, and replacing them with their own partisans. Soon, almost all the churches in Moscow, and approximately one third of all the churches in Russia came under their control. Despite the new persecutions, however, the overwhelming majority of the faithful remained faithful to their patriarch.

That same month, April of 1923, the Living Church convened the Renovationist so-called Second All-Russian Council, during which they passed resolutions against monastic orders, canonized the elevation of married clergy to the episcopacy, deposed and excommunicated the patriarch, and stripped him of his monastic schema. They then proceeded to abolish the patriarchate and implement radical ecclesiastical renovations. Whichever bishops did not agree with the decisions of the pseudo-synod were forced by the secret police to sign the pseudo-conciliar documents, often with direct threats to their lives and to the safety of their flocks. When the patriarch received a copy of these decisions, he declared that he considered the resolutions uncanonical and illegal, and therefore invalid.

The patriarch understood that the level of ecclesiastical instability had become untenable, and without his presence at this critical time, the results could be catastrophic. Half of the Russian church's hierarchy had already submitted to the Living Church, albeit many of them only after threats and force had been applied, and the Kemalist faction in Turkey had coerced the patriarch of Constantinople to send a statement supporting the decisions of the Living Church council and the deposition of the Russian patriarch. St Tikhon knew that he was needed to stabilize the ship of the church, as it was dangerously close to overturning, and with that in mind, he made a sudden and unanticipated move. On June 16, 1923, he published his famous "Declaration," apologizing for his anti-Soviet activity and his anathematization of the regime, and officially distancing himself from any

St Tikhon with the holy hieromartyr Peter, Metropolitan of Krutitsy.

The Bolsheviks arrest St Tikhon.

internal or external pro-imperial, pro-monarchic factions. He then officially asked for his release.

This astonishing move gave the Soviet authorities a solution to a formidable dilemma. They had already decided on the patriarch's execution, even setting a date, but the People's Commissariat for Foreign Affairs informed the government that the patriarch's execution would do irreversible damage to the regime's public image, as the action would be perceived unfavorably by nearly all the significant political and military figures in Europe and America. There had already been universal public outcry in the foreign presses, denouncing the patriarch's arrest and continued imprisonment. His character and reputation, and his work in both America and Russia, had endeared him to Christians of every denomination, and Christian groups in Europe and America were up in arms, demanding that their political representatives fight for the saint's release. Due to this pressure, the Soviets had postponed his execution several times, but they did not want to be perceived as weak by releasing an enemy of the regime, so the patriarch's letter came at the ideal time.

On June 27, 1923, the martyric saint was finally released. He was barefoot and disheveled, wearing a soldier's coat, and he looked like he had aged significantly. His very appearance, bearing witness to his suffering for the church, was enough to rejuvenate all his flock, and send the Living Church into a sharp and irreversible decline. His decision to write that fateful letter was conclusively validated, when, on July 25, less than a month after his release, he was able to officially anathematize the schismatic Living Church, and reunite the Russian Orthodox Church under his pastoral mantle.

St Tikhon is what exactly what the Russian people, battered by revolution, instability, and bloodshed, needed; they loved him with unparalleled ardor, and recognized his holiness with reverence. The Bolsheviks, recognizing this, named all the Orthodox "Tikhonites."

An American friend visited him a few months after his release, and in a rare publication, wrote the following priceless description of the holy patriarch, which witnesses the vigor which had reanimated him when he was once again able to lead his flock:

> An erect, well-built man in a black robe, grey hair and beard which at first glance make him appear older than his fifty-six years, a firm handclasp, and kindly eyes with a decided trace of humor and ever a hint of fire in the back of them. Those are your first impressions. That, and his beaming smile. The next thing I thought of was how little he had changed in appearance in the two years since I last visited him. He does not look a day older, and his manner, in marked contrast to so many of my friends in Moscow, is just as calm, unhurried and fearless as though he had not passed through two years of terrible uncertainty and stress. He had put on the white silk cowl with its diamond cross and the six-winged angel embroidered above the brow which is the head-dress of the Patriarch on all official occasions, but he had evidently just been sitting down to tea and the arrival of an old friend dispelled any formality. So in a minute the cape and gown had disappeared and we were sitting beside the samovar[91] in his living room ...
>
> It would be difficult to imagine a man better fitted, mentally and temperamentally for the peculiarly difficult task of leading the Orthodox Church through these years of disorder and suffering in Russia. His good-humored friendliness, combined with a kindly firmness have become proverbial in the Russian Church. This is even more true of what Russians call his "accessibility". It is common belief that anyone, be he bishop or priest or the most obscure layman, who has real need of his advice or decision, may get to see the Patriarch ...

But these glimpses of fatherly kindness in the leader of the Russian Church must not be allowed to give a one-sided impression. On account of his good nature a Russian writer has compared him to the first Patriarch of Russia, Job. In view of his proven statesmanship and his fearless insistence upon justice as well as the remarkable skill with which he has held the Church together when everything else in Russia was falling into ruin, it seems to me he more nearly resembles Hermogen, whose influence moved so powerfully in unifying and inspiring Russian spirit to throw off the Polish yoke ...

All those who know Patriarch Tikhon enjoy his well-developed sense of humor. I believe it is this which has helped him retain his poise and cheerfulness through the past three years. He was simple, accessible, loved to joke around, and could embellish even the most ridiculous and tragic situations with humor. In the 1920s he had a sign over his office at Donskoy Monastery stating, "Not available for questions concerning counter-revolution."[92]

I asked him how he had been treated. He told me he had been under "home arrest" for more than a year, had been permitted to go out to conduct service in other churches about once in three months, but aside from this had suffered no personal violence; this in marked contrast to many of the Church's dignitaries who had been sent to jail or even condemned to execution. "They think", the Patriarch smilingly remarked, as he patted my hand confidentially, "Oh, he's an old chap: he'll die soon. .... we won't bother him". "Wait and see", he went on, shaking his finger, schoolmaster-fashion, "I'll show them, yet". And the roguish twinkle in his eyes, remarkably young in contrast to his grey hair, gave you confidence that when the present nightmare has cleared in Russia, her Church's leader will be found ready to take a most active part in the affairs of the new day.[93]

Despite his release, and his quick dispatching of the Living Church, the general chaos, anarchy, and terror which prevailed everywhere in Russia, but particularly in Moscow, did not allow him to openly exercise his patriarchal duties. Additionally, the Bolshevik desire for the annihilation of the church had not subsided, and when their demands were not met, they would threaten the patriarch with the assassination of his bishops and priests. Indeed, many Russian clerics faced the firing squad in those turbulent years, martyred for refusing to cooperate with the anticlerical, secularist objectives of the state. The patriarch himself survived three known assassination attempts. The first, on October 21, occurred while he was celebrating the Divine Liturgy. The assassin mistook Metropolitan Peter Polyanskiy for St Tikhon, and in the confusion, neither was killed. The second attempt on his life occurred less than a month later, on November 9, when his apartment was broken into, and again, the assassins fired at the wrong person. This time, however, the shots did not miss, and the saint's episcopal assistant of more than twenty years was murdered in cold blood. The shock and grief further exacerbated the nephritis from which the saint had been suffering, and which had worsened significantly during his imprisonment. The last attempt came soon after the first two. As the saint was kneeling at his murdered attendant's grave at the New Donskoy cemetery, two bullets whizzed by, which barely missed him.[94]

The constant, unrelenting, torturous psychological pressure finally began to take its toll on the patriarch's health. Seeing the church which Christ had placed in his care being decimated, and hearing the daily reports of the horrors which were taking place across the land he so loved, and to which he had devoted his whole soul, broke his tender and fatherly heart. On January 12, 1925, a physician sent to examine him ordered immediate and complete bed rest, away from work. He was admitted to the Bakunin clinic shortly afterwards, suffering from myocarditis, pyelonephritis, and angina pectoris. Dr Bakunin himself originally refused to admit him, fearing reprisals from the Bolsheviks, who had made it clear they desired the patriarch dead, but the next day, "Citizen Belavin," a seemingly poor, old, sick man of no note, was admitted.

On April 5, St Tikhon celebrated the Divine Liturgy for the last time. On the night of April 7, already in a critical condition, he said, "Now I will fall fast asleep and for long. The night will be long, long, dark, dark … "[95] A little before midnight, he asked what time it was, and when they told him that it was 23:45, he answered "Glory to God!," and proceeded to make the sign of the cross three times, whispering "glory to You, o Lord." He was not able to finish. His hand fell from his forehead, and his lips stopped. His martyric soul flew to God.

The holy patriarch's funeral took place at the Donskoy monastery on April 12, 1925, with fifty-eight bishops presiding. Over a million faithful crowded every street and alley, and tears and cries could be heard from every corner of the town.

The translation of his relics took place on February 19, 1992, at which time the saint was discovered to be incorrupt.

The holy passionbearer tsar Nicholas II and St Tikhon.

Tsar Nicholas II visiting Yaroslavl in 1913, during the period in which St Tikhon (on the right) was archbishop of Yaroslavl. The visit was made during the celebrations of the 300-year anniversary of the Romanov dynasty. Behind the tsar are his daughters, who were murdered along with their whole family on July 4/17, 1918.

Saint John Kochurov of Chicago

THE FIRST HIEROMARTYR OF THE RUSSIAN REVOLUTION

His memory is commemorated on October 31

APOSTOLIC ZEAL

It is October 31, 1917, in Tsarkoye Selo, a suburb of St. Petersburg, and the scene that is about to unfold will compose a new and glorious chapter in the history of the Russian Orthodox Church. This chapter, and countless others that are to shortly follow, will be written with the blood of the numberless new martyrs of Russia who suffered under the modern Babylonian Captivity of the Soviet regime. Amongst the thousands of hieromartyrs who gave their lives for their flocks, St John Kochurov stands as a bright light, whose sacrifice and love touched the lives of thousands of men, women, and children across continents and countries.

St John was born on July 13, 1871, in Bigildino, a small village in the Dankovsky district of the Lipetsk region. His father, Alexander Kochurov, was the priest of the village church, which was dedicated to the blessed Theophany, and also taught Religious Studies at the small elementary school. His mother, Alexandra Nikolaevna, the daughter of a priest herself, had seven children, three girls and four boys. This deep foundation in the faith, and the spiritual heritage of the generations of priests in the family, helped bring forth fruit of genuine and wholehearted devotion to Christ and His Church in the heart of young John. Both his parents, but especially his father, worked tirelessly to instill the love of God into their children. Amongst all his siblings, John stood out for his piety, goodness, and deep trust in God. His soul was fertile ground, and the seeds that were planted in his childhood grew and blossomed into a spiritual strength that would nourish other souls.

After his elementary and secondary education were completed, John decided to attend Dankov Theological School, and later the Ryazan Theological Academy. He was a model student, both academically and spiritually, and after graduating in 1891, he was accepted into the prestigious Saint Petersburg Theological Academy. It was during his time in St. Petersburg that John realized that the calling he felt was not simply that of a parish priest, but that of a missionary. Indeed, this was the true fruition of all his previous studies and endeavors, and within five years, he would be leaving everything he knew behind to bring the Faith to an unknown and faraway land.

After graduating from the Theological Academy on July 26, 1895, John married Alexandra Vasilievna, the daughter of the deacon of the Cathedral of the Virgin Mary of Kazan in St. Petersburg. Only weeks after their wedding, John was ordained a deacon, and a month and a day after his graduation, he was ordained into the priesthood by the bishop of Alaska and the Aleutian Islands, Nicholas (Ziorov). He was assigned to the Holy Lavra of St Alexander Nevsky, but having expressed a desire to serve in America, he was soon appointed the first permanent priest of the parish of the Holy Trinity in Chicago.[1]

IN THE NEW WORLD

Fr John's arrival in America was a difficult transition. The nearly wholly Protestant world of New York, where he first landed, lay in stark contrast with the Orthodox Russia he knew. Not yet having learned the language, Fr John stayed in New York long enough to receive a warm introduction from the local Orthodox community, and to find his footing on this new continent.

At the time, Orthodoxy in America was in its infancy, and other than the communities which had been established a century earlier in Alaska and California, Orthodox parishes in the rest of the United States were often hundreds, if not thousands of miles apart. Orthodox communities were few and far apart, many of them without a church, and most of them dispersed within large areas, with a multinational and multilingual flock. Being full of zeal and desire to serve, Fr John did not allow any obstacle, linguistic, cultural, or spiritual, to deter him from pouring his soul into his new mission. Having received a small taste of the New World, and the brotherly encouragement of his fellow priests in New York, he quickly left for Chicago and settled into his new parish.

At that time, the Orthodox community of St Vladimir in Chicago was affiliated with the church of the Three Hierarchs in Streator, over 100 miles away, and they both shared a priest. Before his arrival, both parishes were served by another great saint, Alexis Toth. As there was no church building

St John with his wife, Alexandra.

at the time, St Alexis served Divine Liturgy in houses on North Noble Street and Armitage Avenue. Both communities were small, poor, and composed primarily of Carpatho-Russian and Galician immigrants, with a smattering of people from other Orthodox European and Asian countries.

Upon his arrival, St John found that his desire to build a church would be more difficult than expected, and that his mission would require all-encompassing pastoral care. His parishioners were, by and large, living in poverty, working as day laborers. They had no way to financially support either the church or him, and in a December 1898 article in the *Russian American Orthodox Messenger*, he wrote:

> The Orthodox parish of Saint Vladimir's Church in Chicago consists of a small number of the original Russians, Galician and Hungarian Slavs, Syrians, and Bulgarians. The majority of the parishioners are working people who earn their bread by toiling not far from where they live, on the outskirts of the city. Affiliated with this parish in Chicago is the Church of the Three Hierarchs in the city of Streator. This place, and the town of Kengley, are situated ninety-four miles from Chicago, and they are famous for their coal mines. The Orthodox parish there consists of the Slovaks who work there who have been converted from the Unia.[2]

The unique ethnic melting pot of the Chicago and Streator communities demanded a masterful blend of pastoral, liturgical, and missionary skills, and Fr John had to develop dexterity and expertise in dealing with varied cultural and sociopolitical backgrounds. He soon excelled not only in tending his extant flock, but also in bringing many more to the faith, and in his first three years in Chicago, five Catholics and eighty-six Uniates were brought into the Orthodox Church. He worked to stabilize and secure the Orthodox community, and founded two Orthodox Mutual Aid Societies in Chicago and Streator, the Brotherhood of Saint Nicholas, and the Brotherhood of the Three Hierarchs. These charitable institutions worked to assist the communities around them, not only spiritually, but also with information, education, food, clothing, and other material necessities. Fr John also established two church schools, with more than twenty students. During the school year they operated once a week, on Saturday, but during the school holidays they would be open every day. His humble but shining example drew not only the Orthodox in the area, but Eastern Europeans and Russians of all denominations.

Though incredibly busy with all these activities, he also obeyed cheerfully when on May 22, 1899, the Ecclesiastical Synod of the Aleutian Islands and Alaska appointed him to the newly formed three-member Editorial Committee of the diocese, which oversaw all Russian, Carpatho-Russian, and English liturgical publications (the other two members being St Raphael of Brooklyn and St Alexis Toth). The newly arrived Bishop Tikhon, who succeeded Bishop Nicholas, also asked him to be the chairman of the Board of the Russian Church's Mutual Aid Society.

One of the greatest problems the Chicago-Streator community faced was the condition of the buildings which they used for liturgical services and parish functions. Saint Vladimir's Church was on the ground floor of a rented house, and shared a wall with the kitchen and living space of another tenant. St John lived on the first floor with his family and the church reader. The situation was not much different in Streator.

On November 30, 1898, Bishop Tikhon, the future patriarch of Moscow, was assigned to the Diocese of the Aleutian Islands and Alaska, a move that greatly impacted the two Chicago parishes under Fr John. Zealously fulfilling his hierarchical obligations, Bishop Tikhon visited nearly all the Orthodox parishes scattered around the vast territory of the Diocese of Alaska and the Aleutians in an effort to discern the most fundamental needs of the diocesan clergy. This was an unprecedented and exhausting trip, but when he arrived in Chicago on April 28, 1899, Bishop Tikhon refused to rest, going out the very next day to inspect the proposed site of the new church. He then traveled the 100 miles to Streator and back, celebrating vigil at St Vladimir's church on April 30. The following morning, after celebrating the Divine Liturgy, he approved the minutes of the meeting of the committee for the construction of the new church in Chicago, which was chaired by Fr John, though the limited financial resources of the Chicago-Streator parish would not allow for construction to begin.

Fr John had now been in North America for over five years, and he felt a strong desire to visit his beloved homeland for at least a brief time. He wanted to be nourished and strengthened by Orthodox Russia, and with new vigor once again to throw himself into the fight. With this in mind, he submitted an application to Bishop Tikhon requesting a short leave. He was granted a blessing to take a sabbatical from January 15 to May 15, 1900, but upon

107

returning to Russia, this faithful shepherd did not forget his American flock, but continued tirelessly campaigning to raise funds for the construction of a church and an Orthodox cemetery in Chicago. At the time, many cemeteries in established cities were set aside for specific religious denominations, and there was no designated place for the reposed Orthodox Christians of the city.

HOLY TRINITY, CHICAGO

Fr John's fundraising efforts, both in Russia and in the United States, yielded fruit, and two years later, on March 31, 1902, Bishop Tikhon came to lay the foundation for the new church. A local newspaper described the service in detail, preserving precious descriptions and particulars:

> Russians Begin a Church.
>
> With ceremonies that were participated in by many visiting churchmen of their faith, 500 Chicago Russians and Syrians yesterday laid the cornerstone of the new Russian Orthodox Church of St. Trinity, which is to be erected at Leavitt Street and Haddou Avenue.[3] The church is to be one of the most pretentious structures of the Russian Orthodox faith in the United States. The cost will be $80,000. Half of this amount will be contributed by the czar of Russia, and much of the remaining 15,000 was subscribed in the fatherland.[4]
>
> The Right Reverend Tikhon, Bishop of Aleutia and North America officiated at the service, he was assisted by archimandrite Anatoly,[5] head of the Russian mission school at Minneapolis, and the Rev. Fr John Kochuroff of the parish of Chicago.
>
> At 9:00 o'clock in the morning, the communicants of the church assembled at the Chapel at 13 South Center Ave. to attend mass celebrated by Bishop Tikhon. At 11:00 o'clock the churchmen formed a line and marched from the Chapel to the site of the new church. Robed in his vestments, Bishop Tikhon read the prescribed service of the Orthodox Church, then walking around the cornerstone and the foundation line of the building he sprinkled holy water and made an appeal for God's blessing on the church and its parishioners.
>
> He read sections from several of the psalms, to which the attendants responded in their own tongue. Then moving away from the cornerstone, the bishop walked to the spot where the altar was to stand and with oil and water he blessed it as he had done the boundaries of the church and parish

Left: 1905. The church of the Holy Trinity. The belfry was still under construction.

Below: 1905. St John giving a sermon inside the church.

house. A wooden cross was set in position where the altar is to be, and this will be left as a symbol that a church is to stand on this site.

The service concluded with a hymn by a sextet from Minneapolis and a prayer for the tsar, the president of the United States, the Synod, and the Bishop of Aleutia and North America ...

On the cornerstone was the following inscription:

In the name of the Father and of the Son and of the Holy Spirit.

This church was founded in honor and memory of Saint Trinity, in the reign of the most pious autocrat Nikolai Alexandrovich, emperor of all the Russias, Theodore Roosevelt being president of the United States of North America, the Right Reverend Tikhon, Bishop of Aleutia and North America. In the year 7410 from the creation of the world.

Fr John had that rarest of pastoral gifts, a practical and serious nature when dealing with complex and demanding finances and accounting. He was able to manage the construction of the new church, overseeing the project to completion in a single year. Twelve months and $50,000[8] later, Bishop Tikhon was once again in Chicago for the consecration of the new church, named for the all-Holy Trinity.

On March 16, 1903, the *Chicago Daily Tribune* wrote:

With the mellow light of many hundred candles reflected from the rich gilt of the sanctuary, with the waving of censers and solemn chanting of choir and congregation, while priests in white tunics offered prayer, the Russian orthodox church, toward which Czar Nicholas contributed, was consecrated yesterday morning.

Bishop Tikhon of San Francisco officiated, assisted by the parish priest - the Rev. John Kochuroff [sp] ...

Features were blessing the church with water, prayer by the bishop in front of the sanctuary, clothing of the bishop in episcopal vestments at the dais near the entrance to the church, censing and anointing the inner walls of the altar and church.

After the benediction long life was proclaimed to the Imperial house of Russia. to the president of the United States, the most holy synod, the Rt. Rev. Mr. Tikhon, the founders and parishioners of the temple, and all the people.

The bishop delivered an address in Russian, and the Rev. Mr. Kochuroff [sp] spoke in English.

The church, erected within the last year at a cost of $45,000, is an example of the Russian-Byzantine architecture, built of stone and concrete. Its interior is not finished. It is the only Russian Orthodox church in the city, and has a congregation of 500.[9]

Two years later, on the tenth year anniversary of Fr John's ordination, Bishop Tikhon reminisced back to the construction of the church, and the years 1903–1904, and addressed him as follows: "The year has been filled with the most vivid of impressions, sometimes agonizing, sometimes good. A year of endlessly fundraising in Russia, a year of sleepless nights, worn-out nerves, and countless woes. And here is the testimonial of your care: a temple made with hands, in the image of a magnificent Russian Orthodox temple, shining with its crosses in Chicago, and the peace and love not made with hands that are springing up in the hearts of your flock!"[10]

SERVICE AND ACKNOWLEDGMENT

On May 6, 1903, with Bishop Tikhon's recommendation, Fr John was awarded the prestigious Order of St. Anna, 3rd Class, for his tireless labors, not only for his parish, but for the whole Orthodox Church in America. Indeed, his prominence only rose, and with that, his already-numerous responsibilities multiplied. In February of 1904, he replaced St Raphael of Brooklyn as head of the Editorial Committee of the Diocese of the Aleutian Islands and Alaska, as St Raphael had been elevated to the episcopacy. The very next year, he participated in the preparatory organizational meetings for the first-ever Pan-American Orthodox Clergy-Laity Conference of the Russian Church in America. These meetings took place in the church of the Archangel Michael in Old Forge, Pennsylvania, under the leadership of the newly consecrated bishop of Brooklyn, St Raphael.

Though the actual date of his ordination had been August 27, the large number of clergy present at the convention wished to honor the anniversary of Fr John's first decade as a priest, and on July 20, 1905, the holy priest was given the gift of a gold pectoral cross.

The speeches which followed offer us a priceless glimpse into the saint's life and ministry in America, highlighting his struggles and sacrifices, as well as his accomplishments and triumphs:

The church of the Holy Trinity in Chicago, 1933.
The church looks the same to this day.

Directly after your study at seminary, having left the motherland, you came to this strange land to expend all your youthful energy, to devote all your strength and inspiration to that sacred concern to which you were attracted in your vocation. A hard legacy was waiting for you: the church in Chicago was located then in an untidy church setting, in a wet, half-ruined building, the parish, with its loosely defined parish membership scattered over the huge city with a heterodox population torn asunder by the wild beasts—all that could fill the soul of a young laborer with great confusion, but you bravely accepted the task of selecting a precious spark from the pile of rubbish to fan the sacred fire into a small group of faithful!

You did not think of yourself: calamities, illnesses, the poor location of your house, with its ramshackle walls, floors, and cracks that let in the elements, with destructive effects on your health, and the health of your family members. . . . Your babies were sick, your wife was unhealthy, and bitter bouts of rheumatism seemed to wish to destroy your confidence, to exhaust your energy. . . .

We greet you, remembering another of your good deeds, the performance of which is plaited as an unfading laurel in the crown of honor of your decade of sacred service: we have in mind here your sacrificial service in the office of Chairman of our beloved Mutual Aid Society, in the office of editor to our enlightening missionary publishing house, and in spreading wide our evangelical efforts—organizing the parishes in Madison, Illinois, and Hartshorne, Oklahoma.

To complete your tribute, let us mention another circumstance, which magnifies the valor of your labor and the grandeur of its results. The remoteness of your parish in Chicago has torn you from your bonds with your colleagues in America, depriving you during these years of the chance to see your brother priests ... You were bereft of that which for the majority of us adorns the missionary service through which we pass.

How touching, and how great a degree of isolation was yours, is witnessed by the fact that you had to baptize your children yourself, because of the absence of the other priests around you ... Let this Holy Cross we present serve you as a sign of our brotherly love, and the image of our Lord's Crucifixion on it permit you to accept the hardships, misfortunes, and sufferings that are so often met with in the life of a missionary priest, and let it encourage you to more and more labors for the glory of the Giver of Exploits and the Chief Shepherd, our Lord Jesus Christ.[11]

Less than a year after this celebration, the Holy Synod granted Fr John one of the most honored priestly orders, acknowledging his immense service and historic contributions to the Diocese of North America and the Aleutians. On May 6, 1906, he was elevated to the position of archpriest.

This marked a new period in the holy missionary's service: having become one of the most respected archpriests of the diocese, Bishop Tikhon who valued him highly involved him more and more deeply in resolving the most pressing issues of diocesan administration. In May 1906, he was appointed dean of all the churches in the Eastern States, and in February 1907, he became one of the most eminent participants of the first North American Orthodox Council, which was being held in Mayfield, PA.

PROFESSOR IN RUSSIA

From 1903 to 1907, the Chicago-Streator parish was transformed into one of the most self-sufficient and flourishing parishes in the Diocese of the Aleutian Islands and Alaska. However, no matter how successful the results of Fr John's service in America may have been, his deep, fervent homesickness for his beloved Russia, which he had only seen once in over a decade, increased. That, as well as the necessity of providing his three older children with an undergraduate education in Russia, compelled him to consider the possibility of continuing his missionary ministry in his native land.

A significant circumstance which led to his finally submitting an application for transfer back to Russia was the insistent request of his elderly and seriously ill father-in-law, a priest in the Diocese of Saint Petersburg. The aged cleric had followed the news of Fr John's endeavors and successes in America, and dreamt of handing over his own treasured parish to a priest like him.

Finally, on May 20, 1907, Fr John's application was approved, and he was granted a release from the Diocese of North America and the Aleutians. The Kochurov family immediately began preparing themselves for the move back to Russia. His beloved father-in-law, however, who had been so instrumental in their return, would not live to see the fulfillment of his dream; the week before their departure, Matushka Alexandra received news from Russia that her father had passed away.

In July 1907, the family was ready, and Fr John finally faced the reality of leaving the Chicago-Streator parish, which was so dear to his heart, and into which he had lovingly and energetically poured twelve years of his life. He set out for an unknown future in his motherland, not knowing where and how his services would be needed. He was, however, determined to leave everything to the Lord, and began this new chapter as he had begun the last one, with complete faith and trust in God.

Fr John's return to Russia marked the commencement of his service in the Diocese of Saint Petersburg, but it was also the beginning of a new spiritual challenge, which called on him to apply the pastoral skills he had earlier acquired in America to the field of theological education.

In August of 1907, the Saint Petersburg Church Consistory assigned him to be the second priest at the cathedral of the Holy Transfiguration in Narva, a town approximately 100 miles southwest of St. Petersburg. Although today Narva is located in the country of Estonia, at the time it was a part of the Russian Empire. Two months later, by order of the chief of the Saint Petersburg Department of Education, he was hired as a teacher of religious studies at both the male and female gymnasia in Narva. Starting on October 20, 1907, and for the next nine years, the education of the youth became the main focus of the saint's service to the Church.

Life in small, provincial Narva, where scarcely half the population was Russian Orthodox, brought back memories of the familiar atmosphere of America, where he had to live and serve in a social environment permeated by strong heterodox influences. However, working as a teacher in two schools where the Russian cultural and Orthodox ethos indisputably dominated, made Fr John feel that he was breathing in a genuine Russian Orthodox life reminiscent of his childhood.

His teaching schedule consisted of sixteen hours a week at the male gymnasium and ten hours at the female one. This required a significant effort, as teaching different classes to students of different ages, different abilities, and different backgrounds requires not only a thorough knowledge of the breadth of the subject, but also the skills to make the knowledge both accessible and interesting to all the student groups. However, just as the twelve years he spent at the Chicago-Streator parish had transformed him from an inexperienced beginner into one of the most authoritative priests in the diocese, so his nine years of teaching made him a most effective and conscientious educator and experienced Orthodox preacher.

After five years of teaching in Narva, Fr John's efforts were rewarded on May 6, 1912, when he was awarded the cross of the Order of Saint Anna, 2nd class. Four years later, his achievements in the field of theological education were also recognized, and he was also awarded the cross of the Order of Saint Vladimir, 4th class.

The worldly honors he was given, deserved and appreciated as they may have been, were nothing in comparison to his joy at being able to have all four of his eldest sons attending the Narva gymnasium, where he had the opportunity to personally teach them the laws of God and truths of the Church, and where they were able to receive their spiritual upbringing under his immediate guidance. This was especially important for him in a time where he saw that many of his compatriots, even within the church, were stepping away from the path of Truth and Tradition.

During this time, Fr John was still officially attached to the Holy Transfiguration Cathedral in Narva. However, his job as a teacher did not allow him to fully participate in the parish life of the church, let alone liturgize on a regular basis. Being a priest, first and foremost, this led to a sadness in Fr John, and a strong desire to fully return to his calling. He expressed this desire to the church authorities, and in November of 1916, the Saint Petersburg Church Consistory transferred him to St Katherine's Cathedral in Tsarskoye Selo. Fr John was assigned to be the second priest there, and he joyously and gratefully took the job, fulfilling his dream of becoming a parish priest in his beloved motherland.

TSARSKOYE SELO

Tsarskoye Selo, literally "Tsar's Village" was a relatively small town, but one with great historic significance. Fewer than fifteen miles from the center of St. Petersburg, it was a remarkable incarnation of a whole epoch in the history of Russian culture, happily combining the qualities of a quiet provincial town with those of the resplendent capital. The last royal family of Russia, the Romanovs, resided at the Alexander Palace in Tsarskoye Selo in the last years before their murder.

St Katherine's Cathedral occupied a special place in Tsarskoye Selo. The largest of all the churches, it served the villagers and townspeople, while the other churches, which were far smaller, primarily served the imperial court and the military bases.

In becoming a member of the Tsarskoye Selo clergy, Fr John was unknowingly moving to the center of history. He and his wife and five children (the oldest son, Vladimir, was at the time fulfilling his military service) were warmly and respectfully received by the flock of Saint Katherine's, and from

Detail from a group picture taken at an unknown hospital.
The little girl may be the saint's daughter.

the first months of his ministry there, Fr John showed himself a zealous and inspiring liturgizer, and an eloquent and well-informed preacher. Orthodox Christians from all over the town, as well as the surrounding region and countryside, would flock to the Cathedral to hear him preach.

It seemed that so successful a beginning of parish service would open a new and peaceful chapter in Fr John's life. However, history intervened, and the chapter that had opened with so much promise and joy would close with bloodshed and a martyric death.

The cataclysm of the February Revolution exploded in Petrograd just three months after Fr John's move, and as Tsarskoye Selo was a primary imperial residence, it was immediately drawn into the treacherous vortex of the unrest. Riots had already taken place in the military headquarters of the town during the first days of the Revolution, and in March, the royal family was imprisoned at the Alexandrovsky palace. This home confinement lasted for months, and every day brought the town closer to the attention of the most extremist revolutionary elements, the very elements which had propelled the country toward civil war and the eventual complete collapse of the Russian political, religious, and social structure. These developments gradually poisoned the formerly quiet atmosphere of Tsarskoye Selo, and changed the daily lives of the townspeople from peaceful routine to fear-filled anarchy. Most residents attempted, in any way they could, to avoid provoking the deadly rage of the incendiaries.

During all these troubled months, Fr John continued to preach hope and love from the ambo of Saint Katherine's, as he strove with every fiber of his wounded heart to reignite feelings of peace and reconciliation into the souls of his flock. Full of zeal, and inspired by the Holy Spirit, he repeatedly called on his parishioners to pray, to turn away from the clamor and politics, and to examine their own spiritual life, constantly reminding them that repentance and turning back to God would be the only hope for their suffering country, which stood on the brink of utter destruction.

PROTOMARTYR

In October of 1917, the Bolsheviks seized power in St. Petersburg, taking over the city. The reverberations were quickly felt in Tsarskoye Selo, when armed groups and naval detachments of the Red Guard began marching toward the town to attack a division of Cossack troops stationed there who were still loyal to the Tsar. On the morning of October 30, 1917, the Bolshevik forces began to shell the town with artillery fire. The residents of Tsarskoye Selo, like most of all Russia at the time, did not know the extent of the Revolutionaries' progress, or that their country was now involved in a civil war, and so when the horrific sounds were followed by the fire of weaponry raining down on them, many people ran to the nearest churches, including Saint Katherine's, in hopes of finding solace and consolation in prayer. The clergy of the cathedral proved equal to the dreadful task which now faced them, and in a church flooded with worshipers, they offered a special Moleben[12] seeking an end to the civil conflict. Afterwards, the dean of the cathedral and his two brother priests, including Fr John, decided to organize a procession through the town, praying for the cessation of the fratricidal battle.

The pages of the newspaper *All-Russian Church Social Messenger* published the testimony of a certain newspaper correspondent who was at the scene, describing the litany as follows:

> The Sacred Procession had to be relocated under the conditions of an artillery bombardment, and notwithstanding any predictions it was rather crowded. The lamentations and cries of women and children drowned out the words of the peace prayer. Two priests delivered sermons during the procession, calling the people to preserve tranquility in view of the impending trials. I was fortunate enough to understand clearly that the priests' sermons did not contain any political tinges.[13]

The procession continued as twilight turned into darkness. The congregation began to light candles, passing the flickering flame to one another as they chanted. It was precisely at that time that the Cossack garrison was seen withdrawing from the town. The citizens were now completely defenseless against the violent Bolshevik army waiting to attack.

On the morning of October 31, the Bolshevik forces entered Tsarskoye Selo, encountering no opposition. The day which was dawning was to prove the last in the earthly life of St John, and the first of his sacrificial glorification, in which his name was forever sealed in the history of the Russian Church as the first martyr of the Communist Revolution.

The brutality and carnage which ensued revealed the atheist and antitheist character of the Bolsheviks, and was documented by both residents and journalists following the events, but perhaps most tragically, Fr John's oldest son, who was present at his father's harrowing last moments.

One of the witnesses to these deadly events wrote a letter the day after, narrating, in simple but profound words, the last, painful moments in Fr John's earthly journey.

> Yesterday, when the Bolsheviks, together with the Red Guard, entered Tsarskoye Selo, they began to make the rounds of the apartments of the military officers, making arrests. Fr. John (Alexandrovich Kochurov) was conveyed to the outskirts of the town, to Saint Theodore's Cathedral, and there they assassinated him because of the fact that those who organized the sacred procession had allegedly been praying for a victory by the Cossacks, which surely was not, and could not have been, what actually happened. The other clergymen were released yesterday evening. Thus, there has appeared another Martyr for the Faith in Christ. The deceased, though he had not been in Tsarskoye Selo for long, had gained the utmost love of all, and many people used to gather to listen to his preaching.[14]

A journalist from St. Petersburg, who had also been present, published a more detailed account of that horrific day, and the atrocity and savagery he encountered as he followed the soldiers.

> The priests were captured and sent to the headquarters of the Council of the Working and Soldiers Deputies. A priest, Fr. John Kochurov, was trying to protest and to clarify the situation. He was hit several times on his face. With cheers and yelling the enraged mob conveyed him to the Tsarskoye Selo airdrome. Several rifles were raised against the defenseless pastor. A shot thundered out, then another, after which the priest fell down on the ground, and blood spilled upon his cassock. Death did not come to him immediately … He was pulled by his hair, and somebody suggested, "Finish him off like a dog." The next morning the body was brought into the former palace hospital. According to the newspaper "The Peoples' Affair", the head of the State Duma, together with one of its members, saw the body of the priest, but the pectoral cross was already gone from his breast … [15]

This cross, a gift from a loving brotherhood in faraway America, was meant to be a legacy of his service, and an heirloom and relic for his children and grandchildren. Years earlier, across oceans and continents, he had venerated it in front of his fellow priests, uttering the following words: "I kiss this Holy

Cross, a gift of your brotherly love for me. Let it be my support in times of tribulation. I will utter no pathetic comments about my intention not to be separated from it even till my grave: that would have a grandiloquent sound, but would not be prudent. It does not have any place in a grave. Let it remain here on earth for my children and posterity as a family Holy Relic, and as a clear proof that brotherhood and friendship are the most sacred things on the earth ..." [16]

The cross, indeed, did not join him in the grave. It was ripped from his neck by the greed of the bloodthirsty barbarians and never seen again. The legacy that was left for his family, however, transcended any material object, it was an inheritance of martyrdom, a bequest of sainthood, and an endowment of sanctity.

He was buried in the crypt of the Cathedral of St Katherine, where he had so faithfully and devotedly served in the last months of his temporal sojourn.

The diocesan council of St. Petersburg quickly published an encyclical regarding the events. This became the first official recognition of Fr John's martyric death for the faith.

> Dear brothers,
>
> On October 31 of this year the town of Tsarskoye Selo suffered the martyrdom of one of the good shepherds of the Petrograd diocese, the Archpriest of the local Cathedral, John Alexandrovich Kochurov.
>
> Without any blame or justification for this on his part, he was seized in his apartment, conveyed to the suburbs, and was there, in an open field, shot by the possessed mob ...
>
> It was with feelings of profound sorrow that the Petrograd diocesan council received this news; the grief has been considerably augmented by the realization that, with the Archpriest's demise, a large family is left behind, consisting of six members who now are without food, shelter, or any means of subsistence ...
>
> God is the Judge of the cunning villains who violently ended a life that was still young. Even if they flee unpunished from trial at the hands of men, they can never evade the judgment of God. But our obligation now is not only to pray for the soul of this innocent sufferer, but with all our sincere love to attempt to treat the deep and incurable wound that has been inflicted on the very hearts of his poor, bereaved family. The diocese and the diocesan clergy are directly obligated to provide for the martyred

pastor's orphaned family, to give them the opportunity to live in basic material comfort, and to provide the children with a proper education ...

The diocesan Church council, being moved by the loftiest of sentiments, now appeals to the clergy, parish councils, and all the Orthodox faithful of the Diocese of Petrograd with an ardent entreaty, asking most earnestly, for the sake of Christ's love, that you stretch forth a brotherly helping hand, and by whatever amount you can offer, support a poor family which has been left at the mercy of fate. Great is the need, and it should not be delayed! ...

His martyrdom is, for each of us, a dire reminder, an ominous warning. We therefore must be ready for anything. And to prevent the situations of destitution we now see, we must prepare, between the times of trial, an assistance fund to be allotted for the defenseless, persecuted, and tormented clergy, so that in such cases and in similar ones they may have material aid from their kindred in spirit ...

The dean's special lists will be sent to each parish in the diocese for the collection of donations, both from the parish and from Church funds, to help the family of the deceased Archpriest John Kochurov, and also to establish a special fund for assisting clergy and their families in similar cases ...

An immense task requires means commensurate with it. The diocesan Church council hopes that with God's help such means will be found. The modest offering of the diocese and clergy, made voluntarily and laid on the Christian conscience of each person, will provide an opportunity to dry the tears of the unhappy orphans, and to make a beginning of that sacred brotherly assistance, for which our clergy have a great need, particularly now ...

It has thundered; now is the time to make the sign of the Cross![17]

A few weeks later, on November 26, Metropolitan Benjamin served the Divine Liturgy for the feast of St Katherine's at the Cathedral in Tsarskoye Selo. The Liturgy ended with a fervent exhortation, during which the metropolitan, a future hieromartyr himself, appealed to the people for unity, love, and brotherhood during the troubled times in which they were living.

Speaking in regard to the assassination of their beloved priest, he noted that though sorrow is appropriate, it is more appropriate to follow St John's

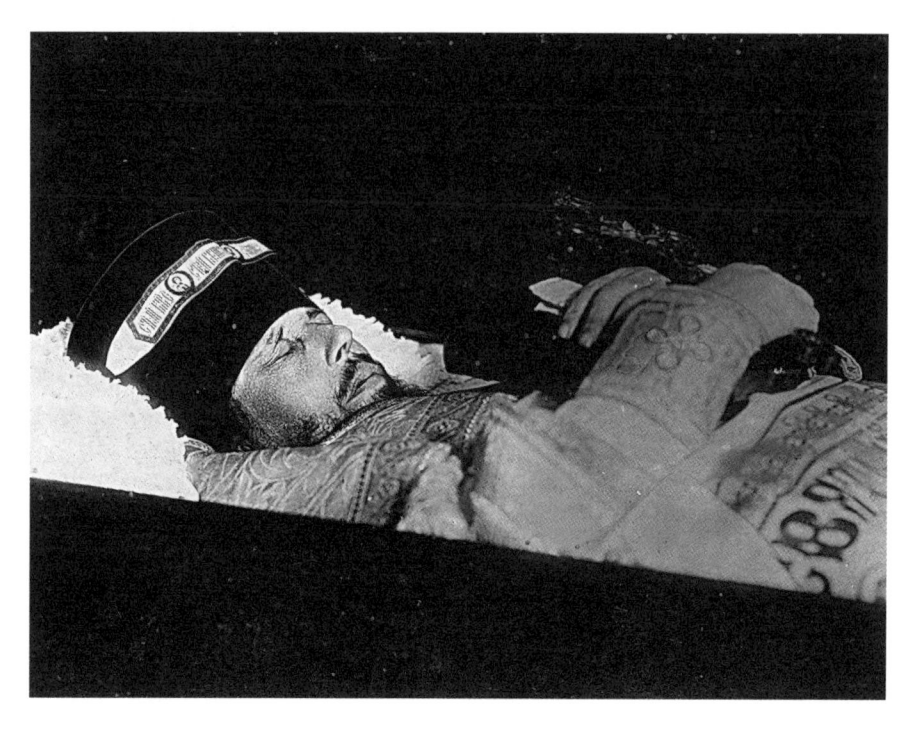

St John, after falling asleep in the lord. Photo from his funeral service.

example, to love God and our neighbor, to fight for peace and reconciliation, and to be prepared to courageously lay down our lives for Christ.

The sermon had a strong effect on everyone, and tears flowed freely on hundreds of faces. Following the Liturgy, the metropolitan led the congregation to St John's tomb in the cathedral crypt, where they chanted the memorial service. After the service, the metropolitan visited the rectory, where he met with the saint's family.

The All-Russian Local Council, which was taking place in Moscow at the time, was where most bishops and archbishops received the news of Fr John's death. Shocked, horrified, and saddened, the members encouraged the council president, Patriarch Tikhon, to compose their letter of condolence to the saint's family. The patriarch knew Fr John very well, and had come to respect and love him during the many years they had worked together in the Diocese of North America and the Aleutians. Expressing the council's genuine conviction that the Orthodox Church had just gained a new saint in the martyred priest, the patriarch dispatched an epistle of sympathy to Alexandra Kochurovna, the slain priest's widow:

It is with great sadness that the Most Holy Council of the Russian Orthodox Church has received a report concerning the martyrdom of Father John Alexandrovich Kochurov, who has fallen victim while zealously fulfilling the obligations of his rank. Joining our prayers with those of the Holy Council for the repose of the soul of the slain Archpriest John, we share your great grief, and we do that with a special love, because we knew well the deceased Archpriest, and have always held his inspiring and strong clerical activity in high estimation.

We bear in our hearts the sure hope that the deceased pastor, adorned with the wreath of martyrdom, now stands at the Throne of God among the elect of Christ's true flock. The holy Council, with earnest sympathy for your bereaved family, has decided to petition the Holy Synod to give you the proper assistance.

May the Lord help you to endure the trial sent to you by the ways of God's Providence, and preserve you and your children unharmed amid the storms and calamities of our time.

We invoke God's blessing on you and on your family.

—Patriarch Tikhon [18]

Saint Alexander Hotovitzky of New York
MISSIONARY AND HIEROMARTYR

His memory is commemorated on December 4

DESTINED TO PREACH TO THE NATIONS

The holy new martyr Alexander was born on February 11, 1872, in the historically vibrant town of Kremenets, in the Ternopil Oblast.[1] The city, once part of Kievan Rus, and today part of Ukraine, had been annexed by the Russian Empire less than 100 years before the saint's birth, and contained strong Cossack, Polish, Hungarian, Lithuanian, and Jewish elements. Alexander was born into the pious family of Archpriest Alexander Hotovitzky, Dean of the Volhynia[2] Theological Seminary. His father was beloved by both his students and his flock, and would be remembered for decades to come as a good shepherd to the Orthodox inhabitants of Volhynia. Alexander received a good Christian upbringing from his parents, who instilled a love for the Orthodox Church and for the people of God in their young son. He was educated at the Volhynia Seminary and the Saint Petersburg Theological Academy, from which he received a Master's degree in 1895.

During his time in St. Petersburg, Alexander met and became a spiritual son of Bishop Nicholas (Ziorov) of the Aleutian Islands and North America, who was visiting Russia at the time. The young student was taken by the bishop's piety and holiness, as well as his stories of the missionary heroes serving in the spiritual wilderness of the New World. It was during this time that he began considering a life of mission, rather than a more comfortable and stable one as a parish priest in his homeland.

After graduation, Alexander was sent to serve abroad, in the Diocese of the Aleutians and North America, where he was tonsured as a second reader for the newly established St Nicholas Orthodox Church at 323 2nd Avenue in New York City. The church was little more than a modified house, which ill-suited the liturgical needs of the faithful, but for the time being, it was the best the community could offer.

To make matters more difficult, one year later the parish priest decided to return to Russia permanently. Seeing the vacancy, Bishop Nicholas decided that it was time to ordain the young reader. This house church, now so meager and humble, would one day—once the Russian Episcopal See moved from San Francisco to New York—become the Russian Cathedral of the Americas. This was the destiny which Providence had ordained for the young man, and the goal for which God had prepared him from his earliest years.

In January of 1896, Alexander was on a brief visit to St. Petersburg, during which he married Maria Scherbuhina, a graduate of the Pavlovsk Institute in Saint Petersburg. A month later, upon the couple's return to New York, the young reader was ordained to the diaconate, and on February 25, 1896, Bishop Nicholas, whom he would always remember with gratitude and love, elevated him to the priesthood. He was just twenty-four years old. His ordination took place at the Diocesan Cathedral in San Francisco, and in his address to the newly ordained priest, Bishop Nicholas spoke these words:

> Your special sense of decency, your good upbringing, your noble idealism, and your sincere piety immediately caused me to look favorably upon you and compelled me to single you out among the young people, with whom you used to visit me in Saint Petersburg ... I could see that you had that special spark from God, which makes any service an action truly done for God's sake, and without which a vocation becomes soul-less and dead work ... Your first experience in preaching has shown you the power of this kind of inspiration: you saw how the people gathered around you and how attentively they stood and listened at length to your discourses ... Why did these people listen to you rather than going to hear other preachers? Clearly the spark which burns within you attracts the hearts of these people like a magnet.[3]

THE WORK

A week after his ordination, the young priest returned to New York to assume his pastoral duties at the parish where he had previously served as reader. His position was a challenging one, as he was required to provide not only spiritual guidance, but also legal, cultural, and political expertise, as the congregation was largely made up of immigrants, who were not familiar with

St Alexander at a young age.

the American justice system, or the way America operated, culturally. As a fluent English speaker, he personally managed many of the everyday issues his parishioners had to deal with, helping them through complex and difficult processes.

However, this was only one of the many tasks he set for himself. In that same year, he spearheaded the publication of the official Diocesan magazine, the *Russian American Orthodox Messenger*,[4] a priceless contribution to the witness of the truth of Orthodoxy on the North American continent. The periodical was published in both English and Russian, and Fr Alexander served as editor and frequent author. Being fluent in English, and passionate about bringing the message of the faith to heterodox America, he often published English-language catechetical and expository articles for those interested in Orthodoxy.

Fr Alexander also took it upon himself to replace the small parish church in which he served with something that would better suit the sacramental needs of the flock. In 1899, the Russian Orthodox community in New York numbered 300 people, and the converted house was insufficient for the liturgical life of such a vast number. Under his leadership, what began as a simple sanctuary was soon the architecturally remarkable and majestic St Nicholas Cathedral in New York. The building was to become an adornment of the city. After receiving the blessing from his bishop, St Alexander visited Orthodox communities throughout America soliciting funds for the construction of the Cathedral, and he asked for donations in writing, both in letters and articles, stating that in the largest city in the world, where every religion and denomination had a temple or house of prayer, there was a need for an Orthodox church, both for the liturgical needs of the Orthodox faithful, and as a witness of the truth and beauty of the faith to the heterodox. It had to be architecturally Orthodox, so that its very appearance would be a visible reminder of God's presence and its Orthodox identity. In 1901, he also traveled to Russia for this purpose, meeting with St John of Kronstandt, who blessed him and his endeavors. Hierarchs, rich Slavs, and even the Tsar donated various amounts, Nicholas II giving 5,000 rubles.[5] However, the work was not easy, and in letters to his bishop, St Tikhon, who had replaced Bishop Nicholas the previous year, Fr Alexander spoke of the difficulties he faced, primarily due to the large-scale corruption in all levels of Russian bureaucracy. Finally, the ceaseless exertion took its toll, and the hard-working missionary fell ill, needing to request a leave of rest until his health was sufficiently restored to allow him to return to America.

This was not his last trip to Russia; many more journeys were needed to gather the amount necessary for the construction. However, the visionary saint did not focus solely on the narrow scope of his own church, or even his own city, but aimed to inform the Russian people and Church hierarchy about the all the vital and extraordinary work that was being done throughout the length and breadth of the New World. He solicited funds not only for his own project, but for many other churches throughout the American continent which desperately needed help, including the Syro-Arab church of St Nicholas in Brooklyn.

His unremitting and tireless efforts yielded fruit, and on May 6, 1901, the day of the Tsar's birthday, the cornerstone was laid for the foundation of the church. A silver commemoration plaque was laid upon the foundation, and Fr Alexander exclaimed "Long Live the Tsar of Russia and the President of the United States."[6] The church, which is still open today, is located on 15 East 97th Street in Manhattan.

The small but beautiful church, replete with Russian architectural elements, with seven domes and a red brick façade, was completed in the fall of 1902. It could hold 950 people, and contained classrooms, a community hall, offices, a printing press, a kitchen, and dining areas. It owed its existence exclusively to Fr Alexander, who collected the funds, chose the location, bought the land, hired the architects, led them in the correct drawing up of the plans, and spearheaded the work at every step. In the annals of St Nicholas Church, which in 1903 became the Diocesan Cathedral, it is recorded that "This Cathedral was established and constructed in the City of New York in North America, under the supervision and through the efforts and labors of the most honorable Archpriest Father Alexander Hotovitzky in the year of Our Lord 1902."[7]

On November 10/23, 1902, the church was consecrated. A journalist from the *New York Times* who was present at the celebration wrote:

> With all the pomp of its rites, the magnificence of the vestments of its clergy, in the presence of the members of the Russian Embassy, and before a crowd of worshipers that occupied nearly every inch of standing room, the new Russian Orthodox Church of St. Nicholas was consecrated yesterday morning. The edifice at 15 East Ninety-seventh Street was decorated at the

entrance with the red, white, and blue of the American flag and the white, blue, and red of Russia.

Delegations of Russian societies marched into the church carrying their national flag, the colors of their adopted country, and a religious banner bearing pictures of the Saviour, the Virgin Mary, and Saints ... There were lavish decorations of palms and chrysanthemums. On either side or the doors ... are pictures of the Madonna and the Saviour ... Two golden crosses and insignia yesterday for the first time flashed in the sunlight, which came pouring in through the stained glass windows of blue and yellow. Hundreds of candles about the altar added their light and many of the congregation carried other candles, which they burned during the service, which lasted for three hours and fifteen minutes.[8]

In 1903, St Nicholas church became a cathedral, when St Tikhon—then Metropolitan of the Aleutian Islands and North America—transferred the episcopal seat from San Francisco to New York. Fr Alexander's church now became the official cathedra of the diocese, and as the parish priest, he became a member of the diocesan board. The next year, he wrote the following letter in the New Year edition of the *Russian-American Orthodox Messenger*:

Happy New Year

Pitiful is the man, who remains unmoved by the mysterious moment of the birth of a new year. To go to bed and to sleep on the thirty first of December feeling no difference in one's usual mood, and to rise from the bed next morning, the first day of a new year, still feeling as usual! To sleep a dreamless sleep, to get up without dreams, with which a man's soul longs to dilute occasionally the tediousness of his everyday life ... Such people must be wooden indeed!

Yet they exist. They pass through the boundaries of time, appointed by the Supreme Power, indifferently, as indifferent as the needle of a watch. Mechanically it approaches the dividing line of midnight, calmly it goes ahead into the future without giving a thought to the past. These people do likewise.

"Where is the change that occurred?" they will say. "Everything is exactly as it was, the flow of life is the same, and the order of hours is also the same."

Yet there are many people who would feel themselves extremely unhappy, if the monotony of their existence was not allowed to be varied by the boundary of a new year.

Some people may maintain, that there is no sense in being moved by the mental contemplation of the newly begun period of life, other people may laugh at this feeling of mine—yet my soul has tasted the familiar emotion, dear to me from my childhood, and I approach the invisible boundary of the new period, with a natural awe, an awe which does not mean fear of the future alone, but hope also and faith in the future.

This tremulous feeling of hope is the foundation of our noblest aspirations. A man feels renewed, almost regenerated. New forces seem to have entered our organism, and the heart feels alert with a ray of new courage. And one feels afraid that one might import into this atmosphere of renovation the suffocating closeness of bad habits, formed in past years. It is as if someone has put a stream of new paint, which pleases our eye, on the gray background soiled by use—and so we feel reluctant to destroy all this newness, to have it soiled and mouldy again.

This is how it should be. The New Year's greeting we hear from our friends ought not to be an empty sound for us, it ought to find a response in our hearts, our wills, in the whole of our beings.

Involuntary our thought dictates to us the program of our work for the new year. We long to reach "happiness", in the great and the holy sense of the word, which is in harmony with the church of Christ. And our soul, trusting in the grace of the Lord, feels within itself the promise of a good and a blameless life.

It is by the innate interpretation of the boundaries of time, that can be explained the universal new year custom of forming good intentions and resolutions. These good intentions have been suggested to us long ago in the words of the God-Man himself. Waiting for the first moments of the New Year, open the pages of the Sermon on the Mount.

Being humble, gentle, truthful, being kind and making peace, accepting suffering for Christ's sake,—all these are as many suggestions for our achievement, for the perfectioning of our wills, for the carrying of the light into the kingdom of vanity, passion, falsehood, pride, greed and cruelty, for the building up of supreme and indestructible happiness.

And the more fervent in our devotion to the commandments of Christ, as compared to what we were capable of a year ago, the happier shall we be in the coming year, the more happiness shall we be able to give to our neighbors.

So let the Lord move us to a good life and good achievements not only until the evening decline of the coming "new year," but of the whole of our earthly life as well.

A happy New Year to you, friend readers!

A.H.[9]

From 1898 to 1907, Fr Alexander served under the omophorion of Bishop Tikhon. St Tikhon, who in the tragic year of 1917 was to be elevated to the Russian see as patriarch of Moscow, valued his priest's sincere piety, charismatic personality, pastoral love, and multifaceted theological erudition, and so assigned him many different tasks, which required extensive travel throughout the United States and Canada. The spectrum of Fr Alexander's ministry was quite broad and very fruitful. He was particularly successful in missionary service, primarily amongst the Uniates who had recently emigrated from Central and Eastern Europe. The work of St Alexis Toth, who had brought back hundreds of thousands of Uniates to the true faith, was inimitable, but Fr Alexander poured himself into the sacred task with the same zeal and passion. There was a great need for shepherds who would take the large flocks which were now reunited to the Church and guide them through the initial stages of the process until they were established and safe. Fr Alexander was one of those shepherds. Through his efforts, Orthodox parishes were established in Philadelphia, Yonkers, and Passaic as well as other large and small towns throughout North America.

In addition to these responsibilities, he also actively participated in the establishment of the Russian Orthodox Church Mutual Aid Society (ROCMAS), which provided material aid to Austrian Carpatho-Russians, Macedonian Slavs, Russian troops in Manchuria, and Russian prisoners-of-war in Japanese internment camps. He served as treasurer, first secretary, and president of the society at various times through the years, and he took special care to send crosses, prayer books, and other liturgical and spiritual objects for both the soldiers and the prisoners of the 1905 Russo-Japanese conflict. As if all that were not enough, in 1903 he also began a tenure as diocesan treasurer.

He closely collaborated with other Orthodox priests in America in representing the Orthodox Church in American religious institutions and meetings, and he authored a stream of articles, as well as serving at official

135

dialogues between the Episcopalian and Orthodox Churches. He served on the committees to raise funds for Orthodox liturgical and spiritual publications in the English language, and in 1908 became the head of the Office of Russian Émigrés to New York and the Association of Russian Migrants of America. His multifaceted missionary work would bring many to the light of the Orthodox faith.

CANADA

US president Theodore Roosevelt was a significant catalyst for the end of hostilities in the Russo-Japanese war.[10] Fr Alexander was present as a member of the Russian clerical delegation at the ceasefire and peace negotiations which took place in Portsmouth, New Hampshire. After the negotiations were over and the peace agreement signed, the saint presided over a celebratory service giving thanks for the peace. Members of the St Nicholas Cathedral choir chanted.

It is widely accepted that St Alexis Toth wrote the first chapters in the history of Orthodoxy in Minnesota. In the same way, St Alexander wrote the first chapters of the history of Orthodoxy in New York. But not just New York. In 1906, Patriarch Tikhon received a letter from some Russian émigrés living in Montreal, Quebec, asking him to please send someone to lead them and organize their liturgical and spiritual life. The patriarch sent Fr Alexander, asking him to stay through Great Lent, and do whatever he could to help the Orthodox faithful. Fr Alexander did, indeed, travel to Canada, and celebrated the very first Slavonic-language Divine Liturgy at the Syro-Arabic church of St. Nicholas, which St Raphael of Brooklyn had established some years earlier. He founded the Russian Orthodox Brotherhood to care for the needs of the Russians in the area, and upon his return to New York arranged for the transfer of the first permanent priest in Montreal, at the Russian parish of Sts Peter and Paul.

While he was in Canada, he received a letter from Bishop Tikhon asking him to visit the cities of Halifax and Sydney in Nova Scotia and meet with Orthodox Christians there about the possible establishment of a Russian community or communities in the Maritimes. Halifax was the major port of entry for immigrants to Canada, and the steel mills of Sydney employed large numbers of migrant workers, so there were large numbers of Orthodox believers in those areas.

On February 26, 1906, the tireless missionary celebrated the tenth anniversary of his priesthood. Bishop Tikhon addressed him with these inspired and celebratory words:

> As you remember your ordination as a priest of God at this anniversary, you are doubtless unwillingly contemplating how you have used your God-given talents, and asking yourself if the Grace of God was bestowed on you in vain and how far you have advanced on the path of moral perfection. As you judge yourself in this way, you are at the same time the judge and the accused. In order for a judgment to be fair, the testimony of onlookers, the witnesses, must be heard. Now they are speaking before you—listen to them. Thanks be to the Lord! We just heard their eloquent and heartfelt testimony praising you. For myself as your superior, I can testify that you have proven to be trustworthy, and have justified the expectations which were hoped for at your ordination.[11]

Both the Russian Church and the Orthodox in America honored, loved, and admired Fr Alexander. His reputation grew both in North America and abroad. The Tsar himself showered him with distinctions and accolades. The archpriest's character, humble, and full of love for both God's Word and His people, increased in renown through the years, and his sphere of influence and activity only grew. On February 29, 1914, he was invited to the White House to meet with President Woodrow Wilson. He was met by the president, his family, the Russian Consul, and many other politicians and staff. Fr Alexander spoke a few words, in fluent English, and gave the president a gift, *The Service Book of the Holy Orthodox, Catholic, Apostolic (Greco-Russian) Church*, by Isabel Hapwood. Before departing, he invited the president and the other individuals present to attend a service at the Cathedral and enjoy the wonder of Orthodox hymnody.

Fr Alexander's dedicated service in America ended on February 26, 1914, exactly eighteen years after his ordination to the priesthood. The Holy Synod in Russia assigned him a new, and equally challenging, task, this time in Finland, where the archbishop had requested his help.

In his farewell address, the priest took leave of his flock with the following words: "Farewell, American Orthodox Rus—my dear Mother, the Holy American Church. I, your ever-grateful son, bow fully to the ground before you. You gave birth to me spiritually, you nurtured me, from your depths you inspired me by your strength. Through the shining witness of your founders, through the enlightened apostolic teachings of your preachers, through the fervor of your faithful flock, you have given me the greatest possible joy—to be your son."[12]

Fr Alexander's North American mission had been rife with difficulties and sorrows, and during his farewell liturgy, Metropolitan Platon (Rozhdestvensky) shared one of the many instances of the faithful priest's sacrifices for the Church.

> One morning, during the years we worked together, you came to my room and, without saying much, unbuttoned your shirt, revealing a very large, bluish, bloody abrasion on your chest. That wound from a fanatic, who in a fit of rage attacked you wildly with a stick, followed the meeting of Russian people at which you had encouraged your own ethnic brother to renounce the pernicious Unia with Rome … My entire being was shaken to the core and I was profoundly moved, for before me at that moment was a genuine example of witness for Christ.[13]

His parishioners were no less heartbroken at the loss of their beloved pastor, and bade him farewell with the following words:

> With the very pain that one can imagine that a person would experience in the separation from him not only of body parts but also of soul, the whole of Russian Orthodox America is forever saying goodbye to you … Will the Russian American Orthodox ever forget you, the most glorious of her pastors? No! Never! You will live forever in the history of Russian America, in the grateful hearts of faithful sons, in your great labours in participating in the creation of the American Orthodox Church, which, we believe, at the Last Judgement will intercede for you with the Righteous Judge: may He adorn the glorious head of her beloved son with an imperishable crown.[14]

FINLAND

From 1914 to 1917, Fr Alexander served as a priest in the city of Helsinki, where the majority of the population was Protestant, primarily Lutheran. Fr Alexander's assignment there was not by chance. Although Finland (then the Grand Duchy of Finland) was at that time part of the Russian Empire, the Orthodox clergy there had to exert great efforts to protect the Orthodox from the proselytic expansionism of the Finnish Lutherans. The Lutherans based their efforts on nationalism, and the ethnic sentiment which prevailed at the time, as Finland was in the middle of a divisive and all-encompassing battle for independence from the Russian Crown. Using the opportunity that the events presented, Lutheran missionaries claimed that Orthodox priests were there as agents of the Russian state, sent to work for the political powers of Russia, and hostile to Finnish independence, and as such, must be shunned as enemies of freedom and subversive advocates for Finnish subjugation.

Fr Alexander was well-versed in dealing with hostile religious factions, and his long and valuable experience in America made him an effective advocate for Orthodoxy in the new country. Having learned of his success with the reintegration of Uniates within Orthodoxy, Sergius (Stragorodsky), Archbishop of Finland and future patriarch, assigned him to the Uspensky Cathedral of the Dormition of the Virgin Mary, and made him overseer for all the Orthodox churches in the Helsinki.

Just as he had in America, the future saint poured his heart and soul into his new mission in Finland, starting an Orthodox periodical, and composing many of its articles, dealing with religious issues and clarification of the Orthodox faith. In his three years there, the magazine published nineteen issues.

Just as he was settling in, however, the Russian Revolution sparked a flame which would turn into a holocaust. The February 1917 coup ignited what would be the worst crisis the Church of Russia had faced in three centuries, and the Mother Church needed as much of its talent as it could gather back home. All true men of God, spiritual luminaries, and respected clergy were needed in Moscow, and Fr Alexander was immediately recalled home.

RUSSIA

In August of 1917 Fr Alexander was permanently transferred to Moscow, and assigned as assistant priest at the magnificent and splendid Cathedral of Christ the Saviour. Here he was once again under the direct guidance of St Tikhon, with whom he had already been closely associated in America. The patriarch was glad to have him by his side during the difficult time he faced, and relied on the archpriest's delicate grace and diplomatic skills.

Fr Alexander participated in the deliberations of the All-Russian Local Council of 1917–1918, which began the same month he arrived from Finland. The Council took place at Christ the Saviour Cathedral, and began with a celebratory Divine Liturgy at the Cathedral of the Dormition in the Kremlin on August 15/28, its feastday.

When the synod began, Fr Alexander was one of the first to recommend reestablishing the Russian Patriarchate, nominating St Tikhon for patriarch. Later, when St Tikhon was elected, Fr Alexander and six others signed as official witnesses to the election.

When the Sobor began discussing the drafting of a message to the Orthodox flock concerning elections to the State Council, he stated that, as the fate of Russia was at stake, the Church, and especially the Synod, should not shy away from the struggle to save the nation. The faithful should be educated on the issues, and they should be encouraged to vote.

In a speech regarding the Sobor's efforts to restructure and reorganize the Russian Church, he outlined his preliminary plans for order and healing in the internal life of the Church. Seeing that certain members of the synod were passive and indecisive in their resolutions, he stated with some bitterness, "It seems as if there were builders who were furiously preparing blueprints, plans and so forth for the construction of an edifice and at the same time were calmly observing the destruction brick-by-brick of this edifice by enemies."[15]

In October of 1918 the Bolshevik Revolution succeeded in upending the Russian world, and establishing a new atheist, communist regime. The bloody Civil War soon followed, which would soon see millions dead, and the entire machine of state come to a complete halt. During those difficult years, Fr Alexander collaborated closely with St Tikhon in the administration of the Moscow diocese. Any ecclesiastical or pastoral work at that time was accompanied by much grief and danger, and like most of the active clergy and monastics of the era, he was subjected to interrogation and imprisonment. In May 1920 and November 1921 Fr Alexander was arrested and jailed for brief periods. He was repeatedly interrogated, accused of violating the decrees concerning the separation of the Church from the state, and the school from the Church, by holding church school for the children. Tragically, this was only a small foretaste of what was to come.

The Bolshevik Revolution did not only have political repercussions, but it also led to an economic disaster. The loss of over 5 million lives during the civil war and the upheaval which followed led to a food shortage. The cessation or destruction of the extant means of food production, transfer, and distribution led to a national famine, such as had not been seen in centuries. Beginning in the spring of 1921, the populace began starving, hundreds of thousands dying in the streets. In 1922, the church was subjected to harsh tribulations when, under the pretext of famine relief, the Soviet Regime violently confiscated all ecclesiastical treasures including sacred vessels, icons, relics, and other holy objects. These treasures were sold, and the proceeds went not to the hungry, but to munitions and arms for the Red Army in the continuing Civil War.

During the famine, heeding the appeal of the patriarch, the Orthodox Church made constant and generous donations to assist the starving, setting up food banks and personally delivering supplies to hundreds of thousands of Russians. Indeed, the patriarch issued an order instructing that all non-liturgical objects, and any and all monetary assets with no sacramental value be voluntarily handed over. However, when he also issued a statement forbidding the cooperation of the clergy in surrendering sacred vessels for non-ecclesiastical use (based on canon law), a slanderous campaign against the Church was begun in the press. St Tikhon was arrested, and a wave of court cases took place throughout Russia, in which priests, deacons, monks, nuns, and lay men and women were accused of counterrevolutionary activity. During these trials many faithful servants of Christ were sentenced to death and shed their blood as martyrs and hieromartyrs.

During these harrowing times, Fr Alexander was unwaveringly guided by the statements and directives of the holy patriarch. Funds to assist the starving were collected at Christ the Saviour Cathedral. At the same time, measures were undertaken to protect the sacred objects of the church. Clergy and parishioners of Christ the Saviour Cathedral met at Fr Alexander's apartment in order to make decisions and draft a resolution concerning the state decree.

A draft of this decision, prepared by Fr Alexander, protested against the violent confiscation of church valuables, and a general assembly was convened on March 23, 1922, at Christ the Saviour Cathedral to decide on whether or not to publish it. This meeting adopted the final text of the resolution, which demanded guarantees from the state that all donations be used to save the lives of the starving, and protested the constant and vitriolic publications slandering the Church and the hierarchy. The drafting of this document was deemed by the authorities to be criminal counterrevolutionary activity, and before it was even presented to the authorities, Fr Alexander was arrested.

THE TRIAL

After two court cases in St. Petersburg and Moscow regarding the confiscation of liturgical and sacred objects, in which the church was accused of treason and which resulted in the executions of a large number of clergy and laity, a new highly visible trial began in Moscow on November 27, 1922. In this trial, the state accused the church of supposedly "attempting to retain in their hands possession of church valuables and, through the resulting starvation, to topple the Soviet regime." This case had an additional underlying purpose of inciting the populace into a frenzy of hate against the Orthodox Church, and in this way strengthening the core of the atheist, communist regime.

A total of 105 clergy and laity were on trial. The most significant part of the indictment concerned the activity of the clergy and laity of Christ the Saviour Cathedral.

The indictment stated:

> The main organizers and leaders of this criminal activity were Priest Hotovitzky, chairman of the council of parishes in this area, Priest Arseniev, rector of the Cathedral, Priest Zotikov, Priest Gromoglasov, former lawyer Kayutov, former deputy minister Shchepkin, the merchant Golovkin, and engineer Anohin. When the decree of the Supreme Central Executive Committee concerning the confiscation of church valuables was issued, they began their preliminary activities under the leadership of the priest Hotovitzky, who repeated to secretly gather the above-named people at his apartment in order to plan with them the measures which they proposed to enact to achieve their criminal intentions.[16]

The case was in court for two weeks. After the detailed indictment was read, questioning of the defendants began. Fr Alexander remained calm and composed during the questioning, as he tried to protect the other defendants. Following the interrogation of all the defendants and witnesses, at the court session on December 6, the infamous prosecutor Vishinsky asked the court for a sentence of death for thirteen of the defendants including Archpriests Alexander Hotovitzky, Nicholas Arseniev, and Sergius Uspensky, and Abbess Vera (Pobedinskaya) of the Novodevichy Women's Monastery. Vishinsky requested that the other defendants be sentenced to prison.

On December 11, the defendants were given an opportunity to say a final word to the court. In his comments, Fr Alexander did not try to save himself, but rather attempted to obtain leniency and mercy for his brother clergy, "I direct your attention to those who were at the meeting in my apartment: some of them are old and the others are very young and guilty of nothing.

A photograph with a handwritten note and signature by the saint, 1919.

This was a completely ordinary meeting, it was not counter-revolutionary and it cannot by any means be characterized as a dark plot."[17]

On December 13, the verdict of the revolutionary tribunal was announced. It was milder than the bloodthirsty verdicts delivered at previous trials held in St. Petersburg and Moscow regarding the confiscation of church valuables. Each of the main defendants, including Abbess Vera, Archpriest Sergius, and Fr Alexander, was sentenced to ten years in prison, the confiscation of all their personal property and the deprivation of their civil rights for five years. The others were sentenced to lesser terms of imprisonment.

After the holy Patriarch Tikhon resumed his administration of the Church and made several statements regarding loyalty to the governmental authorities, many hierarchs, clergy, church leaders, and laity, who had previously received sentences from the judiciary in conjunction with the confiscation of church valuables, were granted amnesty. Fr Alexander was among those freed in October 1923. Following his liberation, he was not assigned to a parish but served by invitation at various churches in Moscow.

The freedom was short lived. In September 1924, a new wave of persecutions arose. Fr Alexander, whose name had been placed on a government list of threats to the state, was characterized as follows: "A priest and preacher with a post-graduate education, very active, zealous and influential among the Tikhonites.[18] His outlook is anti-Soviet."[19]

THE END

On September 9, 1924, Fr Alexander was subjected to yet another round of interrogations, in which he calmly stated: "In my religious convictions, I consider myself to be a Tikhonite. My relations with the Patriarch are intimate rather than just strictly administrative, but lately, I have avoided meeting with Patriarch Tikhon, as I felt that this might inconvenience him due to my conviction in conjunction with the confiscation of church valuables. I have never expressed an opinion concerning the restoration of the former government, and such a thought has not even crossed my mind." [20]

Finally, by a decision of a special meeting of the administration of the Department of State Political Management, the long-suffering priest was sentenced to three years of exile in the Turukhansk region in Siberia.[21] His already failing health was further weakened by his sojourn in the far north, but he was able to survive, though barely, in the Arctic climate, and eventually return to Moscow, where, upon his return, he was raised to the rank of protopresbyter. In the 1930s, the new protopresbyter served at the Church of the Deposition of the Holy Robe of the Theotokos on Donskoy Street. One of his parishioners preserved a priceless memory from that time:

> In 1936, Father Alexander did not preach, as he was apparently forbidden to do so. In 1936-7, I was present many times when Father Alexander served. He was a tall, gray-haired priest with gentle facial features, who looked extremely intelligent. Gray, trimmed hair, a small beard, very kind gray eyes, a high-pitched, loud tenor … pronounced exclamations distinctly and with inspiration … His appearance reminded me of many priests who were exiles from the western regions … Father Alexander had many parishioners who greatly revered him … Even today, I remember Father Alexander's eyes. It seemed as if his glance penetrated your heart and embraced it with affection. I had the same feeling when I saw the holy Patriarch Tikhon … The same light also shining in Father Alexander's eyes was testimony to his sanctity.[22]

Despite all he had suffered so far, the final stage of his martyric journey was still ahead. In the fall of 1937, he was arrested again during the new persecutions of the Great Purge.[23] The extant documentary evidence of his life ends here; however, a large number of witnesses testified to his death as a martyr in a concentration camp. The place of his burial remains unknown.

Saint Raphael of Brooklyn

His memory is commemorated on February 27

HIS BEGINNINGS IN A LAND OF MARTYRDOM

On July 9, 1860, fanatical Muslims poured into the Christian district of Damascus; the massacre which followed was unspeakable. Three days later, over 20,000 Orthodox and Maronite Christians would be lying dead in the streets, alleys, and churches of the city.

In the middle of the nineteenth century, the area which comprised the territory of Syria was under the rule of the Ottoman Empire. It included not only the modern country of Syria, but also the lands which make up present-day Lebanon, Palestine, Israel, and Jordan. With the decline of the Ottoman Empire, European powers began playing an ever-increasing role in the politics of the Muslim-majority empire, forcing changes to the laws which had held religious minorities in social and political subjugation for centuries. The European powers had insisted on the abolition of the dhimmi system,[1] a demand which the weakened Ottoman Sultanate was forced to agree to. This caused riots and uprisings amongst zealous factions of Muslims in every corner of the empire. In the last millennium, the Christians of the area had been sporadically, though consistently, persecuted, and massacres were not unheard of. These political changes, however, had reignited long-standing religious hatreds throughout the region, and on that summer day, tensions exploded, as hundreds of Muslims flooded into the Christian neighborhoods, going into homes, stores, and churches, and slaughtering any Christian in sight. Several hundred Christians barricaded themselves in the Cathedral of the Holy Dormition of the Theotokos, and seeing that they were unable to broach the church, the Muslims set it alight, burning everyone inside alive.

None of the major Orthodox churches in Damascus survived, and though the fate of the Christian men was horrific, the fate of the women was even worse. The ones who were not raped and killed were stripped and dragged through the streets naked, their bodies being sold to Bedouins for a few shillings. The Turkish police, the official law enforcement in the region, energetically participated in these crimes, calling on Christians who were in hiding to come out, on the pretense that they would rescue them and transport them to a safe location outside the killing zone. As soon as any Christian heeded the call, however, they found that the police were as eager and bloodthirsty as the mob, indiscriminately killing men, women, and children en masse. When the slaughter ended on July 11, 380 villages, 560 churches, and 40 monasteries, many of them ancient, lay in ruins.[2]

This was the tragic background in which our father among the saints, Raphael, was born. His parents, Michael Hawaweeny and his second wife Mariam, were well-established pious Orthodox Christians living in Damascus. Seeing the tide of unrest, they took their three children and fled for Beirut (in Lebanon) before that tragic July day. Miriam was pregnant, and on November 8, 1860, her baby was born, which she named Rafla (Raphael in Arabic) in honor of the holy archangel, whose feastday the birth fell on.

Rafla was baptized three months later, on the feast of Theophany, and in the spring of 1861, the family was able to return to Damascus. The young boy attended elementary and secondary school at his local parish academy, where he excelled, earning the admiration of not only his peers, but also his teachers. In 1874, however, just as he had completed the school year with honors, his father informed him with a heavy heart that he could no longer afford the tuition, and that the bright and eager student would have to abandon higher education and learn a trade through which he could financially help his struggling family.

God had other plans, however, and help came from an unexpected source; a deacon named Athanasius Atallah (later metropolitan of Homs), recommended young Raphael to then Patriarch Ierotheos of Antioch, who accepted the boy into the Patriarchal school, which prepared young men for the priesthood. Raphael was elated, as his mother, who was the daughter of a priest, had always encouraged her young son to follow the clerical calling.

Raphael moved into the grounds of the school, where he completed his education. On September 14, 1874, the day of the Elevation of the Holy Cross, he was tonsured a reader, and three years later, in 1877, his academic excellence was recognized when he was selected to be a substitute teaching assistant at the academy. He was only seventeen years old.

The following year he was appointed Lecturer in Arabic and Turkish for the Patriarchal school, and on March 28, 1879, following his desire for the monastic life, he was tonsured a monk by Patriarch Ierotheos.

The patriarch asked the bright young man to serve as his personal secretary and attendant, a high honor, but one that would take him away from his beloved teaching. He obeyed, but having had a deep thirst for learning and knowledge from his earliest days, he jumped at the opportunity when Patriarch Joachim III of Constantinople asked the Antiochian prelate to send one deserving student to study at the Theological School of Halki on a full scholarship. Ierotheos hesitated, as he did not want to lose the young monk who had made himself so indispensable to him, but with the encouragement of a notable Damascene Syrian then residing in Constantinople, Dimitris Nicholas Shahade, he agreed, and on July 6, 1879, Raphael boarded a ship for the City of Cities.[3]

THE BEGINNING OF THE JOURNEY

Upon arrival in Halki, the young monk submitted to the necessary physical examination before being accepted into the school. To his astonishment, however, he was deemed too weak and sickly to endure the rigors of the academic studies that would be required of him, and therefore turned away. His sorrow at these news was so great that he almost fell into total despair, but God once again intervened through the same Nicholas Shahade who had helped him before, and after a long conversation with the Dean of the seminary, Raphael was accepted on a provisional basis.

The ecumenical patriarch, Joachim, asked a Constantinopolitan merchant to supply Raphael with 18 Ottoman lira per year for his books and personal necessities. In his diary that year, the young monk wrote: "of that amount, I had two lira to spare, after all expenses were paid. I sent one to my father and one to my mother, so that they would be pleased with me."[4]

Raphael recompensed his benefactors with his academic excellence, and at the end of the first year, the young seminarian was at the top of his class, something which surprised and pleased both the patriarch and his instructors. In 1883, however, Patriarch Joachim resigned, and the merchant who had been supporting Raphael refused to continue his financial aid. The distraught monk mentioned this difficulty in a letter to his former teacher, Athanasius Atallah, now an archimandrite and proistamenos[5] of the monastery of the Prophet Elijah at Dhour El Choueir, in Lebanon. Fr Athanasius sent an epistle

151

St Raphael as a seminarian at the theological school of Halki.

St Raphael as a young hierodeacon, 1886.

explaining the situation to fellow archimandrite Chrysanthos Saliba, later metropolitan of Arkadia.

This holy man, notable in his own right, was born Halil Saliba in the city of Bteghrine in Lebanon. He served as an archdeacon at the Patriarchate of Antioch, and as abbot at the monastery of St George in Tripoli, Lebanon. Shortly before his death in 1889, he was ordained metropolitan of Arkadia. It was he who took it upon himself to send the young scholar the same 18 Ottoman lira per annum.

During his seminary years, Raphael expressed the first signs of his later lifelong dissatisfaction with the Hellenocracy of the Patriarchate of Antioch. Specifically, when the new patriarch of Antioch was elected, he and some other students protested the decision, claiming that the new patriarch, Gerasimos, a member of the brotherhood of the Holy Sepulcher, bribed his way to the Patriarchal Throne. The school authorities were forced to discipline the students for these protests, but for Raphael, the sentiment only grew.

On December 8, 1885, Raphael was ordained to the diaconate in the school chapel, and in July of 1886, the young deacon received his degree in Theology with excellent marks. He then immediately returned to his homeland, where he was placed under the service of Metropolitan Chrysanthos, his former benefactor, something which gave him exceeding joy, as he would now be able to repay the debt of gratitude he owed.

In July of 1886, Deacon Raphael accompanied the metropolitan on a tour of all the villages of the metropolis of Arkadia, and only when the tour was finished did he ask for leave to go and see his parents in Damascus. During his visit to his home town, he was asked to give a sermon at the Cathedral every Sunday, and his presence brought joy to a congregation that felt him as their own.

After twenty-eight days at home, Raphael returned to the metropolis, which was preparing for the visit of Patriarch Gerasimos. Burying any feelings of disapproval toward the Primate, the young hierodeacon assisted in the preparations, and when the patriarch arrived, he was always by the side of the two hierarchs, serving them joyously and tirelessly during the entirety of the visit. Indeed, the patriarch of Antioch found himself so impressed with Deacon Raphael that he asked Metropolitan Chrysanthos to allow him to take him with and make him his personal assistant, and instructor at the theological school he was planning to build. The metropolitan agreed, and the new member of the patriarch's retinue followed him to Laodicea, Cilicia,

Antioch, and Lebanon. He was soon chosen to be the patriarch's official spokesman, giving sermons when Gerasimos could not be present himself. After completing their visits to the patriarchal dioceses, they returned to the Patriarchate in Damascus on September 13, 1887.

IN RUSSIA

The young deacon's thirst for knowledge had not been quenched, even now, and he longed for further education, so he asked the patriarch to permit him to enroll in graduate studies at a university in Russia, promising to return upon completion and serve as the patriarch's Russian translator. The primate acquiesced, and on September 17, 1888, Raphael was accepted as a student at the Theological Academy of Kiev. The next year, wishing to replace Christopher Jabara, the Arab proistamenos at the metochi[6] in Moscow, Patriarch Gerasimos ordered the young deacon to take over as head of the Antiochian representation in Moscow. At his request, Bishop Sylvester ordained young Raphael to the priesthood in the chapel of the Academy on the July 16, 1889. A month later, Metropolitan Ioanikii of Moscow raised him to the rank of archimandrite and confirmed him as the head representative of the Antiochian Church in Russia. Archimandrite Raphael's aptitude was admirable, and after two years, he was able to reduce the debt of the Antiochian representation from 65,000 to 50,000 rubles.[7] He also arranged for twenty-four Syrian students to come to Russia to further their theological training. Feeling a warm zeal in his heart for his native Syria, he poured himself into filling the spiritual and material needs of his people.

When Patriarch Gerasimos resigned from the See of Antioch in order to assume the See of Jerusalem, Archimandrite Raphael saw it as an opportunity to return the rudder of the Church of Antioch to Syrian hands. Wishing to restore the administration of the Antiochian patriarchate to its own native clergy and people, Archimandrite Raphael began a letter writing campaign, reaching out to Antiochian bishops, priests, and laymen, and even writing articles for Russian newspapers, drawing attention to the plight of his native land. His efforts failed, however, when in November of 1891 Metropolitan Spyridon of Tabor, a Greek Cypriot, was elected to the throne of Antioch. The saint could not accept the appointment, and along with many other Arab hierarchs, believed that the election was, again, the result of bribes. He refused to commemorate the new patriarch during services, and continued to write articles and letters in defense of the Antiochian cause, opposing Patriarch

Spyridon's elevation. As a result, he was suspended from both his priestly functions and those as a representative of the Patriarchate. Fr Raphael accepted this measure, but continued publicly decrying the patriarch.

At this point, the patriarchs of Antioch, Jerusalem, Constantinople, and Alexandria petitioned the Tsar to stop the archimandrite's activities, which he agreed to do. In the process, the Syrian monk's name was dragged through the mud, and many accusations were hurled against him, so much so, that even some of his closest friends began doubting his character.

Abandoned by all, and not being able to bear the injustice of the smear campaign launched against him, Fr Raphael sought refuge in the bishop of Dimtrovsk, who was assistant bishop of Moscow and proistamenos of all the Moscow monasteries, and also sent letters to Konstantin Pobedonostsev, the assistant to the Tsar's Council of the Empire and Chief Procurator of the Holy Synod of the Church of Russia. The latter did, indeed, encourage the Holy Synod to conduct a thorough investigation of the allegations against Fr Raphael, which was immediately begun.

Once the investigation was completed, Fr Raphael was exonerated, and the bishop of Dimtrovsk published the following excerpt from the findings:

> I testify with certainty that Archimandrite Raphael, former head of the Antiochian metochion in Moscow, according to official reports from the two general superiors of the Moscow monasteries, Archimandrite Gregorii and Archimandrite Sergii, has led a blameless life and he still maintains good behavior in his spiritual life. Further, that during his tenure as head of the metochion his efforts and activities were based on noble intentions.
>
> —ALEKSANDER, Bishop of Dimtrovsk
> Vicar to the Archdiocese of Moscow
> Moscow. February 13/25, 1893[8]

The maligned archimandrite sent a copy of the entire findings to friends in Damascus, and encouraged them to show it to the clergy of the city. Eventually, Patriarch Spyridon wrote to Pobedonostsev, asking him to persuade Fr Raphael to ask for the patriarch's (his) forgiveness. Not wishing for the conflict to continue, especially now that the Church of Russia was involved, Fr Raphael apologized via signed telegram in 1893, and the suspension was lifted. Upon his request, he was released from the jurisdiction of Antioch and allowed to transfer to the Church of Russia in perpetuity.

In November of the same year, he moved to Kazan, taking a position as instructor of Arabic at the theological academy. He remained there until 1895, when Providence propelled him to the calling for which it had been preparing him for since infancy; the mission which, though he did not know it at the time, would change history, and lead him to the path of holiness.

THE NEW WORLD

Archimandrite Raphael's passionate writings, along with his reputation as an ardent and dedicated priest and excellent spiritual father, had carried his fame beyond the country, beyond the continent, across the ocean, to the New World. A great number of Syrian émigrés had settled in New York, and in 1895, they had formed the Syrian Orthodox Benevolent Society of New York, with the goal of establishing a church and hiring a permanent priest. They soon invited St Raphael to oversee the Arab Orthodox community of New York, offering a salary of $50 a month.[9]

The saint answered the call, and after consulting with his fellow clerics, accepted the position, with the understanding that the new parish they were to build would be under the jurisdiction of the Russian Patriarchate, which he was now under, and not the Patriarchate of Antioch. The community agreed, and the saint began preparing for the 5,000-mile trip across the Atlantic.

During that period, the bishop of the Aleutian Islands and Alaska, Nicholas (Ziorov), happened to be in St. Petersburg, and happily agreed to make all necessary arrangements for Fr Raphael's transfer to the United States. In the transfer letters, the Holy Synod of Russia clarified that the patriarch of Antioch did not object to the archimandrite's move, and placed him, and a Syrian deacon who was to accompany him, under the omophorion[10] of Bishop Nicholas. The Synod also set aside 1,800 rubles annually[11] to provide for their needs, 1,200 for the saint, and 600 for the deacon.

Knowing that his Syrian compatriots in New York did not have a church built yet, Fr Raphael began gathering all the sacred objects necessary to furnish a church for liturgical purposes. During his trip from Russia to New York, Bishop Nicholas and St Raphael stopped in Austria, Hungary, the Netherlands, France, and England, where they visited all the famous cathedrals and museums, but also made a point to celebrate the Divine Liturgy. Finally, in London, they boarded the ship bound for New York.

Archimandrite Raphael arrived in New York on November 2, 1895, and was welcomed by a delegation of Arab Orthodox Christians, who were eagerly awaiting their shepherd from Russia. A September 15, 1895 article by the *New York Times* described the scene:

> Among the foreign colonies in New York the Syrian colony is one that is attaining importance, as it has been steadily growing in numbers for several years past. The number of Syrians at present residing in the city is estimated at 10,000 and in the United States at 150,000. Of course, nearly all of them are Christians, either Maronites or members of the Orthodox Church, and should they keep on coming to this country at the rate they have been, it will not be very long before only few Christians would be left in Syria. The natives will all be Mohammedans and Druzes.[12] To what extent the industries and trade of that country will be affected by the loss of this thrifty population can hardly be determined at present, for the Christians of Syria have certainly been the mainstays of industry and commerce there, as well as of agriculture ....
>
> The Russian Bishop of Alaska, whose Episcopal Seat comprises all the United States, has been taking a great deal of interest in the Syrians of the Orthodox Greek church who are in this country, and has quite recently prevailed upon the Russian Emperor and Synod to appoint a Syrian priest who studied in Russia as pastor for Orthodox Syrians in this country, under the supervision of the Russian See. The success of the Russian Bishop of Alaska was first published in the Syrian colony yesterday, and has created a great deal of rejoicing. The name of the Syrian Russian priest is the Rev. Archimandrite Rafael Hawaweeny, a native of Damascus, and is he expected here next month.[13]

Providence had selected St Raphael to gather the dispersed sheep of His flock in America. At that time, Orthodox Syrian immigrants did not have anyone to care for their spiritual nourishment and well-being, and many of them had left the faith and joined other denominations. Others ignored religion completely, losing interest in any spiritual activity. It was in this climate of a spiritually starved diaspora that the saint arrived, and on November 5, his first Sunday in America, he assisted Bishop Nicholas in serving the Divine Liturgy at the Russian church.

A few days after his arrival, Fr Raphael found a suitable place for a chapel, on 77 Washington Street in lower Manhattan, and furnished it with the liturgical items that he had brought with him from Russia. He refused

NEW YORK CELEBRATION OF THE BIRTH OF THE RUSSIAN PRINCESS.

FOR THE CZAR'S BABY DAUGHTER.

Imposing Spectacle in the Russian Church, with Bishop Nicolas Officiating.

A scene of ecclesiastical splendor in rare contrast with the plain exterior of the edifice in which it was presented was shown in the Orthodox Russian Church yesterday morning.

The church is at No. 323 Second avenue, an ordinary three-story and basement brick dwelling house. The front parlor serves as the audience room and the back parlor as the chancel. No pews or seats of any kind are provided, but a congregation which filled the front room almost to suffocation and crowded the hallway and staircase, remained standing throughout a service which lasted for nearly three hours.

The light of many candles made the place insufferably hot, and some of the priests in the gorgeous and heavy robes and vestments seemed on the verge of fainting before the long ceremony was ended.

Bishop Nicolas, of Alaska, who has recently returned from a visit to Russia, was the celebrant of the high mass which preceded a second service designed to be in commemoration of the birth of the new Crown Princess of Russia. It was expected that a telegram would be received officially announcing the birth of the royal infant before the service ended, but for some unexplained reason the telegram did not arrive and the Bishop being therefore unofficially informed of the birth of the child was unable to offer up the prayer he had intended to say for her.

Assisting the Bishop during the services were two mitred abbots, or Archimandrites, as they are called in the Greek Church—Raphael of Damascus, and Theoclitus, who was at one time an instructor of the son of the King of Greece. The monk Inonentius also took part in the ceremony, his black hat and long black veil furnishing a striking contrast to the magnificent robes of the Bishop and the abbots. The Russian Consul-General Oldrovsky was one of the congregation and officiated in passing the contribution plate.

At the conclusion of the services the entire congregation passed before the Bishop in single file, each person pausing to kiss both his right hand and a golden cross which he held in his left hand.

The article from the New York World newspaper covered the visit of Bishop Nicholas to the chapel of the Syrian Orthodox on November 6/18, 1895. During the service there were prayers for the newborn daughter of Tsar Nicholas II, the later passionbearer, Olga. In the amazing sketch which accompanied the article one can see St Raphael on the top left, and Bishop Nicholas in the foreground, on the lower right.

financial assistance and the salary offered by the Syrian Orthodox Benevolent Society, working tirelessly without pay, with paternal devotion for the flock that Christ had entrusted to him. Four days after their arrival, Bishop Nicholas came and blessed the new chapel, dedicating it to Saint Nicholas of Myra, and they celebrated the service of the blessing of the waters.

St Raphael immediately began his pastoral duties, hearing confessions, celebrating the Divine Liturgy, teaching faith classes, and comforting his flock in the difficulties of their lives. He moved across the Brooklyn Bridge, to 120 Pacific Street, and many Syrians who had previously been renting rooms in lower Manhattan moved across the bridge to be closer to him.

On Sunday, April 5, 1896, the Syrian community in New York celebrated Pascha for the first time in their new chapel. For many of them, it was their first Paschal service since leaving their native land. The *New York Herald* immortalized the service in their article titled "The Syrians Celebrate Easter."

> The Syrian community gathered about 200 strong shortly after midnight last night to welcome Easter Sunday with national services in their little Chapel on the second floor of number 77 Washington St. It was the first service of the kind in America, as the congregation was only organized about six months ago. The room was decorated for the occasion, and was brilliantly illuminated with tapers. Before the altar stood a beautifully embroidered "Burial of Christ"[14] received six days ago as a present from Tsar Nicholas the Second to be used especially on this occasion …
>
> They filed in singly, the men and the women, and as they entered each dropped one coin or several in a receptacle by the doorway. Then they passed over to the Czar's gift, nearly all kissing the prostate figure of the dead saviour, beautifully portrayed in colors on the top and surrounded by heads of the Saints, the whole set in fine relief, on which the inscription was elaborately embroidered in gold with Russian characters. With many genuflections they then passed to their places, the women all sitting on one side of the room while the men who stood through the service and who greatly preponderated, occupied the other.
>
> Candles, a little less than a yard long, were placed in the hands of each by an assistant, and were lighted by those nearest, and these were held burning throughout the services, and their combined light added to that of the fixed tapers, illuminated the Chapel as though by electricity.

The Archimandrite took his place before the figure of Christ at midnight, with his back towards his congregation when the service opened and commenced a solemn chant which was taken up by the choir. He was dressed in a flowing black robe and wore the cylindrical hat of a Greek priest, flaring at the top and with no brim. This headgear was also shrouded in black. He is a man of medium build, with black hair falling down about his shoulders, and a full beard ... [15]

APOSTOLIC JOURNEYS

Initially, St Raphael remained in New York. It was not long, however, before he heard of smaller communities of Arab Christians scattered throughout the length and breadth of North America, so in the summer of 1896, he began the first of several pastoral journeys across the continent. On his own initiative, he visited thirty cities between New York and San Francisco, seeking out the lost sheep in cities, towns, and villages, many of whom had not seen a priest or received the Holy Sacraments in years. He fed the spiritually hungry people with the Word of God in each place where he stopped. He performed marriages and baptisms, heard confessions, and celebrated the Divine Liturgy in the homes of the faithful where there was no church building. He would preach, and his words fell like rain on the parched souls of the faithful, who welcomed him like Christ Himself.

During his first cross-continental journey, the archimandrite had seen first-hand the need for an Arabic prayer book, containing the prayers and services of the Orthodox Church, but published in America. With the blessing of Bishop Nicholas, St Raphael took on the challenge, and in 1898 published his first book in the New World, an Arabic language service book called *The Book of True Consolation in the Divine Prayers*. This book of liturgical services and prayers was very useful to priests in celebrating the divine services, and also to the people in their personal prayer life. Bishop Nicholas announced the publication in the *Russian American Orthodox Messenger* periodical, started by St Alexander Hotovitzky in New York just two years earlier, and recommended that any priest who had Arab speakers in his parish purchase the book.

The saint's ascendency continued throughout 1897, when the Ecclesiastical Synod of the Russian Episcopacy in America created a three-member panel to inspect Russian, Carpatho-Russian, and English Orthodox publications in the New World. The members of this committee were Sts Raphael, Alexis

St Raphael as an archimandrite, immediately after his arrival in America, 1895.

Toth, and John Kochurov. At the end of that year, recognizing his services to the Church and the Russian Empire as professor of Arabic at Kazan Theological Seminary during the reign of Tsar Alexander III, now-Tsar Nicholas II honored St Raphael with the Cross of the Order of St. Anna, 3rd class,[16] for his exceptional exertions.

In May of 1898, St Raphael began his second pastoral journey, which lasted five months. It was during that trip, on May 6, 1898, on the occasion of his (the Tsar's) birthday, that Tsar Nicholas II honored St Raphael with the Cross of the Order of St. Anna, 2nd Class. Bishop Nicholas awarded him the medal during a majestic ceremony in the San Francisco Cathedral.

Completing his second pastoral journey across America, St Raphael came to realize that his own visits once a year were insufficient, and priests were needed to establish parishes and rejuvenate the spiritual and liturgical life in the scattered Arab communities across the States. The Arab-speaking parishes needed more frequent access to the sacraments of the Church, so that same year, he sent messages to Antioch asking for more priests and laymen interested in the priesthood. With the support and assistance of Bishop Nicholas, his letters were answered, and soon the Patriarchate of Antioch began to send priests and young theologians, who greatly assisted in the new mission.

In December of 1898, knowing he was soon to leave for Russia to take up his new post as metropolitan of Tver, Bishop Nicholas gave his faithful archimandrite a parting gift, signifying his respect and acknowledgment of the achievements that the saint had accomplished in such a short time; it was a gold watch, engraved with both his and St Raphael's names on the inside.

A few days later, he was on a ship back to Moscow, and in a few days, his replacement had landed in New York. It was Bishop Tikhon, later saint and holy patriarch of Moscow.

Archimandrite Raphael welcomed the new ruling bishop in America, and on December 15, three days after landing, Bishop Tikhon came to celebrate the Divine Liturgy at the Syrian church of Saint Nicholas. Raphael told his people that their new bishop was one who "has been sent here to tend the flock of Christ-Russians, Slavs, Syro-Arabs, and Greeks which is scattered across the entire North American continent."[17]

MINISTRY WITHOUT BORDERS

In March of 1899, St Raphael received permission from Bishop Tikhon to start collecting funds to build a new church to replace the chapel, which was located in an old building on a dirty street, and for an Orthodox cemetery. He published fundraising petitions in almost all the Arab-language newspapers in the United States, as well as sending letters to all the metropoles of the Patriarchate of Antioch. A month later, he left on yet another pastoral tour, this time stopping in forty-three different cities and towns. Traveling by land and water, and undeterred by the obstacles and difficulties before him, he spent seven months in the northeastern, southern, and midwestern United States. He performed weddings and baptisms, and blessed the weddings of Orthodox people who had been married by non-Orthodox clergy. He chrismated children who had been baptized by Catholic priests, and traveled to Greek and Russian parishes, which were not being served, celebrating the services and hearing confessions in fluent Greek and Russian, to the great surprise and amazement of the congregations.

The unimaginable difficulties facing the saint as he visited community after community across the vast North American continent cannot be described, but with deep faith and trust in God, he faced and overcame every challenge in his path. He conscientiously cared for not only his existing flock, but for any new recently arrived fellow Arab, or ones who had moved away. He located Orthodox Christians wherever they were, and made sure to keep them under his paternal care. Indeed, soon the fruits of his labors began to be apparent, not just in the fulfillment of the spiritual and liturgical needs of the Orthodox Arab immigrants, but also of the increasing awareness which his ministry raised in non-Orthodox circles. The saint's love extended to all God's children, and many Americans, learning about his arrival in their towns and cities during his third intercontinental trip, attended the services and followed his sermons with interest. Many of them asked for more information on the Orthodox faith, having never encountered it in any form in the Protestant-majority religious landscape.

He also cared for his fellow Arab Maronite Christians, who, long forgotten by their own ecclesiastical authorities, sought his guidance, counsel, and spiritual nourishment.

The *Russian American Orthodox Messenger* published a nearly day-by-day account of his trip. Reading these, one can see how many faithful went to confession in every city and town, how many attended services, how many sacraments the saint performed, the issues he discussed, and a plethora of additional information that shows the saint's desire to serve his flock. Many of the entries are solely descriptive, but some delve into detail, and it is those entries which truly remind one of the proto-Christian period of the apostles and their first followers. In a time before automobiles, when travel outside the large metropolitan areas could only be accomplished by horse-drawn carriages, on dirt tracks and uneven surfaces, often for hours at a time, with no amenities or comforts, a journey such as the saint undertook was a truly heroic, and at times even martyric, feat. The following entry brings a sense of awe and reverence.

> September 7/19—On Tuesday he continued on to Kearney, NE, where he arrived at midnight, eight and a half hours later than scheduled; nevertheless, nearly the entire Arab community was still gathered at the station to greet him. During the open coach ride to the home in which he was to stay, Raphael caught cold, but still stayed up until 4:00 A.M., talking with the people. In the morning he was too exhausted to serve Liturgy, so he substituted the Typica service.[18] By evening he felt stronger, and set out in the company of fifteen Arabs by buckboard to visit an outlying ranch. They sang church hymns and folk songs the whole way, and arrived at 1:00 A.M. The host kissed the ground in front of Raphael, then his feet and hands. Raphael was greatly touched by this display. The man's wife was also very happy finally to have the opportunity to confess her sins and see her four children baptized. Raphael slept on their small divan (while the rest of the party spread out on chairs and the floor). In the morning they celebrated Orthros, blessed water to sanctify the cabin and the rest of the

property. In the evening they returned to Kearney; the remaining ranchers gathered there to meet him.[19]

The owner of this isolated ranch was a man named Nicholas Yanney; the reason he lived so far away was because he was a man of solitude and prayer. Yet a tragedy was soon to upend his entire life, and set him on a new path. When he was just twenty-nine, his wife had a complication while delivering their fifth child. Neither mother nor baby survived, and the drastic loss put him on a trajectory which eventually led to his becoming one of the greatest priests and missionaries on the entire North American continent. During the Spanish Influenza which ravaged the country, Fr Nicholas visited the faithful, administering them the sacraments on their deathbeds, and ministering to them. He contracted the disease, and died in 1918, faithful and selfless to the end.[20]

AN ARAB PATRIARCH

During the five months of this third missionary journey, St Raphael performed ninety-five baptisms and seventy-three weddings, and during forty-five Divine Liturgies he communed 650 men, women, and children. After every Divine Liturgy he held faith classes, preached, taught, and spent his time with the faithful of the area, discussing, answering questions, and comforting. He also managed to raise nearly $5,000[21] for the church and cemetery in New York. He wrote to his new bishop, asking that he be allowed to contact the Holy Synod in Russia and other Russian philanthropic organizations to ask for assistance. Bishop Tikhon not only permitted it, but donated $125 of his own money toward the work. He also encouraged St Raphael to write to the Tsar of Russia, who loved the Church and her saints, and explain the situation. Indeed, the pious Tsar once again showed his love for the mission of God, and immediately sent $1,027 for the building of the new church.

On November 11, while still in Pennsylvania, St Raphael received a telegram after church informing him that Metropolitan Meletios (Doumani) of Laodicea had been elected patriarch of Antioch, and that the appointment had been approved by the Sultan (Syria then still being a part of the Ottoman Empire). With great joy St Raphael told his people that for the first time in over 170 years, a native Arab had been chosen as primate of the Antiochian Church. His elation was overwhelming, as he saw the desire of his heart, and the cause which he had so passionately espoused, and for which he had suffered so much, come to fruition.

After the new patriarch had been installed, the metropolis of Laodicea in Syria petitioned the new primate to install Archimandrite Raphael as his successor on the now-vacant episcopal throne. The Patriarch, however, stated that the Holy Synod could not elect Fr Raphael because his work in the New World was invaluable to the Church, and there was no one who could replace him.

In the years that followed, the saint received multiple requests to return to his homeland. In 1901, Metropolitan Gabriel of Beirut wrote to him, asking him to be his auxiliary bishop, but Archimandrite Raphael declined, saying that he could not leave his American flock, and that he believed he was where God wanted him to be. In December of the same year, he was elected bishop of Zahlé in absentia. Patriarch Meletios sent a telegram congratulating him and asking him to return to Syria, but after thanking the patriarch for the honor, the saint again declined the office.

Learning of these eminent offers, his New York parishioners quickly sent a letter to Bishop Tikhon, asking him to ensure that their shepherd remained with them. An excerpt from the letter read as follows:

> We have sent a petition to the Holy Synod of Russia and another to the Holy Synod of Antioch praying that he [Raphael] will remain with us and that he will continue the work which was so much blessed under his hands. He was the good gift of the Holy Synod of Russia to their loyal children the Orthodox Syrians, and we trust that we will not lose this gift. We earnestly pray you to use your influence towards that same end, and to send the echo of our voices to the Holy Synod of "Petersburg" and add your mighty word on our behalf ... [22]

The letter clearly illuminates the love which the Syrians in the New World held for their spiritual father, but it proved superfluous, as the saint himself had decided to spend the rest of his life tending his American flock.

St Raphael's desire to acquire a parish cemetery was fulfilled in August of 1901, when he was able to purchase a section of the Mount Olivet cemetery on Long Island for the exclusive use of the Orthodox Syrian faithful of New York. A month later, he was again honored by the Tsar with the medal of the Order of St. Vladimir, 4th class. [23] The event caused a news frenzy in his home country of Syria, where the press congratulated him at length for his slew of honorary achievements in the Russian court.

MEXICO

Many Syrian refugees moving to the Americas had found a new home in Mexico. These Orthodox faithful lived without a priest until October of 1900, when a Syrian deacon from New York moved to Mexico and wrote to St Raphael, informing him of the situation in the country, and asking his advice on how to get the sacraments to the Syrian faithful in his new homeland. Upon receiving his letter, the saint immediately responded, letting him know that under the care of the Russian bishop of North America, there were five itinerant priests ordained to travel to any and all underserved areas in the continent, and as long as there were three or more families, the community could request a visit from one of these priests. Informed of his response, the Syrians in Mexico quickly wrote directly to the saint, asking him if he would be willing to come down himself, a request to which he joyfully acceded. Scheduling his visit for January of 1902, he arranged for another Syrian metropolitan to take over his duties, and sent a telegram to the Syrian community in Mexico, informing them of his impending arrival.

On January 17, 1902, he boarded the steamship *Monterey*, which was to travel to Mexico via Havana, Cuba. The saint was able to disembark in Havana long enough to visit an Arab merchant and his employees. The weather during the first part of the trip was cold, but after crossing Florida and Cuba, it became milder. Finally, on January 24, the saint arrived in the Port of Progreso in the northwest part of the Yucatán Peninsula. There, he was greeted by an Arabic representation, which had rented a train specifically to take the saint to Mérida, the state capital, 40 kilometers away. Upon arrival, he was welcomed into the home of a wealthy Orthodox Arab, and that same night, he was visited by members of the Arabic community, who wished to welcome him and pay their respects. In a show of gratitude and joy, they lit the sky with fireworks, celebrating his arrival.

The next morning St Raphael asked to visit those who had not been able to make it the night before. There were also many ongoing feuds between members of the community, due to various personal or professional reasons, and he immediately set himself up as negotiator, trying to solve the situations and relieve the tensions within the community. On that Sunday he celebrated Divine Liturgy at the house in which he was staying, and nearly all 300 of the local Christian Arabs attended, not only Orthodox, but also Maronite and Melkchite. Amongst the congregation were also some local Mexicans, who, hearing about the saint's arrival, came to hear him and learn more about the Orthodox faith. The majority of Orthodox Arabs partook in the sacraments of confession and Holy communion during his stay, and his sermons on the importance of love and harmony amongst Christians did not fall on deaf ears.

Surveying his diary entries from the period, we see that his three-week stay in Mérida yielded a wealth of spiritual fruit. He performed four weddings, fifty baptisms, and celebrated four Divine Liturgies. In an unexpected twist, many Spanish-language newspapers in the Catholic-majority country covered the saint's visit, describing it in glowing terms. It turned out that only after his visit did they realize that the strange, Arab-speaking migrants were not Muslims, but Christians like themselves. After that, the Syrian community took on a much more integrated and important place in the Mexican society of Mérida.

Before his scheduled departure, the saint was invited by two families who lived further away in the Yucatán, asking him to visit and baptize their children. The first village was Peto, 85 miles inland, and almost at the south end of the region, but the saint, ignoring the difficulties and discomforts of the journey, joyously agreed. When he arrived, the whole village, including the mayor and the Roman Catholic priest, were expecting him. A mariachi band was also there to welcome the visitor. Peto's twenty Arabs welcomed the saint with flowers, and then the whole procession, including the mayor and Catholic priest, accompanied the saint in a panegyrical procession to the house where he would be staying.

The next morning, all the Orthodox faithful in the village came to receive confession and holy communion. During the Divine Liturgy, the saint baptized ten children. The Mexican villagers came and brought their children to be blessed, and a local colonel came to him with his fiancée, asking the saint to wed them. The saint explained that he could not, as they were Roman Catholics, and recommended that they find a priest of their own faith to perform the ceremony.

The day after, the saint took leave of Peto and traveled to the village of Tekax, 30 miles away, where the second family resided. He was accompanied by many of the villagers from Peto, along with the Roman Catholic priest. The saint joked that the priest had not left him alone for a single hour during the entire trip. After ministering to the sacramental and pastoral needs of the family in Tekax, the saint was ready to depart for Mérida, from where he would take the train to the port. It was then that he received an urgent telegram from the colonel in Peto, asking if the "good father" could receive him and his future wife into the Orthodox Faith. The saint answered immediately, asking them to meet him in Merida. There, he catechized them on the foundational tenets of the faith, and after assuring that they were ready, and receiving their confession of faith, he baptized and married them.

In his diary, St Raphael wrote that the province of Yucatan was "good soil," upon which the seed of the Orthodox faith would yield much fruit, if sowed properly. The Catholic faith there was mostly superficial, and the Mexican residents had been deeply impressed by the holy sacraments. Many had told him they were very interested in Orthodoxy, trying to convince him to stay, but his pastoral obligations in America did not allow it, and finally, on February 24, 1902, a month after he had arrived, the saint boarded the ship which would take him back to New York. This was his first and last visit to Latin America, but he would never forget it, and seven years later, at the first opportunity, he arranged for the installation of a permanent priest in Mexico.

THE CROWNING OF HIS EFFORTS

Despite St. Raphael's ardent wish to build a church for the Syrian community in New York, the inflation which characterized the beginning of the twentieth century in America meant that construction would cost nearly $19,000,[24] a sum beyond the economic capability of his flock. That did not stop him, however, and in the fall of following year, the parish purchased a former Swedish Lutheran church on 301–303 Pacific Street in Brooklyn, a few blocks from the saint's home, and had it refitted for Orthodox worship. On Sunday, October 27, 1902, surrounded by the great joy of the faithful in attendance, Bishop Tikhon consecrated the new church in honor of St Nicholas. When the procession arrived at the doors of the church, Archimandrite Raphael greeted Bishop Tikhon in Russian, saying: "Blessed are you, O reverend master, who comes in the name of the Lord to consecrate this new church founded by the piety of your Syrian spiritual children ... Blessed are you, O reverend master, who comes in the name of the Lord. Through your prayers the Divine Grace comes upon this new house and makes it truly the house of God and a fountain of grace and blessing to everyone who enters it in faith, respect and godly fear. Amen."[25]

Many local newspapers wrote lengthy articles about the event, which caused a great deal of wonder. The *Sun* described the ceremony thusly:

> A procession such as seldom seen in the country formed outside the residence of Archimandrite Raphael, 120 Pacific St, Brooklyn, yesterday morning, then marched up two blocks to 299, the new Church of the greater New York's Syrian Orthodoxy.
>
> At its head was a Greek wearing the elaborately decorated jacket and the flaring short skirt, ribbon bedecked stockings, and the side arms typical of his country. Following him came ten deacons in richly embroidered robes and carrying religious and national banners, while behind them walked Archimandrite Raphael and Archbishop Tikhon of Alaska and North and South America. The latter had come from San Francisco especially to attend to the ceremony.
>
> In the rear came a great part of the 2,000 Syrian members of New York's Orthodox Greek church, some wearing sack suits, others frock coats, and not a few attired in the low-cut waistcoat and white tie of evening dress.
>
> They were dedicating their new church, their first real church, for their old quarters at 77 Washington street, Manhattan, where they had worshipped for the last ten years, had been merely a makeshift. The former quarters were merely rented, the new church has been bought outright. It cost fully $14,000, and all of this amount, with the exception of $1,500 from the Russian church and a contribution from the Syrian Catholics in the city, has been cheerfully given by the big merchants of the race in Broadway and their humbler countrymen in Washington street.
>
> When the procession entered the church, it crowded it to the doors. As there are no seats except along the sides of the building, most of the congregation stood up. Russian bankers rubbed elbows with men who trundle pushcarts six days out of seven.
>
> In the center of the floor stood the clergymen surrounded by the deacons. Around them in a closely packed circle were gathered the congregation. Candles were passed to the worshippers, who lighted and held them while the priests chanted prayers and psalms in a guttural minor key. The language employed was sometimes Arabic, but more often Russian, the tongue of the Archbishop. The odor of incense filled the air. After a prayer intoned in the body of the church, the train moved into the inner temple. The latter was separated by a wooden partition from the

congregation, but through three doorways could be gained partial views of the Archbishop as he blessed the holy table, sprinkled it with oil and holy water and placed upon it the embroidered altar cloths, testaments, and silver candle sticks.

At length the Archbishop accompanied by an attendant carrying holy water emerged from the temple, passed through the interior of the church and then about its exterior sprinkling its walls. The ceremony closed with an address in Russian by Archbishop Tikhon.[26]

After the service St Tikhon addressed his flock with these words: "I congratulate you, O Orthodox Syrians ... the early Christians, like you, celebrated the divine services in small houses and sometimes in caves, until they could build great and amazing temples. Truly "this is the day which the Lord has made; let us rejoice and be glad in it" (Ps118:24). Your joy, O Syrians, is our joy we the Russians, and today your joy is fulfilled."[27]

Immediately following the consecration, there was a Divine Liturgy, which commenced at 11:40 a.m., and ended at 2:00 p.m. At the end of the liturgy, the Syrian flock revealed a gift they had purchased for their shepherd and father: a pectoral cross, a symbol of their recognition of the sacrifices he had made for them and for the Church. Moved, St Raphael said: "'Not to us, O Lord, not to us, but to Thy name be the glory' ...[28] 'I planted, Apollos watered, but God gave the growth. So neither he who plants nor he who waters is anything, but only God who gives the growth.'[29] It is true that I worked a lot and endured even more grief in seeing this church realized; but no matter how much I worked and however much grief I endured, I consider myself only to have done my duty as a priest and servant of God ... Can we servants of God and spiritual pastors expect anything in this life except labor and grief? Is that not to what we dedicated our life, in order to work without recompense, for the good and the salvation of our neighbors? 'So you also, when you have done all that is commanded you, say, We are unworthy servants; we have only done what was our duty' (Luke 17:10)."[30]

At the end of the services, there was a festive gathering in the parish hall, in the basement of the new church. There, they toasted Tsar Nicholas II, President Theodore Roosevelt, Antiochian Patriarch Meletios, the Holy Synod of Russia, the bishop of the Aleutian Islands and all America, Tikhon, and lastly, Archimandrite Raphael. The parish sent a telegram to Tsar

Nicholas, thanking him, and at 5:00 p.m., the celebration continued at the saint's house. Thus, St Raphael's second major project was completed.

BISHOP RAPHAEL

St Raphael had already indelibly made his mark in the history of Orthodoxy on the North American continent, but the zenith of his ministry and struggles for the Kingdom of God were still ahead.

As the number of parishes in North America grew, Bishop Tikhon found it impossible to visit all of them, and he began a major reorganization process within the diocese in order to administer it more efficiently. As part of this reorganization, Fr Innocent Pustynsky was consecrated as Tikhon's first auxiliary bishop, and given the title Bishop of Alaska. Bishop Tikhon's plan, which he submitted to the Russian Holy Synod, asked to transfer the See from San Francisco to New York, as most parishes and faithful were concentrated in the east, and proposed that Archimandrite Raphael be ordained a bishop and made his second vicar, after Innocent of Alaska. Impressed by St Raphael's spirituality and leadership skills, he also asked to retain him as head of the Syro-Arab Orthodox Mission in North America.

Indeed, on February 18, 1904, the Holy Synod of Russia unanimously elected Archimandrite Raphael as Bishop of Brooklyn, and approved by the Tsar, the letter made its way across the Atlantic. The Holy Synod informed Patriarch Meletios of the news, and he, pleased with their decision, sent a congratulatory epistle to the saint. St Tikhon published the following letter, announcing the new diocese, with the church of St. Nicholas in Brooklyn as its new Cathedral:

> The Russian Spiritual Authorities have always dealt with the needs of Orthodox Syro-Arabs, and the establishment in North America of the Vicariate of Brooklyn is a new confirmation of this attention. I sincerely congratulate our Orthodox Syro-Arabs, that henceforth in the person of Archimandrite Raphael, they will have their own national bishop. All Orthodox Arabs in America are placed under his immediate authority, and the name of the Bishop of Brooklyn is to be commemorated at prayers, along with that of the Diocesan Bishop, in all Syro-Arab parishes in North America. [The liturgical celebration of] Archimandrite Raphael's election will take place on February 28/March 12, in the New York cathedral, and his consecration on February 29/March 13, the third Sunday of Great Lent,

171

St Raphael, after his episcopal ordination.

in the Brooklyn Syro-Arab church. Father Raphael after his consecration as bishop will be freed from his duties as censor of the *Amerikanskii Pravoslavnyi Vestnik*, and is thanked by the Diocesan Authorities for his work as censor. Censorship of the *Vestnik* is assigned to the member of the Censorship Committee, Priest John Kochurov. —Bishop Tikhon.[31]

On the third Sunday of Lent, 1904,[32] St Raphael became the first Orthodox bishop to be consecrated on American soil. Bishop Tikhon and Bishop Innocent of Alaska officiated at the service at Saint Nicholas Cathedral in Brooklyn, which was packed with faithful. The new bishop's vestments were a gift from Tsar Nicholas II. Many New York newspapers, as well as reporters from other cities and even states, covered the historic occasion, some of them going into great detail. These priceless articles, some of which described the entire ceremony from beginning to end, preserved the memory of an event that changed the course of Orthodox history in America. The following excerpts give a small glimpse into the glorious day:

> New York yesterday enjoyed an extremely interesting spectacle, not common anywhere, and unique in America, the ordination of a Bishop in the Orthodox catholic Church of the East, commonly called the Greek Church. The Right Reverend metropolitan Tikhon Bishop of Aleutia and North America was recently granted two coadjutor bishops by the Holy Synod of Russia, in view of the immense extent of his diocese and of the great growth of his church in the United states, Canada, and Alaska. The first of these to don the mitre was Archimandrite Innokenty, who was consecrated Bishop of Alaska in Saint Petersburg. His arrival on Tuesday last made it possible to ordain to the bishopric the archimandrite Rafael, rector of the Syro-Arabian church in Brooklyn, to have charge of all the Orthodox Syrians in the States, Canada, and Mexico, numbering about 20,000.
>
> The first part of the ceremony … was performed in the Russian cathedral on east 97th Street on Saturday evening. The gorgeous ceremonial and robes, the fine singing, and large, deeply reverential audience (which included many Americans) would be well worth detailed description did space permit. At the conclusion of the service, Bishop Tikhon came from the sanctuary arrayed in his purple silk mantle and wearing his short pall.[33]

173

Archimandrite Raphael Hawaweeny of the Syrian Arabic Greek Orthodox Church was consecrated yesterday morning in the little edifice where the distinguished Syrian pastor has spent the last seven years working for the establishment of the church in America. The services were followed by a mass, conducted by the newly consecrated Bishop who is the first Bishop of his church in America ...

At 10:30 o'clock the little church was crowded to the doors. Believers from all over the country were present to witness the ceremony. Dignitaries of the church from various cities as well as officiating priests of the order were present, taking part in the services which lasted 2 hours and a half ...

A chorus of male voices chanted a processional while bishops Tikhon and Innocent, dressed in the purple, covered with the golden gilt vestments of their stations, walked slowly out of the royal gate and through a lane formed by the spectators to a small platform in the middle of the auditorium. Following the bishops was archimandrite Raphael accompanied by archpriest Toth who decorated the candidate with three imperial orders and then presented him to the waiting bishops. In Russian, Greek, and Syrian Bishop Tikhon asked the candidate to make confession of faith. He responded in all three languages repeating the confession.[34]

"In accordance with the decision of the Holy Synod at St. Petersburg, a third bishop was added yesterday to the Russian Church in America ... Raphael Hawaweeny, Archimandrite, pastor of the Syrian Arabic church of Brooklyn, became Bishop Raphael, the first of his faith to be consecrated in America."[35]

Long before the hour set for the ceremonies, Pacific Street between Smith and Hoyt streets was crowded from corner to corner by people who wished to see the procession from the home of the archimandrite ... Every hue and color was represented in the procession, which moved slowly to the church. Two policemen had a busy time in preventing the curious from obstructing its progress. At the entrance of the church was another great crowd. Inside every foot of standing room was occupied.[36] At least 2,000 worshippers jammed the building, so that with the heat of hundreds of burning tapers, three women fainted just before the actual consecration of the new bishop ... The nominated Bishop knelt while the bishops placed their hands on his head and invoke the Holy Ghost to descend and bless him. Bishop Raphael ranks as the Bishop of Brooklyn and second prelate in the Aleutian diocese.[37]

NEW STRUGGLES

Following his ordination, Bishop Raphael redoubled his pastoral labors, dedicating his entire being to the nourishment of his flock. To that goal, he announced his intention to publish a magazine, which he called *Al-Kalimat* (The Word). This would serve as the official publication of the Syro-Arab mission, and would help bring the people and parishes of his diocese closer together. He knew that he could not visit all Orthodox faithful across North America, but through the ministry of the printed word, he could preach the word of salvation even to people he would never meet. Recognizing that the future of the Orthodox Church in America was English-speaking, he wrote portions of the magazine in English. The first issue was published on January 1, 1905. The introduction read:

> We called our magazine Al-Kalimat—The Word, first in the name of our Saviour and Redeemer Jesus Christ, the Word of God, and second in order to indicate one of our three priestly duties, the duty of teaching and preaching the word of salvation everywhere, and especially within our God-saved diocese in accordance with the commandment of the Apostle Paul (see II Tim. 4:1-5).[38]

The content of the new magazine was to be exclusively spiritual. *Al-Kalimat—The Word* would focus on five primary topics:

1. Dogmatic truths
2. Ethical teachings
3. Ecclesiastical subjects, both historical and contemporary
4. A chronicle of the diocese
5. Official pronouncements

Through the pages of this work, St Raphael desired to enlighten the faithful on dogmatic and ethical issues, to inform them about the situation in other Orthodox countries, and to spread the spirit of love amongst a widely dispersed flock. He had no intention of meddling in pointless polemics and critiques of other Christian denominations or of political movements. His purpose was solely spiritual: to build up the Arab Orthodox across America in the faith. This purity of intentions is one of the primary reasons *The Word* continues to be published to this day.

His new episcopal position did not stop him from continuing his missionary journeys across America, during which he baptized, confessed, married, liturgized, and preached the word of God. Once, on the return trip to New York from a grueling cross-country missionary journey, St Raphael arrived by train in a Midwestern town late one evening and, carrying his own luggage, quietly made his way to a nearby hotel to await a connecting train early the next morning. "Physically exhausted from several months of travel and living out of suitcases, St Raphael found himself in the unique circumstance of not having the name or address of a single contact in the area; thus he could, at long last, enjoy an evening of undisturbed and well-deserved rest. Instead, after placing his luggage in the simple room, St Raphael went out to roam the dark streets, hoping to discover even one Orthodox Christian to whom he could minister. After several hours and numerous inquiries, he happened upon a handful of young Orthodox Arabs and joyfully spent the entire night and early morning hours comforting them in their loneliness, offering them fatherly counsel and advice, instructing and encouraging them in the faith, and hearing their confessions. Only at the last moment did he reluctantly leave their company in order to rush back to the hotel, retrieve his suitcases and hurry to his train. Out of breath, he arrived at the station in time to board the train as it pulled away from the platform. But before he closed his eyes to steal a few minutes of rest on the crowded and noisy train, St Raphael carefully inscribed in his notebook the names and addresses of his new-found spiritual children, placing next to each a notation of what he promised to send—to one a prayer book, to another an icon, to yet another a prayer rope, and, to all, assurance of his paternal love, prayers and blessings."[39]

In April of 1905, he blessed the groundbreaking of a new Orthodox church in Boston, and in May of that same year, he was once again honored by Tsar Nicholas with the Cross of the Order of St. Vladimir, 3rd class. Two months later, in July of 1905, Bishop Raphael participated in a groundbreaking event in the history of Orthodoxy in America: the consecration of The Holy Monastery of St Tikhon of Zadonsk, the first Orthodox monastery in the contiguous United States, and its adjoining orphanage, in South Canaan, Pennsylvania.

On July 16, he traveled to the site on which the monastery would be built, a farm near Mayfield, Pennsylvania. As Archbishop Tikhon was in San Francisco, he presided over the blessing of the grounds and the commencement of the work. At the train station, he was greeted by the proistamenos of the planned monastery, Hieromonk Arseny Chagovtsov (later bishop of Winnipeg), and the members of the local Orthodox community. The welcome was warm and joyous; as soon as the train pulled into the station, the community band began to play. Four fraternal societies in full traditional costume, with their leaders donning dress swords, officially greeted the hierarch. The men then lined up on either side of the path leading from the train to the carriage that would take Bishop Raphael, Fr Arseny, and a third priest, to the site, forming a sort of honor guard. The faithful of the area had gathered along the main road leading to the Orthodox church in Mayfield, and Fr Raphael blessed them as the carriage drove past. At the church, he was greeted by the children of the parish school dressed in their Sunday best. The entrance to the church was filled with faithful holding the cross and fans. It was like the entire populace had gathered at the church to celebrate this historic moment.

The parish priest greeted the hierarch, blessing him with the cross, and after putting on his episcopal mantle, St Raphael entered the church, which was richly decorated and brightly lit with candles. As he entered, the congregation chanted "Axion Estin."[40] The bishop venerated the icons, and then sat on the throne to hear the priest's greeting, which started in this way:

> Your Grace, fortunate is the flock in Mayfield to greet you joyously this day of your arrival in our midst. We have not yet recovered from the feelings of joy we experienced at the recent visit of our first hierarch, Archbishop Tikhon, and now the Lord has given us this opportunity to receive and greet with proper festivity Your Grace, and once again to see a hierarch and to hear the celebration of the hierarchical service. You have come to us as the first hierarch of the Syro-Arabian Church in America, in order to share with the Russian people the joy of the opening of the orphanage and the establishment of the Holy Community ...[41]

He responded, expressing his gratitude and joy at being able to represent Bishop Tikhon in such a watershed moment in Orthodox history, and then, once again greeting the faithful, departed. The next day, Sunday, July 17, 1905, he celebrated the Divine Liturgy at the Mayfield church, and then accompanied Fr Arseny to the site where the monastery was to be built. The carriage trip took three long hours, but when he arrived at the farmhouse, which temporarily served as the orphanage, he celebrated the evening service, in the presence of Sister Maria, the head of the orphanage, the children, and members of staff, along with some local Orthodox farmers. Some non-Orthodox residents of the area also joined them, and came back again the next day when the saint celebrated Matins and blessed the orphanage. Fr Alexander Hotovitzky, who was soon to be martyred for his faith during the Soviet Purges, joined him in celebrating the Divine Liturgy out in the open, in the spot where the cornerstone of the first building of the monastery was to be laid. Over 100 people were in attendance.

TRIALS

As with all saints, so with St Raphael, the cup of temptation was always close by. The biggest of these temptations came shortly after his ordination to the episcopacy, in mid-August of 1905.

Through the previous months, a hostile fight had broken out between the Orthodox Syrian newspaper, and that of the Catholic Maronites. The constant vitriolic interchanges had forced the saint to call on the two sides to put an end to the fighting. The publisher of the Maronite newspaper, however, known for his extremist views, took this call to peace as the long sought-for opportunity to attack the saint. He began to publish scandalous, defamatory articles, casting aspersion on the saint's moral character. At the same time, the hierarch began receiving death threats, and was forced to have parishioners accompany him everywhere he went, particularly at night, to protect him from possible attacks. Indeed, the conflict between the Orthodox and the Maronites had spilled out onto the streets, and the brawls resulted in several serious injuries for both sides.

One night, as he was on his way to visit a parishioner who had been injured during one of these altercations, St Raphael found himself in the middle of yet another such street scuffle. The police were called, and they arrested everyone in sight, including the bishop, who by this time had passed through and was on his way to the parishioner. The officer who arrested the saint claimed, for reasons no one was able to decipher, that the saint not only had a gun, but that he had aimed it at him and fired, though he claimed the gun had misfired and therefore he was unharmed. St Raphael was imprisoned overnight, but the next morning he was released on bail.

The case was taken to court, where it remained until December 7, when all charges were dropped. During this time, and for some time after, Bishop Raphael continued receiving death threats, and began to be followed by suspicious-looking individuals. The case did not escape the notice of the local newspaper, which published the following:

> Despite threats against his life, Bishop Rafael Hawaweeny of the Syrian Greek church officiated yesterday at the services held at the church, on Pacific Street. A guard of detectives was on hand. The congregation was the largest since the troubles of Bishop Hawaweeny with the anti-church element began. The bishop declared that he readily forgave his detractors and said that he regretted their ungodliness. He also called upon his congregation not to raise an arm in his defense, as the laws were ample protection against the attacks that were being made on him and his parishioners.[42]

FOUNDATIONS FOR THE FUTURE

For the next ten years, Bishop Raphael tended his growing flock. His ministry had accomplished three major milestones, which would leave their mark in the history of Orthodoxy in America: the acquisition of Saint Nicholas Cathedral and parish cemetery, *The Word* magazine, and the ordination of the first bishop on the American continent.

Taking heed of St Paul's words, "I press toward the mark for the prize of the high calling of God in Christ Jesus,"[43] he didn't rest on his laurels, but always looked to the future, organizing new projects and fighting with ever-renewing strength for the salvation of his flock. Indeed, with the growth of his New York community there came an increase in the number of children, and he was concerned about their future. He wanted to establish an evening school to educate them in a Christian atmosphere, as he knew that the future of the Church in America depended on the instruction of the youth. The next generation of Orthodoxy would not depend on first-generation immigrants, but on their American-born children, who considered America, and not Syria, their home. He wanted to keep both their national and their religious identity alive, all while respecting and preparing them for the English-speaking world in which they lived. This began with the issue of language. Children who did not speak Arabic, and therefore did not understand the Arab-language church services, were already choosing to attend non-Orthodox churches where services were conducted in English. Even worse, several first-generation immigrants who had been enticed by missionaries of other

Christian denominations while still in Syria now chose to send their children to Protestant and Catholic Sunday schools.

Seeing the danger, Bishop Raphael saw the absolute necessity for using English in worship and in education, and began several programs to address the problem. He had become fluent in English himself, adding it to the large selection of languages he already spoke, and he knew that the future of the Arabic community in America was English-speaking. With the help of Fr Ingram Nathaniel Irvine, a former Episcopal priest and recent convert to Orthodoxy, he began a widespread program to incorporate English into both the services and the community life of the Syro-Arab mission. Fr Ingram, who had been received into the church and ordained a presbyter by Bishop Tikhon in October of 1906, recommended an all-English Divine Liturgy and sermon once a month, as well as at least four English-language articles in *The Word*. Additionally, there would be an English-language Sunday school every Sunday. This coincided with the publication of *The Service Book of the Holy Orthodox Catholic Apostolic Church*, translated by Isabel Hapgood, which contained a compilation of Russian Orthodox services translated into English. St Raphael recommended the use of this book in all of his parishes throughout the United States.

In a sermon delivered from the ambo of the Brooklyn Cathedral, St Raphael called the community to a General Assembly to discuss the spiritual and financial issues of the diocese, amongst which was the new Orthodox school. He published the invitation in the pages of all Arab-language newspapers in America, setting the date for the assembly on June 26, 1906. When the day came, the parish hall was overflowing with people, all of who supported their bishop's planned projects. Four years later, toward the end of 1910, the dream which had been born in that assembly was made reality in the form of a night school, which operated daily from 4:00 to 6:00 p.m., and which taught, amongst other things, liturgics, chant, Orthodox doctrine and practice, and Arabic.

Seeing the need to expand in order to house all these new organizations, St Raphael oversaw the purchase of a large three-story building directly next to the cathedral. This structure would house the central offices of the Brooklyn Diocese, along with the night school, Sunday school, and orphanage, as well as serve as the vicarage. This purchase cost $16,000[44], and after a down payment of $4,000, they received a five-year loan at 6 percent interest for the remainder.

The saint preached ceaselessly, inspiring thousands with his words. His sermons were noted for combining practicality with instruction in the Divine Word, and like iconography, taking the Divine and making it accessible to the human. On the Sunday of the Canaanite Woman, 1907, he delivered the following sermon to his flock:

> Beloved, in this age irreligion and atheistic principles have almost become universal because of the striving of individuals and peoples in most corners of the globe after money, which has come to be considered the only source of true happiness …
>
> And so some people ask, "what is the benefit of unceasing prayer, since God very often does not answer our prayer no matter how much we cry out to Him with hope?" They say that we should abandon lengthy prayers, the repetition of which does not benefit us in any way but only robs us of our precious time!
>
> We agree with the people who say this insofar as very often one prays to God with all warmth and faith but God does not respond immediately and at all times. But what is the best thing for us to do in this case? Is it to abandon prayer, as they say, and turn our attention to work or is it to persist in it without weariness or boredom? There is no doubt that no one can answer this question for us better than our heavenly Teacher, the Lord of wisdom and of right behavior. Our Lord and God Jesus told His disciples a parable about how "it is necessary to pray at all times without tiring" of prayer. He said, "There was in a certain city a judge who did not fear God nor regard man. Now there was a widow in that city; and she came to him, saying, 'Get justice for me from my adversary.' And he would not for a while; but afterward he said within himself, 'Though I do not fear God nor regard man, yet because this widow troubles me I will avenge her, lest by her continual coming she weary me.'"[45]
>
> So see how the Lord teaches us through this parable that we should pray at all times without tiring or boredom and that even if God is slow to respond, He will inevitably fulfill our requests that we make earnestly and persistently.
>
> Perhaps someone might ask, "Why is God slow to fulfill our requests which are often for healing a beloved child or a dear relative who is suffering on the bed of sickness and injury?" We reply that this is in order for God to test our faith and our love for Him. We have seen the episode of the

Canaanite woman that was read to you today. It is that one day while Jesus was outside the land of Genesareth, on His way to the area of Tyre and Sidon, a Canaanite woman appeared, Syro-Phoenician by race and pagan by religion.[46] She had come out of that region, crying in a loud voice and imploring Jesus, saying, "Have mercy on me, O Lord, Son of David, for my daughter is severely afflicted." In order to test her, Jesus remained silent and did not reply with even a word. But she continued to run after the crowd, begging for Jesus' mercy, tears streaming from her eyes like blood, until the entire crowd felt pity for her and Jesus' disciples went to Him and said, "Send her away, for she cries out after us." Jesus refused their request and said to them, "I was not sent except to the lost sheep of the house of Israel." The woman finally went up to Jesus "and worshiped Him, saying, 'Lord!'" But Jesus did not help her or even dry her tears with a comforting word. He replied with words sharper than a blade, comparing her as a foreigner in race and religion to a dog. He said that He saw no good in turning His care from the people of His race and religion and focusing it on foreigners, saying, "It is not good to take the children's bread and throw it to the dogs." But rather than acting like a fool or becoming angry at these insulting words and in sorrow and despair leaving Jesus, she replied with all patience and calm, "Yes, Lord, yet even the dogs eat the crumbs which fall from their masters' table." When Jesus had become certain—indeed, the crowd was made certain—of her great faith in Him, He answered, "O woman, great is your faith! Let it be to you as you desire." And truly Jesus fulfilled her request, as the Evangelist says, "her daughter was healed from that very hour."[47, 48]

On March 26, 1907, St Tikhon returned to Russia, as he had been elected the new archbishop of the historic city of Yaroslavl. He was succeeded by Archbishop Platon, who had recently arrived from Russia, and on August 20 of that year, St Raphael, along with representatives of the clergy and laity of the Arabic communities of New York, greeted their new primate. During the speech which followed, St Raphael spoke about the history of Orthodoxy in America, and invited the new archbishop to celebrate Divine Liturgy at the cathedral in Brooklyn on Sunday, September 16.

The next two years saw two more honors bestowed upon the faithful Syrian shepherd. Having served, in one of his many positions, as president of the Red Cross in Syria, he was awarded a medal for his significant donation

The last known picture of St Raphael, 1914.

of $2,000^{49}$ for the relief of the victims of the 1905 Revolution in Russia. This distinction was conferred upon him in March of 1908, by Maria Feodorovna, mother of the tsar, and then president of the Russian Red Cross. In June of the following year, Tsar Nicholas II awarded him the Cross of the Order of St. Anna, 1st class, an honor usually reserved only for hereditary nobility.

THE END

St Raphael's earthly journey was destined to be a brief one. On October 25, 1912, as he was working in his office, he felt a sharp pain in his stomach. Ignoring it, he continued working, but after an hour, the pain had become excruciating, and he was forced to rest. Another hour passed with no reprieve from the anguish, and his face had now become pallid and weak. This was the beginning of the illness which would claim his life. Doctors initially were not able to diagnose the cause of the pain. During this period the saint prayed ceaselessly, "Lord, let thy will be done." Eventually, he was diagnosed with myocarditis, an ailment which causes inflammation in the heart muscles and weakens the organ. At the time, it was most often fatal.

His diocese immediately published an encyclical letter, calling on all the Arabic parishes in North America to hold a service of supplication to the Theotokos for the restoration of his health. Dozens of parishes across the continent gathered on Sunday, November 4, following the Divine Liturgy, to pray for their hierarch. The next day, Monday, the saint felt better, and his doctors noticed a marked improvement. He was allowed to begin receiving visitors, many of whom gathered at the cathedral on November 8 for the feast day of the bishop's patron saint, and for his own birthday. The same evening, Archbishop Platon visited the hierarch to offer his prayers and to congratulate him for a speedy recovery. Two weeks after his initial attack, St Raphael felt strong enough to celebrate the Liturgy in his cathedral. It was Sunday, November 11, and the church was filled with the faithful who had come to see their shepherd.

Having somewhat recovered, he continued his ceaseless missionary activity, not heeding the doctors' orders for constant rest and exceeding care. In January of 1913, he was a concelebrant at the Divine Liturgy marking the opening of the new Orthodox Seminary of North America in Tenafly, New Jersey. The seminary had been moved from its previous location in Minneapolis after an internal reorganization. A month later, on February 21, he attended the celebratory liturgy at the Russian cathedral in New York, to mark the tricentennial anniversary of the Romanov dynasty. Responding to the congratulatory telegram from the saint, Tsar Nicholas asked for his blessing and prayers.

Despite his severely weakened health, and the pain and difficulties which accompanied it, the irrepressible bishop continued his missionary journeys across America, miraculously completing two more transcontinental trips in the years 1913–1914. In total, he had crisscrossed the continent six times, all in the service of the sheep of Christ's flock in the Americas. In the Historical Chronicle of the Diocese of Brooklyn, these six trips are recorded in detail. The numerous States he visited, in which he performed the sacraments, consecrated churches, blessed the plans for new works, preached, taught, and nourished the souls of the faithful. He traveled by land and sea, over mountains and valleys, suffering the heat of the day and the frost of the night, with only one goal: to find and offer spiritual consolation to every Orthodox soul across the continent.

Finally, his body, unable to keep up with the superhuman demands of his soul, gave up. In the last months of 1914, he again fell ill. He spent two months at home, bearing his illness with fortitude, patience, calmness, and courage. The peace which he radiated at this time fooled those who surrounded him. They could not believe that a man who looked so calm was so close to death. But at 12:40 a.m. on February 14/27,[50] 1915, the saintly hierarch peacefully delivered his soul to God. Only then did this shepherd rest.

They called him, but he did not answer. They shook him, but he did not respond. Their father was gone.

That evening, Bishop Alexander, who had replaced Bishop Innocent as head of the Diocese of Alaska, arrived at the saint's residence. With the help of several other priests, they dressed him in his hierarchal vestments and began the reading of the Gospel. The next day was a Sunday, and Bishop Alexander led a procession of priests from the Brooklyn Cathedral to the saint's house. Masses of faithful followed, weeping at their indescribable loss. When they reached the house, they performed a short memorial service, and then carried his body back to the Cathedral. After his body was placed in the center of the church, they began the Divine Liturgy. It was a heartbreaking service, with the priests often unable to speak from their deep sorrow, and the congregation weeping loudly.

The saint's body remained in the cathedral for a week, during which the Gospel was read 24 hours a day, interrupted only during services. Divine

St Raphael's funeral service.

Liturgy was celebrated every morning, and the memorial service was chanted twice a day, in the morning and evening.

On Sunday, February 22, the church overflowed with people, there to honor the saint on the day of his burial. Archbishop Alexander of Alaska[51] presided over the service, concelebrating with the metropolitan of Seleucia, Herman, who was then on a pastoral visit to the United States, and a record-breaking forty-four priests and four deacons.[52] The cathedral could not hold the masses who had come to venerate the saint, and hundreds of congregants stood outside, ignoring the freezing temperature and snowfall.

After the completion of the Divine Liturgy, the funeral service took place. A procession followed, carrying the saint's body through the streets of Brooklyn, the city he had served for so long. Brooklyn's chief of police led the procession, accompanied by two police officers. Behind him were children, dressed in white, carrying wreaths. The priests and congregation followed, carrying the saint's remains. After returning to the cathedral, Archbishop

187

Alexander gave the final sermon, and the saint's body was moved to the crypt, where a tomb had been prepared.

Five years later, St Raphael's relics were moved to the Mount Olivet cemetery he had purchased, and in 1988, they were once again translated, this time to the cemetery of the Holy Resurrection at the Antiochian Village in Ligonier, Pennsylvania, where they remain to this day.[53]

Catalogue of Churches that were established by St Raphael of Brooklyn, along with the date of their consecration is given below. All these churches were under the canonical ecclesiastical jurisdiction of the Diocese of Brooklyn up until his death.

1. St Nicholas Cathedral, Brooklyn, NY, 1895.
2. St Nicholas Church of Canada, Montreal, Canada, 1899.
3. St George Church, Boston, MA, 1900.
4. St George Church, Worcester, MA, 1902.
5. St George Church, Kearney, NE, 1903.
6. St Mary Church (Dormition), Wilkes-Barre, PA, 1904.
7. St George Church, Lawrence, MA, 1904.
8. St Mary Church (Dormition), Johnstown, PA, 1906.
9. St George Church, Glens Falls, NY, 1906.
10. St Nicholas Church of Montreal, Montreal, Canada, 1908.
11. St George Church, Vicksburg, MS, 1908.
12. Archangel Michael Church, Beaumont, TX, 1908.
13. St George Church, Grand Rapids, MI, 1908.
14. St George Church, Chicago, IL, 1908.
15. St John of Damascus Church, Boston, MA, 1909.
16. St George Church, Washington, DC, 1909.
17. St George Church, Mexico City, DF, 1909.
18. St Simeon Church, Ironwood, MI, 1910.
19. St George Church, Michigan City, IN, 1911.
20. St George Church, Charleston, WV, 1911.
21. St Nicholas Church, Cleveland, OH, 1911.
22. Archangel Michael Church, Geneva, NY, 1912.
23. St Elias Church, La Crosse, WI, 1912.
24. St George Church, Pittsburgh, PA, 1912.
25. St George Church, Macon City, MS, 1913.
26. St George Church, Utica, NY, 1913.

27. St George Church, New Kensington, PA, 1914.
28. St George Church, Cedar Rapids, IA, 1914.
29. Archangel Michael Church, Monessen, PA, 1914.
30. St George Church, Toledo, OH, 1914.

Saint Sebastian of Jackson

THE HUMBLE APOSTLE OF THE NEW WORLD

His memory is commemorated on November 30

ORTHODOX OFFSPRING OF AMERICA

This great saint, equal to the apostles, came from humble origins. His parents, Ilija and Jelena Dabovich, were from a tiny village in Montenegro called Sasovići, in the area of Herceg Novi[1] in the southwestern corner of the country, and were the first documented Serbian immigrants on the West Coast. They arrived in San Francisco in 1853, only three years after California had been admitted to the Union, and they settled down in the growing city, opening a wholesale fruit market. The fourth of their seven children, Jovan (John), who would later become St Sebastian, was born on June 21, 1863, during the presidency of Abraham Lincoln. He would come to be the first American-born Orthodox Christian who would be ordained a priest and tonsured a monk in the entirety of North America.[2]

His parents were one of the hundreds of thousands of individuals and families who moved to San Francisco during the period of the Gold Rush, which began on January 24, 1848, when a man named James W. Marshall discovered gold in Sutter's Mill, in Coloma, California. The news traveled with lightning speed, not only across the continent, but across the world, and soon nearly 300,000 people from North America, Europe, and the Balkans were traveling to the remote wilderness of California to make a new life. While most of these immigrants sought to find gold, some others, like young Jovan's parents, saw it as an opportunity to establish a new life in a new land, one that would provide stability and financial security for their children.

Six years before Jovan's birth, an Orthodox Christian community had already begun to form in San Francisco. It was called the Greco-Russian Slavonic Eastern Church and Aid Society, and was made up of Russian, Serb, Greek, and Syrian immigrants who had arrived during the initial years of the Gold Rush. The community did not have a permanent priest, and was not considered an official parish, so the spiritual and sacramental needs of the flock were served by priests on the warships of the Imperial Russian Navy, which were often docked in the San Francisco harbor. These ships were equipped with facilities to perform divine services, and many had fully operational chapels on board, which celebrated frequent Divine Liturgies. It was on one of these warships, the Богатырь (Bogatyr, meaning "knight" or "hero"), that the young Jovan was baptized by Hieromonk Cyril of the Tikhvin monastery. Years later, St Sebastian recalled: "Eventually, the Russian ships weighed their anchors. And there were no more priests here. It would seem that, left without a church or a priest, this Orthodox community should have disappeared from the face of the earth, especially in the rush for gold, for wealth. Through the mercy of God, however, this did not happen. The Orthodox—Serbs, Greeks, and Russians—lived at that time in concord, and supported each other in a brotherly manner. On all major feasts, they gathered together with those who had families, and sang religious and folk songs."[3]

Finally, in 1868, a year after Alaska was sold to the United States, the Russian Diocese of the Aleutian Islands and Alaska appointed a permanent priest to San Francisco. Fr Nicholas Kovrigin, who had previously served at the cathedral in Sitka, was transferred to California, along with reader Vasily Shishkin, and with their arrival, the San Francisco community was finally able to commence regular liturgical services. The first Orthodox chapel in the bay city was inside the house of a local Serbian, Peter Sekulovich, on Mission Street, which, at the time, was located outside the city. They named their infant community "Prayer House of the Orthodox Oriental Church," and the Dabovich family faithfully attended every service. The very first Divine Liturgy in San Francisco was to take place on Pascha of 1868. It also happened to be the very first Divine Liturgy that young Jovan had ever attended on land, and the momentous event imprinted itself on his childish mind (he was only 5 years old at the time). Years later, he was to write: "I remember that first service, to which I went with my mother. We had to walk a long way along unpaved streets. Furthermore, we were mercilessly drenched by rain. At last we reached a small house; we crossed over a ditch (or temporarily excavated gutter) on a plank and entered the church. The 'church' was set up in a divided room. At the end, opposite the entrance, the Holy Antimension lay on a covered table. A little table in a corner served as the table of oblation. I remember two icons on the walls: the Saviour and the Mother of God. There were approximately twenty communicants at that Liturgy."[4]

THE BIRTH OF A MISSIONARY

Jovan was a serious, quiet, and somewhat frail child, whose piety and love for the Church became manifest from an early age. In 1872, when he was nine years old, the newly consecrated Russian bishop of Alaska and the Aleutians, John (Mitropolsky), transferred his episcopal seat from Sitka, Alaska, to San Francisco. Since Bishop John was the only Orthodox hierarch in the entirety of the American continent, this move marked the transfer of the whole American diocesan administration to California. The bishop was fluent in English, and came to America with the intention of not only serving the needs of the Orthodox Alaskans, but also of bringing the Faith to the heterodox on the North American continent. Wanting Orthodoxy to move into the contiguous United States, he moved the diocesan residence to California.

Upon arrival in San Francisco, Bishop John erected a church on Pierce Street, consecrating it for St Alexander Nevsky. Young Jovan now had the opportunity to attend and participate in all church services and sacraments, and this only increased his wholehearted dedication to the Church and his desire to serve God and his fellow man through the Holy Priesthood. He attended the parish's Saturday school and the "Greco-Russian Seminary" (also known as the Mission School) which Bishop John had transferred from Sitka to San Francisco, and there he had the chance to study alongside Aleut natives who had come from Alaska. At the small school, he became proficient in Russian and Church Slavonic, and also picked up a good deal of Greek. Recalling those early days in San Francisco, Fr Sebastian later wrote: "From the time of the arrival of the Right Reverend John, priests, after his example, began to proclaim the word of truth to the flock in San Francisco. A Saturday school for the children of parishioners was opened where they were taught the Catechism and the Russian language .... Michael Vladimirov was choir director and singing teacher. He also taught mathematics at the [Mission] school. Besides the clergymen that taught at the school, Vladyka[5] himself also had seven classes a week, in Holy Scripture and the Slavonic language. A native Greek, Dimitrios Frankiades, from the University of Athens, was teacher of the Greek and English languages. At the time of the Right Reverend John as many as sixteen pupils studied at the bishop's school in San Francisco. Of that number five are now serving in various positions of the local diocese. The Right Reverend John loved his school, one might say, with a singular love."

193

St Sebastian at
a young age.

St Sebastian as a
young cleric.

As he grew into adulthood, Jovan proved a spiritual beacon, and an exceptional man. Those who knew him best told of his lack of ostentation and disdain for wealth, calling him a modern St Nicholas. He deeply empathized with the poor and helpless, identifying with them so completely that he chose to dress in nothing but modest apparel and eat the simplest of meals, often nothing more than milk and cheese. He frequently gave his possessions away to those in need, a pattern which persisted throughout his life.

After graduating from high school, Jovan served at the San Francisco cathedral as a reader, chanter, and teacher. In 1884 he received word from Russia that he was to be sent to Alaska, to assist at St Michael's Cathedral in Sitka.[6] The cathedral had been established in 1848 by the great enlightener of Alaska, St Innocent, who had converted the Tlingit natives[7] in the Sitka area to the Orthodox Faith. After moving to Alaska, Jovan became acquainted with the natives who had been catechized by St Innocent himself during his extensive missionary and apostolic ministry throughout the vast Alaskan region. Inspired by this great example, twenty-one-year-old Jovan began a missionary ministry of his own, manifesting the bright evangelical zeal which would become the hallmark of his life.

Learning from the Orthodox Tlingit in Sitka that there was another Tlingit population to the northeast that had not yet converted, Jovan organized a mission of Tlingit parishioners to preach the Orthodox Faith to the non-Christian Tlingit, who lived over 100 miles away, near present-day Juneau. Indeed, the Juneau Tlingit responded with eagerness to the new faith, and within six years, groups of them would make the long and arduous journey to Sitka to be baptized. Three years later, in 1893, an Orthodox church was built in Juneau, and today, it is the oldest continually functioning church in Alaska. Several years later St Sebastian recorded: "My assistants among the Indians … set out for what was then a very small place, now the sizable town of Juneau, and following special instructions from me, they (and other parishioners) spread the Word and Orthodoxy, and the result of that is the present Church of St. Nicholas in Juneau."[8]

IN THE SERVICE OF THE CHURCH

Jovan was now twenty-five years old, and his desire to wholly devote himself to the service of the Church was fulfilled on December 30, 1888, when he was tonsured a monk by Bishop Vladimir (Sokolovsky), at the San Francisco cathedral.[9] *The San Francisco Daily* newspaper mentioned the event, writing:

"An interesting ceremony took place at the morning service in the Russian Orthodox Church of St. Nicholas yesterday. Rev. John E. Dabovich took the solemn vows of the religious life, being received into the ranks of the monastic order by Rev. Dr. Vladimir, Bishop of Alaska and the Aleutian Islands."[10]

Jovan took the holy monastic vows, and name "Sebastian," as his tonsure took place on the feast of the Roman martyr Sebastian. A new man emerged from the ceremony, one who would fully devote his life to Christ and His ministry. A week later, on the feast of the Nativity,[11] he was ordained into the Holy Deaconate. *The San Francisco Daily* once again noted: "Rev. John E. Dabovich, who was recently ordained a clergyman of the Greek church, was yesterday made Deacon, with the title of Father Sebastian."[12]

Bishop Vladimir, who had officiated over both services, had previously served in the Japanese Orthodox Mission under St Nicholas Kasatkin, Enlightener of Japan. It was from him that the new bishop of the American diocese learned that when the Orthodox Faith is brought to new territories, it must be done in the local languages. He became the first Orthodox hierarch in the New World to preach and serve in English, and required his priests to do the same. As Fr Sebastian later recalled, "The bishop paid special attention in the temple to preaching the word of God in English, which was the language commonly understood. To this end the bishop himself, although not completely familiar with the English language, improvised talks in English, which the people readily heard."[13]

Soon after his ordination to the diaconate, Fr Sebastian traveled to Russia, where he studied at the Theological Academy of St. Petersburg. He stayed there until June of 1892, after which he returned to America. During his absence, a momentous and extraordinary event took place in the United States. In 1891, Bishop Vladimir traveled to Minneapolis, Minnesota, and on March 25, he received former Uniate cleric Fr Alexis Toth and his 350 parishioners into the Orthodox Church. This proved to be only the beginning of a large and steady flow of Uniates returning to the Faith, which proved perhaps the most significant milestone in the history of the Orthodox Church in America in the twentieth century.

On June 8 of that same year, 1891, Bishop Vladimir was elected bishop of Ostogozhsk,[14] and he departed for Russia in October to assume his new duties. His successor was Bishop Nicholas (Ziorov), whose seven-year American tenure was to prove one of the most significant and fruitful in the history of the Russian Diocese in the contiguous United States. The new bishop lost little time in ordaining the exceptional young monk into the Holy Priesthood, and on August 28, 1892, the very first American citizen to be ordained into the priesthood knelt to receive the blessing of the presbyterate. The *San Francisco Morning Call* dedicated an extensive article to the event.[15]

AN ORDINATION SERVICE.

Held at the Greek-Russian Church Yesterday Morning.

A young man born in San Francisco is the first American to take the vows in that faith.

An impressive ceremony.

A very impressive service was held in the Greek-Russian church on Powell street at 9:00 o'clock yesterday morning, and the church was filled to overflowing.

The occasion was the ordination of Sebastian Dabovich, the first American-born to be admitted into the Russian priesthood. Priests have been ordained in Alaska who were born there, but their birth took place when that country was a Russian colony.

The services were conducted by Bishop Nicholas assisted by Father Greenkevitch as priest and Father Soboleff as deacon. The opening chant was from the liturgy of Saint John and sung by the choir of eight boys.

The Russian church differs from other Christian churches by having the services held in the body of the church as well as in the pulpit.

After the first part, which was about the usual Sunday morning service, the Bishop marched to a small dais in the center of the church, followed by the candidate for admission into the priesthood, and the other functionaries who formed a line on either side. The Bishop asked for blessings on the candidate, after which the Cherubic Hymn was chanted. At the conclusion of the singing, the Bishop laid his hands on the head of the young man who was then kneeling at his feet, and an assistant put over his shoulders the robes that he will wear in future whenever he officiates that service. After a blessing was asked, the usual morning service was proceeded with, and the new-made priest took part as an assistant.

Sebastian Dabovich, the new priest, was born in San Francisco of Slavonic parents in 1863 and received his early education in a private school. Later in life he studied with father Johannes and Bishop Nestor. It was his intention from childhood to become a priest, and he has never thought of anything else. In November 1890 he left this country for Russia, visiting several of the cities in that country for a few months, but eventually settling down to study in Saint Petersburg. He also spent some time at Kiev, one of the holy towns of Russia, and a place to which the devout members of the church make pilgrimages. He returned to this country on the 20th of June last, and has spent most of his time since in retirement and preparations for the obligations he was soon to take.

Father Dabovich will preach his first sermon next Sunday morning in English. His subject will be "Love According to Christian Doctrine". Next Monday he will leave for a missionary tour of the coast, to be gone several months. He will visit every town between Victoria and San Diego and says there are over 2,000 of his countrymen that he will talk to.[16]

And so began the great missionary ministry of St Sebastian, one of the most significant workers for the spread of Christ's gospel in the twentieth century, and a man whom St Nikolai, bishop of Ohrid and Žiča, would later refer to as "The greatest Serbian missionary of modern times."[17]

IN THE FOOTSTEPS OF THE APOSTLES

Before his ordination, Fr Sebastian had submitted a report to Bishop Nicholas in which he had estimated that there were some 1,500 Orthodox Christians living in California, Oregon, and the then-territory of Washington. He asked that he be assigned to minister to the parishes, communities, and individuals dispersed across these states, and Bishop Nicholas, recognizing his rare apostolic zeal, granted his request, appointing the young hieromonk to California and the Pacific Northwest. Within a week of his ordination, Fr Sebastian had already departed for his first missionary tour of the West Coast, eventually traveling as far north as Vancouver, British Columbia, and south to San Diego. He traversed over 3,000 miles, paying little heed to the primitive transportation and the tiring journey. While most often traveling by rail or horse-drawn coach, he found that many of the Orthodox communities were far removed from railway stations, and required miles and hours of journeying on foot to reach them. The saintly missionary did not let any of these discomforts deter him, walking miles in the heat, rain, and cold to reach the sheep of Christ's flock. Across the states and regions, Fr Sebastian found poor Orthodox immigrants of many ethnic backgrounds who lived far from Orthodox churches and clergy. As he wrote in a letter to Bishop Nicholas, some of these believers had come under the influence of Protestantism, as those had been the only churches accessible to them, but they welcomed the opportunity to return to their mother Church. He also found many Uniates who called themselves Orthodox, but had acquired "questionable practices"[18] as a result of their ties to Roman Catholicism.

While in the Northwest, Fr Sebastian baptized children and adults, celebrated weddings and the Divine Liturgy, and served all other necessary services and sacraments for the isolated Orthodox of the region. Extremely grateful to their new missionary priest, the flocks in these states began to hope that maybe there was a chance that Orthodox churches would now be established in their areas. Fr Sebastian hoped with them, and prayed that by God's grace, their wish would be fulfilled.

While visiting Oregon, the tireless hieromonk decided that Portland would be the best site for a future church. While there were very few Orthodox in the city itself, Portland was a central location, easily accessible to all believers in the region, like the significant number of Greek fishermen who had settled along the Columbia River and in the port city of Astoria. Further north, in Seattle, he found a group of dedicated faithful, strong and unmoved in their Orthodoxy, who were eager to form a parish. He also found small, dispersed flocks in the communities of Tacoma, Gig Harbor, and Wilkeson, as well as Vancouver and Victoria, in British Columbia. In Gig Harbor, he baptized the Native American wife of a pious Serbian man from Herzegovina; this couple and their large extended family later became founding members of the first Orthodox church in Seattle.

Although he was of Serbian ancestry, Fr Sebastian knew his task was to minister to the Orthodox of all ethnic backgrounds, and to preach the Faith to the non-Orthodox Americans. Being fluent in English, Serbian, and Russian, and knowing some Greek as well, he served as a bridge between the traditionally Orthodox countries of the Old World, and the vast spiritual wilderness of the New. A century later, Bishop Irinej Dobrijević, the Serbian Orthodox bishop of Eastern America, would write: "By every report Sebastian Dabovich was not one to ask about jurisdictional or national affiliation before setting out on long journeys to minister to Orthodox Christians in mining communities, lumber camps, or far-distant towns or villages. He offered his pastoral services with a free hand to anyone who was in need. Just as he gave no thought to his own comforts as a youth, caring more for the needs of others than for his own concerns, Fr Sebastian denied himself all worldly comforts of home, family, or earthly possessions, so that he could provide for

199

the spiritual needs of the Russian, Serbian, Bulgarian, Greek, Syrian, or Arab Orthodox Christians who required his aid."

During Fr Sebastian's 1893 service in the Pacific Northwest, Fr Alexis Toth was constantly traveling back and forth from his parish in Minneapolis to the Uniate community in Wilkes-Barre, Pennsylvania, which he would soon be bringing into the Orthodox Church. Seeing that the division of his time was proving detrimental to both parishes, Fr Alexis wrote to Bishop Nicholas requesting a temporary assistant priest for his Minneapolis parish of St Mary's, so that he could return to Pennsylvania and devote himself fully to completing his work in Wilkes-Barre. Granting this request, Bishop Nicholas sent Fr Sebastian to Minneapolis. The young hieromonk was to remain there for about a year, nurturing the flock which Fr Toth had brought back into the fold. While at St Mary's, Fr Sebastian continued the work of the great Fr Alexis, striving to help the former Uniates enter more deeply into the life of the Orthodox Church. A charismatic minister, he preached eloquent sermons and taught at the parish school. The church choir director and music director of the school, Paul Zaichenko, provided a priceless vignette of Fr Sebastian from that period: "Fr Sebastian Dabovich succeeded Fr A. Toth as parish priest. He was a quiet and pensive monk, always considerate, conscientious, modest. He performed his duties sincerely, and taught the Bible class of the parish school with enthusiasm. He was a tireless and unselfish worker, a humble and a just man before his Lord. He was one of the most worthy workers in the Mission. I knew him back in San Francisco. At that time, he sang in the cathedral choir, of which I was a choirmaster. His aim was his betterment in religious life. As in San Francisco, so too in Minneapolis, he was the example of virtuous living; he always considered it his duty to avoid an evil step. Leading a quiet monastic life, he found great happiness in reading religious books and in teaching students the Holy Bible. He loved children and was always considerate of his parishioners."[19]

While serving in Minneapolis, Fr Sebastian made his first visit to Chicago, where he spent five days assisting Bishop Nicholas in organizing the Russian Orthodox exhibit for the World's Columbian Exposition.[20] The Fair ran from May 1 to October 30, 1893, and featured ethnic handicraft and works of art, parades of people from dozens of different nationalities around the world, in traditional dress and costume, as well as exhibits on different religions, foreign to most Americans. While in Chicago, Fr Sebastian gathered the local Orthodox Serbs and celebrated the Divine Liturgy for them, unknowingly laying the foundation for what was to become the Serbian Orthodox church in Chicago.

APOSTOLIC FRUIT

After less than a year of serving in Minneapolis, Fr Sebastian was recalled to the West Coast to resume his missionary work there. He arrived in San Francisco in December of 1893, but was soon called away again, this time to baptize a Serbian infant in Jackson, California, which was then a gold-mining community near the "mother lode."[21] Seeing that many Serbian miners had settled with their families in Jackson and the neighboring towns, Fr Sebastian immediately recognized the need to build an Orthodox church in the area, and he urged the local Orthodox inhabitants to begin working toward that goal. The Serbs agreed and began gathering the necessary resources, purchasing the land for both the church and an Orthodox cemetery. Things moved quickly, and by December of 1894, the new church had been erected.

On December 16, Bishop Nicholas consecrated the new church, dedicating it to St Sava of Serbia. Although the consecration was celebrated in Slavonic, Fr Sebastian had made sure to translate portions of the service into English so those in attendance not familiar with Church Slavonic could follow along. The new church in Jackson, founded by the first Orthodox priest ordained in the United States, became the first Serbian Orthodox church to be erected in the Western Hemisphere. The small, but picturesque church is still in service today, and has the additional distinction of being the oldest operating Orthodox church in the western (contiguous) United States. Bishop Nicholas gave the new parish a gift of an icon of the Theotokos, which had been sent from the Monastery of St Panteleimon on Mt. Athos. This icon, commonly referred to as the Jackson icon of the Mother of God, is wonderworking.

While remaining based in San Francisco, Fr Sebastian continued his missionary travels throughout the western United States. In Seattle, he organized the community which was later to become the Saint Spyridon Cathedral, and served as their temporary priest, establishing their ecclesiastical and sacramental life. In 1892 and 1895 he visited Wilkeson, Washington, and assisted the flock in founding their new church, which they did in 1896, dedicating it to the Holy Trinity. He served the first ever Divine Liturgy at the Portland church of St Nicholas in 1895.

In August of 1897, Fr Sebastian traveled to Butte, Montana, which was, at the time, the most important copper-mining center in the United States. On

August 15/27, he celebrated the Divine Liturgy for the Feast of the Dormition of the Theotokos. After the service, the missionary hieromonk met with the Orthodox in the area, mostly Serbian copper miners, and discussed the possibility of building a church in the town. Indeed, the faithful embraced the idea, and with his assistance and encouragement, the parish of the Holy Trinity came into being. The new church was completed in 1904, and Fr Sebastian once again traveled over 1,000 miles to celebrate its inaugural Divine Liturgy on the feast of the Beheading of the Forerunner, on August 29/September 1, 1904.

The tireless and devoted missionary visited Orthodox communities of all sizes all across the westernmost United States, in Fresno, Visalia, and Hanford, California, and Bisbee, Arizona, establishing parishes and becoming the impetus behind the building of churches. In recognition of his extraordinary missionary labors, Bishop Nicholas awarded Fr Sebastian a gold cross, a distinction typically reserved for Russian clergy who had served the church for at least ten years. The young hieromonk had not even completed three years since his ordination to the priesthood. Bishop Nicholas explained the reason for this unusual recognition and exception in his episcopal address, delivered at the honoring ceremony:

> With the blessing of the Most-holy Ruling Synod of All Russia and by the assent of the Most-pious Emperor, this high sign of distinction is now bestowed upon you, my beloved brother in the Lord. It is granted to you not only as a reward for your devout ministry in the lower ecclesiastical ranks, but even more so as an encouragement in the ever-greater labors and heroic tasks which you will continue to face in your missionary ministry .... You were not forced to pick up the cross of a monk and a missionary, but did it of your own free will, for your and others' salvation. This made you not your own but Christ's; now you should seek not your own, but the things which are Jesus Christ's.[22]

In 1896 Fr Sebastian made a trip to his ancestral land of Serbia, where he studied theology for a few months. Upon his return to the United States, he was appointed priest of the St Basil Cathedral in San Francisco, and teacher at the church school. This new position did not prevent him from continuing his missionary work, and in October of 1897, he and Fr Alexander Hotovitzky accompanied Bishop Nicholas on a trip to Washington, D.C., serving as translators for the hierarch when he met with President William McKinley. This was the second meeting in the history of the United States between an Orthodox bishop and a United States president, the first being a meeting between Bishop Vladimir and President Grover Cleveland in 1889. In his audience with the president, Bishop Nicholas expressed his concern over the treatment of Orthodox Christians in the new American district of Alaska,[23] and particularly the fact that American trading companies were compelling the faithful to work on Sundays and feast days. The hierarch asked the president to stop the unlawful seizure of church property, which was taking place throughout the Alaskan region, and the president promised to present the matter to Congress.

A SWIFT WRITER AND PREACHER OF GRACE

The year 1898 brought a great blessing for Orthodoxy in America in the form of Bishop Tikhon (Belavin), later patriarch of Moscow and All Russia, who was appointed to succeed Bishop Nicholas as head of the Diocese of the Aleutian Islands and Alaska. On December 23, 1898, St Tikhon arrived in San Francisco, and was met at the train station by Fr Sebastian, and representatives of the various nationalities of the cathedral parish: Russian, Serbian, Greek, and Syro-Arab.

By the time Bishop Tikhon came to America, Fr Sebastian's reputation as a missionary had spread beyond the borders of the American continent, to Europe and Russia. In 1899, hearing about his apostolic zeal and tireless ministry, the Tsar of Russia, Nicholas II awarded the hieromonk the prestigious Cross of the Order of St. Anna.[24] Two years earlier, in 1897, the 32-year-old minister had been awarded the Order of Danilo from Prince Nicholas of Montenegro. *The San Francisco Call* covered the event, writing the following, in its June 7, 1899 edition.

> Information was received yesterday by the Rev. Sebastian Dabovich of this city that the order of St. Anne had been conferred on him by the Czar of Russia. This is the second order presented to the minister during the past two years. He received the handsome order of Daniel of Montegre [*sic*][25] from Prince Nicholas two years ago, and he prizes both very highly. The doctor is of the opinion that the degree was awarded to him through the influence of Bishop Nicholas, who left this city a year ago and had an audience with the tsar, at which he probably recommended the local divine

ORDER OF ST. ANNE CONFERRED UPON HIM

Rev. Sebastian Dabovich, Who Has Been Honored by the Czar of Russia.

INFORMATION was received yesterday by the Rev. Sebastian Dabovich of this city that the Order of St. Anne had been conferred on him by the Czar of Russia. This is the second order presented to the minister during the past two years. He received the handsome order of Daniel of Montegre from Prince Nicholas two years ago, and he prizes both very highly.

The doctor is of the opinion that the degree was awarded to him through the influence of Bishop Nicholas, who left this city a year ago and had an audience with the Czar, at which he probably recommended the local divine by reason of the assistance he had rendered him in his work.

The Order of Daniel, he says, was conferred on him for his kindnesses to Servians and Montenegrin subjects in this city and for the articles he has written on the province of Montenegro and of its struggles against the Turks and other tribes.

Dr. Dabovich is a traveling missionary connected with the Holy Trinity Cathedral. He was born in this city in 1863 and received his early education in the public schools of San Francisco. On graduating from the latter he entered a religious school and upon concluding his studies in 1884 he went to Alaska and served in that country. In 1889 he journeyed to Russia and entered the Theological Academy of St. Petersburg. On graduating in 1892 he returned to this city and took up missionary work, and is engaged in that labor at the present time. He has written a number of books and has also contributed to magazines. His sermons at the Cathedral are extremely popular and cover a wide range of topics on matters pertaining to the Orthodox church

The June 7, 1899 article from *The San Francisco Call* newspaper that wrote about the medal which St Sebastian had been given by the Tsar of Russia. Membership to the Order of St Anna was awarded for a distinguished career in civil service or for valour and distinguished service in the military.

by reason of the assistance he had rendered him in his work. The order of Daniel, he says, was conferred on him for his kindnesses to Serbians and Montenegrin subjects in the city, and for the articles he has written on the province of Montenegro and its struggles against the Turks and other tribes.[26]

Despite his already superhuman missionary work, Fr Sebastian somehow found time to write. Both the quantity and quality of his work were astonishing, and before the curtain fell on the nineteenth century, he had developed one of the first English translations of the Orthodox Divine Liturgy, and had also authored three English-language books: *The Holy Orthodox Church: The Rituals, Services, and Sacraments of the Eastern Apostolic (Greek-Russian) Church* (1898), *Lives of the Saints, and Several Lectures and Sermons* (1898), and *Preaching in the Russian Church: Lectures and Sermons by a Priest of the Holy Orthodox Church* (1899). Not content with this, he also wrote articles on Orthodoxy in Alaska and California, and on Orthodox traditions surrounding the Feast of the Nativity of Christ.

In 1897, as he was finishing his first book, Fr. Sebastian wrote to Metropolitan Mihailo of Serbia,[27] expressing his feelings on his first foray into publishing: "In a few days I shall finish a book, which I am writing in English, 17 chapters and a foreword, about the Orthodox Church, its rites, symbolism, liturgy, and sacraments, and how it differs from the Roman and Protestant churches, etc. If His Grace Nicholas blesses the publication of this book, I think and hope to God that it will be of use to the East and West, since I am fairly well acquainted with both."[28]

Published entirely with money from his own small salary, Fr Sebastian's books bore witness to the missionary vision of their author. As his letter to Metropolitan Mihailo makes clear, they were intended to serve as books of basic Orthodox instruction, written primarily for second and third-generation immigrants from Orthodox countries, for whom English is the mother language, but also to introduce the Faith to the millions of Anglophone non-Orthodox.

While such books are common and widely circulated today, at the end of the nineteenth century they were a rarity and far ahead of their time. Anglicans, Episcopalians, and other heterodox had translated and published some English-language books on Orthodoxy, but the Orthodox themselves had published very few expositions of the Faith in English. Fr Sebastian understood that for Orthodoxy to grow in America, the Faith had to be taught and preached not only in the languages of traditionally Orthodox countries, but also in the language of the New World.

Fr Sebastian's books bear witness to his ardent love for Christ and His Church, the depth of his knowledge of the Orthodox Faith, his careful adherence to the teachings of the Church, his pastoral zeal, his literary and poetic gifts, and his profound sense of spiritual beauty. A large portion of the books consists of sermons which he had preached both in the San Francisco cathedral and in the various mission churches he visited throughout his ministry. These sermons reveal an inspired preacher, whose words could make a listener's soul soar, while at the same time imprint themselves deeply in his heart. *The San Francisco Call* noted this phenomenon, writing: "He [Fr. Sebastian] has written a number of books and has also contributed to magazines. His sermons at the cathedral are extremely popular and cover a wide range of topics on matters pertaining to the Orthodox Church"[29]

His words were powerful; his sermons memorable and effective. One of the many examples of the characteristic liveliness and sublimity of his preaching can be found in a sermon he delivered on the solemn Holy Friday, remembering the Lord's ultimate sacrifice:

> It was our earnest desire to pursue the story of our Savior's trials and His crucifixion; but when I looked on Him whom they pierced, my spirit failed before the terrible sight; I could not watch with Him another hour, and yet I could not leave the hallowed scene. It seemed as though I saw Him brought back from Herod where the soldiers mocked Him. I followed Him through the streets again as the cruel priests pushed through the wild crowd and hastened Him back to Pilate's court. My ears sounded with the cry: "Crucify Him, crucify Him! Give us Barabbas, the robber; let Barabbas go; but Christ, the King of the Jews, Jesus, the Savior, He must die." And there He stood, who loved me and gave Himself for me, like a lamb in the midst of wolves, with none to pity and none to help Him.
>
> As Jesus Christ hung apparently helpless upon the cross, He had only to utter the word, and in a moment more than twelve legions of angels (what an invincible force of energetic beings!) would be ready to succor and defend. But to have shunned all pain and anguish, to have refused the cup which His Father had given Him, to have rejected the cross – this would have been to leave man to his doom; this He could not do. And so, He saved

others, Himself He could not save ... He who prayed, "Father forgive them, for they know not what they do", has stretched out his arms on the wood in order to embrace a sinful world. But no mortal knoweth how the Word was with God, and the Word was God. The Word of God is not bound by death. As a word from the lips dies not entirely away at the moment its sound ceases, but rather gathers new strength, and passing through the senses penetrates the minds and hearts of the hearers, so also the Hypostatical Word of God, the Son of God, in His saving incarnation, whilst dying in the flesh, fills all things with His spirit and might. Thus, when Christ waxeth faint and becometh silent on the cross, then is it that heaven and earth raise their voice unto Him, and the dead preach the resurrection of the Crucified, and the very stones cry out. And the sun was darkened, and the veil of the temple was rent in the midst; and the earth did quake and the rocks rent and the graves were opened, and many bodies of the saints which slept arose.

O sinful man, o nature, bereft of perfection, o reason, a mind earthly winged, down low, stoop thou under cover of repentant shame before the light of this grave. Christian, there is no other place for thee today but by the Cross of Christ. [30]

Fr. Sebastian was an acute and aware observer of the spirit of the times. In another sermon, entitled "The Condition of Society," one can recognize a prophetic vision that remains pertinent today, over a century later. Mourning the birth of new social classes and habits in the New World, the saint wrote:

How long will it thus go on! When will the baptized become active Christians, so that the pastors may give their attention to the conversion of the heathen? What a terrible battle we must fight. Already the fire of hell is in the world. Great cities are multiplying throughout the land. The farmer, as the word is defined in our dictionaries, is a thing of the past. It is now the land-owner with a mansion in the city, a yacht on the sea, and with a private train across the continent. There are comparatively but a few laborers in the fields-too poor to support families. The quiet country homes are becoming few, shall I say precious? I fear not so, because people are fast losing their ability to rightly estimate the value of things. Most of the cities in all the world are overcrowded.

The female portion of the population is most conspicuous. A stupid craze after unwholesome fashions is the one all-absorbing passion of the majority of women ... most of the children in San Francisco are actually brought up in the streets. Oh, how few of them feel the blessed influence of a Christian home! Young men and young women are continually "on the go," as they say. And this "go" is a nervous, unsteady rush to "keep up with the times" And after all their hurry nothing is left but steam and vapor, for they are empty, as empty as the changing and vanishing world can be. Yet they fret and inquire: "Where shall we go to and what shall we see? What shall we do? Oh, what can we do?"

If you promenade along the broad avenue or pass through the narrow lane, if you visit the meeting halls in the city or look into the factories, everywhere you see that same all-devouring gaze of the bold young woman, who stares with a kind of artificial movement of the eyes. And sometimes you hear even so-called Christians say that it is a weakness of character in one who has the downcast eyes of modesty, the blush of innocence. Such people do not know the live sense and fine impulse of a pure conscience. When a young man puffs tobacco smoke or shows his teeth with a disapproving smile in the presence of and at the conversation of older people, then society is wrong; something is the matter with his family.

In view of all this, beloved, the preacher of the Word of God is obliged by a terrible oath he has given before he received the gift in Apostolic succession at his ordination, to present to you the whole of the Truth, not a part of it.

The number of unmarried people is increasing. And there are some married people who say: "We do not want children, because we want to have as much pleasure as possible." This is a false position, for in a Christian marriage ... Christians marry for the sake of God and His law as much as they do for themselves. But Christians who remain single renounce marriage and live holy for the sake of God and Him alone. Thus we find that the family tie is abused, as well as the single state. Courtship of young people just out of school is not to be advised, because it often leads to debauchery. A courtship running through long years also gives occasion to sin and a species of wrongdoing to God, for the heart and its love are stolen from God and thrown away on a man.

Throughout all the long centuries of Christianity there have been in the Church heroic members, young people of both sexes, who by the grace of

God have kept their souls pure and intact … Such persons have had the courage and such unbounded confidence in God's assistance that, although living in the world and its dangers, though threatened by the cravings of their own individual passions and by the temptations of the devil, yet they have succeeded bravely in preserving this treasure even in a frail earthen vessel, have carried it uninjured through life's long journey here below, and have finally presented it to their Lord.

Christian heroes and heroines, you who have imitated or who still do imitate the sublime example of the Most Blessed Virgin, the Church admires your spirit of sacrifice as she does that of the holy martyrs … because you have to combat, to suffer, and to sacrifice your whole life through. With joy and veneration do the angels look down upon you, for you resemble themselves. With motherly affection and with mighty power does the Holy Virgin Mary, when you earnestly pray, throw her sheltering omophorion around you, for you are her pupils and imitators. With the sweetness of divine love the heavenly Bridegroom will fill your heart and more than compensate you for the fleeting, transient, worldly love that you have laid down at His feet. The eternal Judge will find you waiting like the wise and prudent virgins who all through life carry in their hands the pure oblation of love and the burning light of good example. Therefore, faithful to the end, He will invite you to the eternal wedding feast in heaven. Amen.[31]

As a fearless preacher of the gospel in the modern world, St Sebastian bravely castigated the increasing atheism of his day. This is the theme of his sermon, "The Authenticity and Truthfulness of the Gospel," wherein he defends the historicity of the biblical narrative and demonstrates why only the Christian faith contains the full and pure revelation of God. In another study, *The Immortality of the Soul*, he proves that, despite the theories of modern materialists, the soul does indeed continue to live and remain active after bodily death, as it waits for the final resurrection.[32]

Another thing which shines through in the saint's writings is how much he honored and venerated his holy forerunners, Sts Herman and Innocent of Alaska, the missionaries in America. In a miraculous way, he foresaw the official canonization of the humble monk Herman in a book he published in 1898, seventy years before the Alaskan missionary's official canonization. In another book, St Sebastian included a sermon which he had given at the

209

cathedral Church of San Francisco on August 26, 1897, for the centenary of the birth of St Innocent. Indeed, there were people in his congregation while he preached who still remembered the great bishop and Enlightener of Alaska who had reposed in the Lord eighteen years earlier in Russia. After appeals and entreaties from Bishop Nicholas (Ziorov), St Sebastian published the English edition of the life of St Innocent, the book being made available for the 100-year anniversary of the holy missionary bishop's birth. In his sermon on the occasion, St Sebastian said: "I hear them speak the very name of him whom they have come to honor: Innocentius. My whole being thrills with a veneration at the sound of that name ... I become bold and venture to look into the unseen, where I behold the spiritual eyes of our first hard-working missionary, with kindly light beaming upon this gathering and approving of the feeble words of your son."[33] These words attain even greater significance when one realizes they were spoken eighty years before St Innocent's canonization by the Church. Undoubtedly, St Sebastian found heavenly guides and archetypes for his own Apostolic work in the faces of these two saints.

SPEAKING THE TRUTH IN LOVE

It was not merely through his books and sermons that Fr Sebastian sought to introduce non-Orthodox Americans to the true Faith; he spoke tirelessly to countless individuals, engaging them on a personal level, and making friends in all ranks of society, from the common man on the street to the highest strata of American social, political, and religious life. He initiated contact and discussions with members of non-Orthodox churches, expending his greatest efforts toward the Episcopalian Church, which, at the turn of the twentieth century, he saw as the closest and the most receptive to Orthodoxy. He was not alone in this belief. In 1865, when the saint was only two years old, the ober-procurator of the Holy Synod of the Russian Church had noted that an Orthodox church was needed in San Francisco, not only to provide for the residents who were already Orthodox but also "to answer to the growing interest in the Orthodox Faith among American Episcopalians."[34]

Having grown up in San Francisco and having been entrusted with the apostolic ministry of the Orthodox Church on the West Coast, Fr Sebastian now sought to address this need. He met several times with Charles Grafton, Episcopalian bishop of Fond du Lac, Wisconsin. The two men developed a mutual respect for each other, and worked together to organize an Orthodox-

Episcopalian dialogue conference in Fond du Lac. In fact, in November of 1900, Bishop Tikhon, Fr Sebastian, and Fr John Kochurov, a future hieromartyr attended the consecration of a vicar for Bishop Grafton, and three years later, Bishop Grafton made a trip to Russia to experience the full richness of the Orthodox Church firsthand.

In all of his contact with Episcopalians, Fr Sebastian was respectful and understanding, appreciating the points in which Episcopalian doctrine and practice still reflected the historic and apostolic Orthodox Faith. At the same time, however, his stance toward Episcopalianism as a whole was based on the biblical commandment of "speaking the truth in love,"[35] a saying that he took as his guiding principle in reaching out to the heterodox. He deeply felt the weight of his responsibility to carefully present the truth that the Orthodox Church was the only true church of Christ, but to do so with discernment as well as with steadfast conviction. He preached against syncretism and subjectivism in matters of the faith, and he firmly held against sacrificing truth for popularity, writing that "What in human concerns might be called a liberal concession to our opponents, would in religion be a foul treachery, opposite God's truth intrusted [*sic*] to His Church."[36]

This loving but firm conviction when dealing with those outside the Church was evident in many of his writings, but perhaps nowhere more clearly than in "Sincere Religion," wherein he wrote: "This is the principle of all worldly people, and it is a fashion to consider a conscientious religious church-life a downright nuisance, though one is still afraid to call it so. The crowd call it liberal not to make any distinction between the teaching of the different churches, just as if truth and untruth could exist one at the side of the other without any disrespect to God, the Author of truth. It is want of faith and conviction, or rather want of taking an interest in religion, that produces this baleful indifference. It stands to reason that it is sinful to care so little for the revealed truth as to place it on a level with error. You will say, shall we then condemn our erring brethren? By no means. Christ forbids us to judge anybody, for only God knows whether our brother culpably holds the error, or whether he believes it to be the truth. But even if he believes his error to be the truth, error remains error, and never can become truth. Therefore, we must always condemn error, though we may not condemn the person erring, but must pity him that he takes error for truth."[37] Although Fr Sebastian's efforts to bring Episcopalians into the Orthodox Church did not prove successful during his lifetime, St Tikhon later noted that Fr Sebastian

St Sebastian, on the left, with his six brothers and sisters
and their families. In the center is their mother.

was to a large part responsible for making non-Orthodox Christians, and particularly Episcopalians, aware of the teachings of the Orthodox Church.

The saintly hieromonk had a deep interest in Orthodox monasticism, and he frequently introduced the beauty of the cenobitic life to Americans, for whom it was unfamiliar. *The San Francisco Call* covered one such event, noting: "An informal talk was given by Rev. Sebastian Dabovich of the Russian church before the Catholic Club and invited guests last evening at the Occidental Hotel on 'the Holy Mount Athos and Oriental Monasticism,' the subject being one of which little is generally known in this country. Many questions were put to the speaker, and his answers were listened to with great interest by the large audience present, consisting of both clergymen and laymen."[38]

THE JOURNEYS CONTINUE

St Tikhon recognized and appreciated Fr Sebastian's valuable gifts as a missionary priest, and used every opportunity to utilize his talents to the glory of God and the furtherance of His kingdom. In 1900 he appointed the young hieromonk to the North American Ecclesiastical Consistory, which was the diocesan council of the entire American mission, and two years later, he named him head of the Sitka Deanery and superintendent of Alaskan missions. So, after an absence of eighteen years, Fr Sebastian returned to Alaska, where he served until 1903. During his time in Alaska, St Tikhon elevated him to the rank of abbot.[39]

While in Alaska, Fr Sebastian made contact with a group of Serbian and Russian miners in the town of Douglas, near Juneau. He organized them into a parish, and quickly began working to build an Orthodox church for them. Land was donated by the local mining company, and a donation for the church's construction was sent from the Holy Assembly of Bishops in Serbia. Fr Sebastian helped build the church with his own hands, carrying wood, pounding nails, and working with the local Orthodox Christians in every aspect of the labor. Finally, the new church was complete, and on July 23, 1903, Fr Sebastian consecrated it in honor of St Sava of Serbia.

Shortly after leaving Alaska, Abbot Sebastian traveled to Chicago, to resume the work he had begun ten years earlier, founding a Serbian parish in the city. Unlike his previous visit, a decade earlier, he now found many more Serbs in the city, most of whom were eager to build a church. He celebrated the Divine Liturgy for the community, and stayed with them for a week,

Saint Tikhon with the episcopal mantle. In the center is Saint Sebastian and next to him is Saint John Kochurov. Photo from 1900.

Saint Alexis Toth of Wilkes-Barr

Saint Tikhon
as Bishop of Lublin, 1878.

Saint Tikhon
as Bishop of the Aleutian Islands
and North America, 1901.

Saint Tikhon as Patriarch of Moscow and All Russia.

Saint John Kochurov, at a young age, pictured here with his wi

Saint John Kochurov.

Saint John Kochurov at a young age.

Saint John Kochurov in a photo with students and teachers of the gymnasia in Narva.

Saint Alexander Hotovitzky
as a young cleric.

Saint Alexander Hotovitzky and his wife.

Saint Alexander Hotovitzky.

Saint Raphael, in Moscow, 1890.

Saint Raphael, in America, 1905.

Saint Raphael is the first on left in the upper row.
Second from the left on the bottom row is Saint Alexander Hotovitzky.

Saint Sebastian at a young age.

Saint Sebastian
as a young archimandrite.

Saint Sebastian.

Saint Mardarije, on the left as a hieromonk and on the right as a bishop.

Saint Mardarije
as Bishop of America and Canada.

The uncovering of the relics of Saint Mardarije, May 5, 2017.

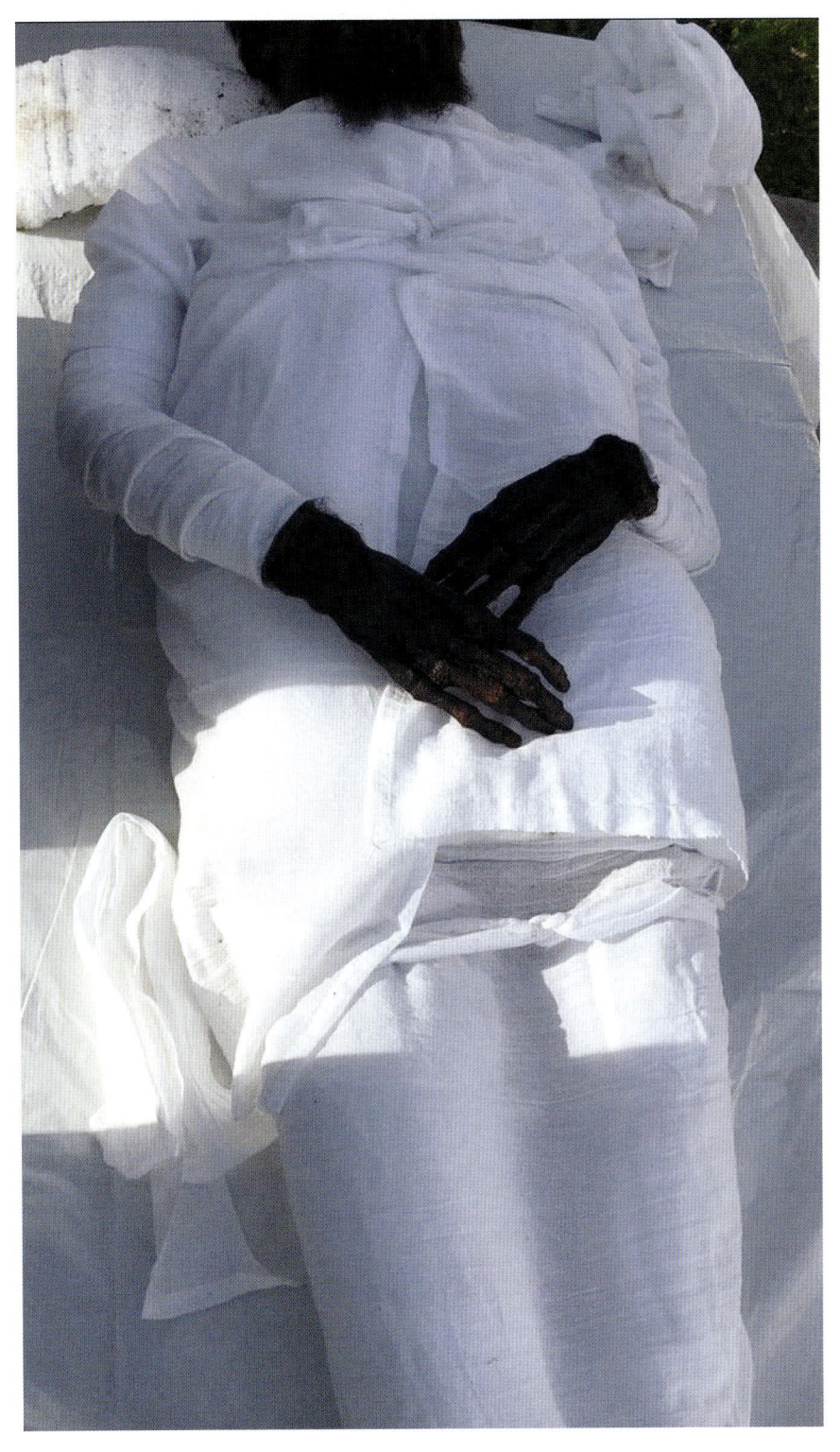

The incorrupt body of Saint Mardarije.

Saint John (Maximovich) at a young age.

Saint John
as Bishop of Shanghai.

Saint John with nuns of the Convent
of the Lesna Mother of God, in Fourqueux, France.
The photo was taken in 1954 or 1955.

Photos from the changing of the holy vestments of Saint John of Shanghai, at the Holy Virgin Cathedral —Joy of All Who Sorrow— in San Francisco, October 25, 2017.

Saint Joseph the Hesychast with his brotherhood.
Elder Ephraim is second from the left.

Elder Ephraim of Arizona
is on the far right.

The holy Elder Ephraim of Arizona.

Ἡ εὐχὴ εἶναι τὸ πιὸ φοβερὸ ὅπλο, τὸ πιὸ ἠρεμιστι-
κὸ χάπι, ποὺ χαρίζει τὴν ψηλάφηση τῶ Κυρίου ἡ
φωνάζει ἡ ψυχὴ ἀπὸ πίστη ἡ βεβαιότητα "Ὁ Κύριός μου
καὶ ὁ θεός μου".—

　　　　+ Ὁ εὐτελὴς καὶ βούλιμος γέροντάς σu +
　　　　　　+ Γερ. Ἐφραὶμ

*The Jesus prayer is the most formidable weapon, the most calming medicine;
it grants us the ability to touch Christ, and the soul cries with faith and certainty
'My Lord and my God!'*

　　　　+ Your unworthy and lowly elder
　　　　　　+ Elder Ephraim

during which he began the negotiations which were to result in the parish of the Holy Resurrection.

In the meantime, Bishop Tikhon had already initiated his organizational overhaul of the diocese. Seeking to best provide for the needs of his multiethnic Orthodox flock in America, and realizing that each ethnic group required special attention and leadership, he sought to create auxiliary bishoprics for the different parishes, all under the jurisdiction of the Russian Diocese of the Aleutian Islands and North America. The Holy Synod had agreed with the hierarch's proposals, and in March of 1904, the Syrian St Raphael (Hawaweeny) was elevated to the newly formed auxiliary episcopal see of Brooklyn. He was to assume the pastoral and ministerial responsibilities for all Syro-Arab communities and parishes in America.

Bishop Tikhon had already decided on St Sebastian as the second auxiliary bishop, and the ideal man to lead all the Serbian communities and churches. In March of 1905, the hierarch established the Orthodox Serbian Mission, based in Chicago, and placed St Sebastian as its head. Having previously visited the city in 1893, 1903, and 1904, the missionary abbot was familiar with the parishes and conditions in the metropolis, and within a few days of his arrival he was able to secure a plot of land upon which to build a church. In a letter to a fellow hieromonk, Protopresbyter Petar Stajčić of the Ravanica monastery, he wrote: "After some days we found a place for the new church, which was located at 8 Fowler Street, on the corner of Evergreen and across from Wicker Park.[40] We put down a $1,000 deposit (donated by Acim Lugonja). The remaining $6,500 was to be paid with interest. We created an improvised chapel immediately, made an iconostasis, and raised a cross on the building, all within several days. The first Liturgy was held, and the church was consecrated to the Resurrection of our Lord Jesus Christ, on the 4th of July, 1905."[41] It was at that very church, on September 18, 1905, that St Tikhon elevated Abbot Sebastian to the rank of archimandrite. Speaking to him during the service, the archbishop said:

> I greet you, most honorable Father Archimandrite Sebastian, with your elevation to the rank of archimandrite and your assignment as head of the Serbian Mission in America. You were entrusted by the diocesan authorities even earlier, as a native Serb, with the administration of one or another of the Serbian parishes here. Now you are being called to a greater ministry: upon you is being laid the care of all the Serbian churches in our extensive

1905, St Sebastian visits the Church of the Holy Trinity in Chigago, and its priest, Fr John Kochurov.

From left to right, St John Kochurov, St Sebastian, and St Tikhon.

diocese and of the spiritual needs of all the Serbs in America. You know how many of them are scattered here, how often they go astray like sheep that have no shepherd, how they end up in a foreign home, and how, having come here for work or to become rich, some of them become spiritually impoverished and, in this heterodox country, lose the great spiritual treasure of the old country: the holy Orthodox Faith, love for the Slavic people, and fondness for their good native customs. Our benevolently solicitous hierarchy, which is always concerned about the needs of the Slavs, who are of one blood with us, desires to have mercy on these people, and is calling upon you now to spiritually guide the Serbs who are living here.[42]

THE WAY OF THE CROSS

During his time as head of the Serbian Orthodox Mission, Archimandrite Sebastian wholeheartedly devoted himself to the needs of the many Serbian communities throughout the country. He also initiated the publication of the *Herald of the Servian Church in North America*, the first Serbian ecclesiastical newspaper in the United States. Shortly after his elevation, St Tikhon asked Fr Sebastian to procure written permission from the Synod of the Church of Serbia for the consecration of an auxiliary bishop for the Serbian Orthodox Mission. The same had happened with Fr Raphael's elevation to the episcopacy, when letters had been sent to the Patriarchate of Antioch for approval, which was readily granted. The Russian Synod had already approved the Serbian auxiliary position, but the hierarchy in Serbia, not being fully aware of the situation of the Serbs in America, refused to approve the request. This was the beginning of sorrows[43] for the missionary archimandrite.

The primary cause of the distress and tribulation which was to follow was the dissension and conflict between Orthodox Serbs in America regarding their ecclesiastical dependence on the Church of Russia. Many Serbian Orthodox reacted badly to this administrative reality, and demanded that they and their parishes and communities be placed directly under the jurisdiction of the Church of Serbia. These individuals began to accuse St Sebastian of being a Russophile and enemy of the Serbs, charges which were completely unjust and unfounded. Contrary to their allegations, Fr Sebastian and Bishop Nicholas (Ziorov) had written to the Church of Serbia almost a decade before, in 1897, asking that the Serbian parishes in America be placed under the jurisdiction of the Metropolis of Serbia.[44] It was the metropolitan of Serbia, Mihailo who suggested that both St Sebastian and the Serbian Orthodox of America remain under the jurisdiction of the Russian Patriarchate, as the Metropolis of Serbia did not have the economic capability to assume the Serbian parishes in America.

The situation which unfolded caused great sorrow and anguish to the saint. On the one hand, he saw the immediate and pressing need for the presence of a Serbian bishop in America, and on the other, he was fully aware of the Church of Serbia's unwillingness to send someone to fill that crucial vacuum. To add to the saint's difficulties, his mentor and ally in his missionary struggles, St Tikhon, was appointed bishop of Yaroslavl, returning to Russia in 1907. The void left by the departure of the charismatic and inspired hierarch would be almost impossible to fill, and finding an equally suitable replacement would prove a formidable task. The future patriarch of Moscow had created a bond of love between all his priests which united them to each other, and which united the flocks to the shepherd. Now this bond was about to break, imperiling that precious unity.

Before he left, St Tikhon made sure to express his love and respect for St Sebastian in a clear and tangible way. St Nikolaj Velimirović, bishop of Žiča and noted Serbian saint, wrote: "Archimandrite Dabovich could have been a bishop even in 1907. The Russian archbishop wanted to consecrate him as a Russian bishop for the Serbian people. But the Serbs did not want it that way. Archbishop Tikhon was sorry about that. He was eager to show his appreciation to Fr. Dabovich for all his wonderful work. Failing to make him a bishop, he did something else. Once when he celebrated the Holy Liturgy in the Serbian church in Chicago, he presented our archimandrite with a precious mitre, which was worth 1,000 roubles[45] [sic] in gold. But Fr. Dabovich quickly sold that precious gift and gave it to the church towards paying its debts. Such a man was he. He was absolutely unselfish."[46]

Metropolitan Platon (Rozhdestvensky), formerly of Chyhyryn[47] succeeded Metropolitan Tikhon. Shortly after his arrival, in September of 1908, he received a letter from St Sebastian, informing him of the situation of the Serbian mission of the diocese. "Last Easter in three churches there were no services, a fourth was closed, and many colonies with a fairly dense Orthodox population did not even hear 'Christ is Risen.' It is impossible to obtain priests anywhere, and in most cases, people cannot give enough to support a priest properly. Now they have promised me in Belgrade that at the next Assembly of Bishops they will raise the question of allocating two scholarships for the Mission, so that two Serbian lads from America may be educated at a seminary in Serbia. But this presents other problems: finding the money to send these lads to Europe. Serbian archpastors in the Old Country with brotherly love expect Your Eminence to organize our part of the Church. The Lord's blessing will doubtless be given to a continuation of the work begun with wisdom, after six years of responsibility, by His Eminence Tikhon, now Archpastor of Yaroslavl."[48]

During the same year, Fr Sebastian, while retaining his position as head of the Serbian Orthodox Mission, served at the Holy Transfiguration Church in Denver, Colorado, which that had been received into the Orthodox Church from Uniatism in 1904. The parish consisted primarily of Russians and Serbs. In September of 1908, Fr Sebastian wrote to Archbishop Platon: "Here the church is fairly large, there is enough land, the debt is small ... Many children. They want a psalm-reader and teacher, who can direct a choir ... Come, Your Eminence, to Denver."[49]

In 1906, the San Francisco cathedral of St Basil had been destroyed in the Great Earthquake[50] and a new cathedral, dedicated to the Holy Trinity, had been built soon after. In July of 1909, the saint traveled to San Francisco to attend the consecration of his hometown's new cathedral. During this period, Fr Sebastian was experiencing a growing sense of futility as head of the Serbian mission. Many of the Serbs in America had made it clear to him that they did not want to support the Serbian mission, or be part of it, calling it a "Russophile agency," as it was under the jurisdiction of the Russian Patriarchate. Much of the frustration and vitriol from these individuals did not stop at the mission, but became personal attacks on the humble archimandrite, calling him a Russophile who served the Russian Church and had placed American Serbian parishes under its jurisdiction.

The reality was that Fr Sebastian was a selfless servant of the Church of Christ in its entirety, and cared only for the spiritual progress and salvation of Christ's flock. Like St Tikhon, he knew that for the Serbian flock in America to flourish, they needed a Serbian bishop and Serbian priests who spoke their language and understood their needs. This was the reason that, at St Tikhon's behest, he had organized the Serbian Orthodox Mission: he had wanted a Serbian bishop consecrated for America. The saint was completely open to Serbian parishes in America being under the direct jurisdiction of the Serbian Church, and had even campaigned for it. However, the Serbian Metropolis was not yet ready to take responsibility for priests and parishes in America, and they had made that clear. Therefore, as far as Fr Sebastian was concerned, the most pressing question was not the jurisdiction under which the Serbian parishes operated, and whether it was Russian or Serbian. He simply wanted them to be under a canonical hierarchy; he wanted to assure their spiritual needs were being met, and he tirelessly worked to ensure that every Serb in America had the opportunity to be nourished by the life and grace of the Church.

Fr Sebastian was now in his late forties, and felt increasing sorrow over the situation with his compatriots. At the end of the first decade of the twentieth century, the needs of the Serbs in America were still not being met. There were nineteen official Serbian parishes in America, and countless other smaller Serbian Orthodox communities, and they were all being served by only eleven canonical priests. Uncanonical priests from Serbia were taking advantage of the situation, roaming the United States and performing services in Serbian communities without permission from any bishop. With no Serbian bishop assigned to America, and with many Serbs not wanting to be in the jurisdiction of the Russian Church, the saintly archimandrite's options were severely limited. He was placed in the unenviable position of having to defend the canonical authority of the Russian Diocese of America over all American Serbs, as that was, indeed, the only canonical ecclesiastical authority at the time. As was expected, this only sharpened the already-hostile animosity of the Serbians under him.

In December of 1909, seeing that the antagonism was causing Serbian priests and communities to avoid him, due to his continued connection with the Russian Church, and finding that the Serbian Orthodox Mission was "left without resources, aid, and, what is more, goodwill,"[51] Fr Sebastian asked Archbishop Platon to relieve him of his duties as administrator. At the same time, he wrote a letter to the Holy Synod of the Church of Serbia, informing them of the situation of the Serbian Orthodox churches in America and asking for their assistance: "Most Serbs have said that they do not want any other jurisdiction, not even Russian, but their own Serbian Church jurisdiction. On this day I am submitting to North American Archbishop Platon my resignation as administrator of the Serbian Mission, for I am exhausted from the effort and cannot oppose a multitude single-handed ... Once again, I caution the Holy Synod that the Serbian Church in glorious, vast America has been left without an administrator, and I urge that a Serbian archpastor be sent."[52] In a report to the Holy Synod of the Church of Russia, Archbishop Platon mentioned his archimandrite's request to be relieved of his duties. In their return letter, which included an official document granting Fr Sebastian's request, the synod spoke glowingly of his numerous and significant accomplishments in America:

> Concerning the Hieromonk Sebastian, His Grace Tikhon of the Aleutians, in his communication to the Holy Synod of June 2, 1902, no. 74, wrote that the appointed Hieromonk, during his service in the Mission, exerted considerable efforts toward:
>
> 1) building holy churches in America (the construction of churches in Jackson and Seattle, and the decoration of the cathedral church in San Francisco),
>
> 2) organizing church-parish life in Minneapolis shortly after the parishioners joined the Orthodox Church,
>
> 3) raising religious and national consciousness among Slavs scattered across America,
>
> 4) acquainting non-Slav Christians (primarily Episcopalians) in America with the teachings of the Orthodox Church, for which purpose he wrote and published, from his meager resources, several books in English, and
>
> 5) translating official documents of the Administration into English.[53]

THE HEART OF AN APOSTLE

After being released from his position as head of the Serbian Mission in 1910, Fr Sebastian served the Serbian Orthodox communities in California. He wrote about them to Archbishop Platon, noting: "The receipts from modest services performed for the many Serbs in the cities of Los Angeles, Fresno and Oakland, I hope, will be enough to nourish me. The new church in Angels Camp is already finished, and to there and to the church in Jackson a new priest, Fr. Jovan Duchich, will soon be coming from Herzegovina. The mission in [Bisbee] Arizona has been reorganized into a parish, and Fr. Samuel Popovich from the Timisoara diocese will be coming to build a new church."[54] The Serbian church communities in these areas had been organized by Fr Sebastian himself. He had established a parish in the mining town of Angels Camp during his early visits to Jackson, and in 1909 the Serbian community there, which numbered about 1,500 people, began building a church. The building was competed and consecrated on August 14, 1910, and was dedicated to St Basil of Ostrog.[55]

The Angels Camp church, as well as those in Jackson and Bisbee, soon received full-time priests from Serbia, so Fr Sebastian settled in the Los Angeles parish he had founded, while frequently traveling to the smaller communities in Oakland and Fresno to minister to their sacramental and pastoral needs. In 1909, under the missionary archimandrite's direct influence, the Los Angeles congregation purchased a large plot of land on the east side of the city, and began building a church and a cemetery. Services were temporarily held in a home chapel while the construction was underway, but in 1911 the church was completed, and Fr Sebastian consecrated it, dedicating it to St Sava of Serbia.

Fr Sebastian hoped to remain at the new Los Angeles church permanently, but it was not to be. In 1912, the Balkan Wars broke out, and the saint felt he needed to help his people during this critical time in their history. He requested leave to travel to Serbia, and upon receiving it, he put all his most precious possessions up for auction, in order to collect money to help the suffering Serbian populace. These prized heirlooms included all the honors and medals he had received through the years for his missionary work, as well as gifts from friends and acquaintances. The auction caused significant waves in the city, and the news quickly spread across the continent. The *Los Angeles Times* wrote about it in detail in their October 12, 1912 edition.

PATRIOTIC SACRIFICE

Bishop[56] Of Orthodox Eastern Catholic Church Will Offer Personal Decorations to Help Serbians.

The Balkan war between the Serbs and Turks has developed many cases of self-sacrifice among the Serbs in and around Los Angeles, but probably none greater than that of Father Sebastian Dabovich, Bishop of the Orthodox Eastern Catholic Church, who has for two years been working among the Slavs and Greeks of this city, to induce them to higher ideals in living. He has built a small chapel on Boyle Heights, and has just begun to get his work on a better footing, when he feels called upon to sacrifice his personal belongings for the benefit of the hospital work in the Serb army.

At the meeting of the Friday Morning Club this morning, in the Woman's Clubhouse, the following historic relics will be offered at auction to the highest bidder above the minimum price named.

A Bishop's gorgeous miter, handmade and painted in Russia by nuns, to be sold to the highest bidder above $100.[57]

A jeweled pectoral cross and chain, made by a Serb jeweler in Bosnia, minimum bid $100.

Twelve sacred hand paintings on panels of steel, minimum $50 for the set.

Beautiful icon of the Savior, which belonged to a Russian nobleman who had it with him in the campaign against Napoleon at Moscow, minimum $50.

Four decorations: Order of Saint Sabbas, from the king of Serbia, Order of Danilo, from the King of Montenegro,[58] Order of Saint Anne, from the Emperor of Russia, a medal from the Emperor of Russia in memory of Alexander III, minimum bid for all $25.

A handsome medium-size hand-made rug made by the Christian peasant girls of Macedonia. Minimum bid $50[59]

While in Serbia, the holy archimandrite served as a chaplain in the Serbian army, and took the opportunity to make pilgrimages to the holy sites in Kosovo and other Orthodox cities in Serbia. While visiting Skopje, Fr Sebastian wrote a letter to Nikola Pašić, the resident of the Serbian Ministry of Foreign Affairs, expressing his hopes that a Serbian diocese with a permanent Serbian bishop would now finally be established in America. It is noteworthy that he named Nikolaj Velimirovich as the episcopal candidate for the proposed see, at a time when the future bishop of Ohrid was still only a hieromonk. The holy missionary discerned the future saint's abilities, perceiving that one day he would be a beacon of the church.

Finally, in August of 1913, St Sebastian returned to America. That same month, he was invited to speak at an Episcopalian conference, and soon after he was asked to be an instructor at the newly established St. Platon Orthodox Theological Seminary in Tenafly, New Jersey. His years of experience teaching in church schools and Sunday schools proved invaluable, as he prepared the new Serbian seminarians for ordination and service at the Serbian parishes throughout the vast North American continent.

While on the East Coast, Fr Sebastian continued to travel to Serbian parishes which still did not have a priest, celebrating the Divine Liturgy, and ministering to the spiritual needs of the faithful. These missionary journeys extended all the way north to Canada, where he served at the Church of St Nicholas in Hamilton, Ontario. He also continued his involvement with conferences and dialogue with the heterodox, always retaining the same charitable yet uncompromising approach to the witness of the verity and exactness of the Orthodox faith and dogma, and speaking the truth in love.

In 1915, while in San Francisco, Fr Sebastian met with St Nikolai (Velimirovich), then an archimandrite. As St Nikolai later recalled, Fr Sebastian was waiting for him at the train station, and after taking him to the Holy Trinity Cathedral, he introduced him to the Serbs of the city. This was the beginning of a close spiritual kinship, which was to last until the death of St Sebastian, who predeceased the author of the Prologue. St Nikolai was later to describe Fr Sebastian as follows: "He was a sincere and convinced believer and a Christian missionary of world-scope. He traveled restlessly and preached and lectured indefatigably. He composed books, wrote articles, epistles, and thousands of private letters to laymen and priests with needed explanations, exhortations and encouragements. He spoke and wrote in Serbian, English, and Russian. His clumsy handbag was always full with New Testaments, religious booklets, printed sermons and tracts. Also with small crosses for boys and girls. All this he distributed freely. He never visited a Serbian family empty-handed. He remembered the apostolic words: 'It is more blessed to give than to receive.'[60][61] During this period, all the Serbian parishes in America had decided to leave the Russian jurisdiction and place themselves directly under the Church of Serbia. The Russian Church would not agree to this new arrangement, and as was to be expected, tensions and rifts began to appear. Fr Sebastian managed to remain relatively uninvolved in the brewing conflict, but this was not enough to save him from the new baseless and unjust accusations. The saint had formerly been resented by the Serbs for being too Russophile, and now he was accused by the Russians of being too Serbophilic. The new Russian archbishop of America, Evdokim Meschersky, trying to keep the Serbian parishes under Russian jurisdiction, began accusing Fr Sebastian of "agitating against the Russian church authorities in America," and St Nikolai of "spreading dissension among Serbian parishes in America."[62] On October 5, 1916, the archbishop convened an Assembly of Serbian Clergy in Chicago, with the purpose of, "sorting out the ambitions of the Serbs."[63] At

St Sebastian near
the end of his life.

this meeting, presided over by the archbishop himself, Fr Sebastian was so directly criticized that he later received a letter of sympathy from one of the Serbian priests present, stating: "With a feeling of profound pain in my soul, I remembered long after our meeting in Chicago ... the personal attacks on Your person at every opportunity. Believe me, the sympathies of the Serbian clergy were never so much on Your side as they are today."[64] Contrary to the accusations, Fr Sebastian's primary concern had never been whether one should be under the Russian or Serbian jurisdiction, but rather the proper and sufficient shepherding of Christ's flock. As St Nikolai later wrote, "during this period of controversy ... Fr. Sebastian ... never engaged in fruitless polemics ... but went on with his apostolic mission all over America from coast to coast. Thus, many times he visited lonely Serbian families in deserts and wildernesses to administer Holy Sacraments and bring consolation."[65]

As World War I continued raging throughout Europe, Fr Sebastian decided that he could not neglect his suffering brethren in Serbia. He asked the Holy Synod of the Russian Church for a permanent release, so that he could join the Serbian Church and serve the faithful in the land of his ancestors. His request was granted in 1917, and Fr Sebastian returned to Serbia to resume his service as military chaplain.

After the war, the saint returned to America, and in February of 1921, he met St Nikolai in New York City. Two years earlier, St Nikolai had been ordained a bishop in Serbia, and his 1921 visit to the United States marked the first time that any Serbian hierarch had come to the New World. Here is how St Nikolai remembered his meeting with Fr Sebastian during that trip: "His poverty amazed me when I met him ... I invited him to lunch. Blushing, he said, 'Thank you; I just bought a roll of bread with my last five cents.' And salary? None. He lived on people's freely given donations. And still, even with empty pockets, he planned new journeys to Alaska, to Japan, and of course to Europe. 'But you are without means!' I remarked. He smiled with his usual childlike and fascinating smile and quoted the Bible: The Lord will provide.[66] And marvelously enough, the Lord always provided for His faithful servant."[67] Fr Sebastian saw St Nikolai as a true man of God, and now that he had been elevated to the episcopacy, the missionary monk firmly believed that he was the best candidate to lead the Serbian Orthodox Diocese in America. By this time, the tensions between the Russian Church and the Serbian congregations in America had ended, following the Russian Revolution of 1917. The ensuing deposition of the monarchy and establishment of the Bolshevik regime had caused a severe rupture, which had effectively ended contact between the newly reestablished patriarchate in Moscow and its American diocese. During the same period, the Church of Greece established its first diocese in the New World in 1921, and the first Greek bishop in America would take his seat soon thereafter.

In the meantime, St Nikolai had been sent to America by the Serbian Assembly of Bishops, and tasked with studying and analyzing the condition of the Serbian congregations in America and determining how they could best be organized. Living through all these historic events, St Sebastian finally felt that his hope of seeing a Serbian hierarch in America could finally be fulfilled. On March 30, 1921, he wrote to Patriarch Dimitrije of Serbia, informing him that "Considering the conditions and problems of the Serbian population in colonies across America, with their churches, organization and needs, it is imperative to undertake as soon as possible the reorganization and unification of our parishes and missions there, so that it truly becomes the Serbian Church in America. His Grace Bishop Nicholai could do this, taking advantage of the present circumstances which are well known to him, especially since he enjoys the sympathies of the authorities there. Asking Your Holiness to confer the blessing in the form of assistance in the struggle for the Orthodox Church in America ..." [68] On September 21, 1921, Metropolitan Varnava, future patriarch of Serbia, nominated St Nikolai for the position of first Serbian bishop of America, and Archimandrite Mardarije Uskokovich, a future saint himself, as his administrative assistant. Many faithful in Serbia, however, objected to the nomination of St Nikolai, as they were unwilling to lose their beloved bishop, so, in 1923 Archimandrite Mardarije was appointed sole administrator of the newly formed Serbian Orthodox Diocese of North America and Canada. In an April, 1923 letter,[69] Fr Mardarije wrote that the hierarchy in Serbia "were thinking of electing as Bishop for the American Church one of the three archimandrites in America, and they are: Sebastian Dabovich, Georgije Kodžić, both from California, and myself. Who will be chosen is a big question."[70]

Finally, in its autumn 1925 meeting, the Assembly of Serbian Bishops elected Archimandrite Mardarije as the bishop of the American-Canadian Diocese. On April 25, 1926, the new hierarch was ordained in the Orthodox cathedral in Belgrade, and in July of the same year he returned to the New World as the first Serbian bishop of America.

THE END OF HIS EARTHY PILGRIMAGE

With Bishop Mardarije's arrival, Fr Sebastian saw the great prayer of his soul come to life, and with that, he decided to dedicate the rest of his life to his missionary ministry. He covered massive distances, traveling all through the globe. From Alaska, and the parishes he established throughout North America, to Russia, and the different small towns in the Balkans, to the coasts of the Black and Adriatic Seas, he traveled tirelessly, spreading the word of God, and ministering to the spiritual and sacramental needs of any who needed him. The wayfaring saint made it all the way to Japan, where the archbishop, St Nicholas Kasatkin,[71] recognizing his talents, asked him to be his successor as hierarch of the island nation. This did not come to be.

During his lifetime, St Sebastian crossed the Atlantic fifteen times and the Pacific nine times. The saint's fifteenth Atlantic crossing, this time to visit Serbia, was to be his last. St Nikolai of Žiča describes the last years of Fr Sebastian's life as follows:

> Patriarch Varnava gave him an apartment in the Patriarchate where he stayed until 1938. Then he moved to Žiča, where he stayed with us for some time, then again to Herceg Novi. On his way to and fro he was steadily accompanied by Rev. Jovan Rapaich, whom he loved most of all and who took true filial care of the old man. Finally, he returned definitely to Žiča, his last resort. He stayed with us until the end of 1940. From there he wrote many letters to his American friends. In a letter to Mr Niko Mussich he wrote: "My body is getting weaker and weaker. I would like to see once more the Golden Gate. All my dearest memories from childhood are concentrated in San Francisco and in the country in which I was born."[72]
>
> I visited him frequently, asking how the brothers served him. His heart was failing. Fr Rapaich was with him day and night. The last time, on my return from the diocese, I went to see him. Sitting in an armchair, he was breathing heavily and spoke in a whisper.
>
> "Do you have any wish, Father?" I asked.
>
> "Only the Kingdom of Heaven."
>
> He spoke no more. These were his last words, representative of his entire career on earth. After that he gave up his spirit. He died on November 30, 1940 ... So ended the earthly pilgrimage of a great servant of Christ and the greatest Serbian missionary of modern times. He was a missionary by words, by deeds, and, what is the greatest of all, by his personal character.

He was a viceless man. Meek and unpretentious, he was positive and constructive in all his words and works.[73]

The saint was buried in the cemetery of the Žiča Monastery. At the time of his death, he owned nothing more than a gold cross, some books, and a few personal mementos. He had long since given away all his possessions to the poor and needy, choosing a life of poverty, simplicity, missionary dedication, and service.

On September 1, 2007, St Sebastian's relics were translated and reinterred at the church of St Savva, in Jackson, California, the very first church the missionary saint had built.

Saint Mardarije of Libertyville

His memory is commemorated on December 12

THE GLORY OF HIS ANCESTORS

Saint Mardarije was born Ivan Uskoković on December 22, 1889, in the tiny, rocky village of Kornet in the Podgorica district of Montenegro. His father, Petar Uskoković, was a respected nobleman of the Lješani district, and his mother, Jela, was from a preeminent and noted family. The young boy's great-grandfather was Duke Stanko Uskoković, who had been a senator in the People's Assembly, a famous hero during the reign of Peter I Petrović-Njegoš[1], and an officer in the Montenegrin army which fought against the Napoleonic invasion of Montenegro. Duke Uskoković was killed at the battle of Dubrovnik in 1813, and was later remembered as a legendary figure in Serbian history.

Young Ivan's baptism took place at the village church of St George, located near the ruins of an ancient monastery that dated back to the Nemanjić dynasty.[2] As the most esteemed and eminent family in the region, known for their bravery and nobility, the Uskokovićs had lived in the area surrounding the monastery ruins for centuries.

Due to his family's status, young Ivan, unlike most of his peers, had the opportunity and privilege of pursuing an education. He received his primary instruction at Rijeka Crnojevića, and later moved to the capital of Montenegro, Cetinje, to continue. When he was just eleven, he asked the then metropolitan of Montenegro, Theophan, to tonsure him a monk. Considering his request as simply the fleeting desires of a child, his wish was ignored, and he moved to Belgrade with his brother, Elijah, to continue his secondary education.

Many years later he would recall his time in Belgrade, where, as a young boy, he would frequent the Cathedral church of the city, feeling a deep and passionate desire within him to serve Christ and devote his life to the service of the Church. The metropolitan of Belgrade at the time was Dimitrije Pavlović, who was later to serve as patriarch of all Serbia. Metropolitan Dimitrije met young Ivan often and discerned a certain zeal and light in the eyes of the child. Recognizing his true and unwavering passion, he gave him a letter for the then bishop of Žiča, Savva (Barac), extolling the student from the mountain village, and recommending him to the novitiate at Studenica monastery. The bishop accepted the Montenegrin teen, taking him under his wing, and after a six-month novitiate, during which the young boy's mettle was thoroughly tested, he was granted his heart's desire and tonsured a monk, taking the name Mardarije, after the famous sixteenth-century Serbian monk and abbot of the Mileševa monastery.

Mardarije was only sixteen years old when he left the world; he had not yet completed his education, and knowing his parents would be against his decision to become a monk, he did not tell them. Not receiving any news from him for several years, his parents came to believe that he had died from some tragic disease. In this way, the young monk sacrificed everything for the love of Christ, forgoing the world, even at such a tender age, in a crucifixional mimesis of his Saviour. A folk poet later described the saint's early life in the following poem:

> He dropped the toy from his boyish hand,
> And fled into the night from his father's haven;
> In Studenica he received his black robe,
> And entirely gave himself to prayer.[3]

IN RUSSIA

In 1906 Mardarije was ordained a deacon, and soon after the Holy Synod of the Church of Serbia decided to send him to Russia for further studies. Initially the Synod wanted to send the young hierodeacon to the famous theological school at the Roman Catholic university of Bern in Switzerland, where many hierarchs had received their education. However, preferring to stay close to a place where the heart of Orthodoxy beat strongly, he petitioned to be allowed to study in the equally prominent educational centers of the Russian Empire. His request was granted, and in September of 1906 he enrolled at the Ecclesiastical Academy of Zhytomyr, near Kiev, and after two years, he requested to transfer to the Chișinău Theological Seminary in Moldavia, which, at the time, was still part of the Russian Empire. He had been seventeen when he began his studies, and was now nineteen, but his ardor had in no way diminished. The warmth of his missionary zeal and pastoral desire to give the public the priceless pearl of the knowledge of God shone through in all his words and actions, and in that same year, despite his tender age, he was ordained a presbyter. He continued his studies at Chişinău, adding pastoral duties to his increasingly busy schedule.

During his clerical rounds, he often visited the orphanage in Chişinău, liturgizing at the Church of St Olga which was located within it, and on March 14, 1910, he gave the following sermon:

> My dear children, I visited your wealthy and valuable library. I saw very many interesting and beneficial books on various topics and saw you often reading these fine tomes. But to my great sorrow and disappointment, I did not see the most important of all books. I looked throughout the library and could not find a single Bible.
>
> You are not to blame for this, nor are your teachers, it is the spirit of the time that is to blame, contemporary society. This wonderful book is very hard to find even in the most eminent homes. It is considered to be an old, boring book whose days have passed. Oh how cruelly are people mistaken! There is no book more valuable than the Bible. There was not and will not ever be another book which can replace the Bible.
>
> There is no book in the whole world which contains so many teachings that can lead one to salvation, so much life and spirit, as the Bible. How many wondrous and miraculous words are contained therein, thousands and millions of words that shine like the sun. When you read the Bible, you cannot help but be amazed and exclaim: "Oh, how Divine, how wonderful!"
>
> The words are like jewels that sparkle in the sunshine, sparkle under the sunlight of eternal love, and tell us of the great miracles of mercy of our great God. But why, dear children, is the Bible such an important and most important book? Because the words of the Bible are not the words of man or of several people, they are the words of God Himself. Man could not write the Bible, man is in no condition to elevate himself to such a height of sanctity and creativity. The author of the Bible is God Himself, though He chose His selected few to inscribe the words.
>
> You might ask: "Didn't we learn that the Bible was written by people, by Moses, by David, Isaiah, the Prophets, the Apostles and the Evangelists?"

Yes, these people held in their hands the stylus, the writing utensil, recording the great revelations, which expressed the greatest and most profound thoughts, truths, the holiest of all sensibilities, inspired by the Holy Spirit. They were inspired by God.

Man did not write down every word and every letter of God, but recorded His thoughts and His will, and laid them down in human tongue. The Bible is a large book, in which the Father of Heaven reveals to His children everything that they need for their salvation. It is a book in which God consoles us in our sorrows and our failings; He gives us strength in our weakness and our despair; He gives us wisdom and guidance.

That is why the Bible is the greatest the most treasured book in the world, and that is why it must occupy the first place in all libraries and among all the books of every house, that is why it must be taken advantage of by us with special attention and love.

If any of you has not received a letter from your father or mother for a long time, from a brother or sister, and when you finally do, then you treasure it and cherish it and read it over and over several times. That is how you should read the Holy Bible. This is not a letter of a father or a mother. It is not from a person but a letter from God, the Father of Heaven. Read the Bible. It will grant you much that is beneficial and necessary in life. It will teach you joy, not to be proud yet not be despondent.

Maybe you cannot afford to buy it. Ask your friends to buy you a Bible, and do not part from it throughout your whole lives. May it be your constant companion in your life's path; it will be your best and most faithful friend. Let it occupy a visible place among your other books. Read it carefully both when you are happy and satisfied, and also when you are sorrowful and when you fall into temptation.

Know that when every last person might abandon you, even your parents, only the Bible will remain with you. It will not betray you even in the most bitter and burdensome moments of your lives. It will give you the teaching of eternal love, of the Father of Heaven, and it will embolden your spirit and your heart.

I have known many people who could not read even the finest books twice, the finest works of great literature of the philosophers and thinkers. They could not find anything of sufficient interest, and so do not reread them. The Bible has a certain characteristic, a property: an exhaustible source of knowledge. That is why it must be read and reread. The Bible contains a great wealth, an inexhaustible source of blessed treasures. The Bible is the only book in the whole world which is of interest to all men, all times, and all peoples.

It is equally interesting for the scholar, the aspiring theologian, and for the lad who can barely read. For you all it must be especially interesting. All of you children, all children wherever they may be, come to love the travels, love the descriptions of the lives of great people, descriptions of the astounding feats of great heroes. You love stories about miracles; you love the songs.

You will find all of this in the Bible—accounts of the travels of the people of Israel through a great desert to the land of Canaan. You will read wonderful pages from the life of the Holy Apostle Paul in Asia and Europe, and his great deeds, his sufferings and labours. You will read in the Bible wonderful pages about the heroic efforts of great men. You will read about Gideon, Samson, David, and others. You will find many miracles contained therein, which will reveal to you the great and wondrous works of God. You will find yourself swept away in reading the Bible.

Read the Bible, my dear children, read it often. In addition to the good and the joy it brings you, you will see that. At first it may seem too difficult and obscure for you, but continue to read. What you won't understand today you will understand tomorrow. Read it, for in the Bible is the key to eternal joy, to eternal life. Amen.[4]

In 1912, after completing his education at the Academy of Chişinău, he graduated with the highest marks and was given the office of Synkellos[5] He immediately decided to enroll in the Saint Petersburg Theological Academy to complete his studies, which he did after four years, receiving his degree in theology. Aside from his theological studies, Fr Mardarije also attended classes in Ecclesiastical Law at the Saint Petersburg Faculty of Law, something which would prove valuable in his future missionary career in the United States and Canada.

During his time in Russia, a friend of his happened to ask him what his plans were for the future. Full of divine zeal and Godly passion, he answered: "Sowing Christian love, spreading peace, quieting passions, preaching good, and turning people into brothers."[6]

He had a special place in his heart for the humbled and marginalized, whom he loved and cared for dearly. Compassion and mercy characterized his entire life, perhaps more than any other of his virtues, and his years were marked by constant almsgiving and works of charity for anyone who had any need. Indeed, God seemed to bring multitudes of such people into his path, and so his daily acts of service and charity became incalculable.

One way in which he expressed his love for the downtrodden was his visits to prisons in Siberia, Turkestan, and Bukhara. Traveling to these remote and forsaken places, he spoke with the prisoners, delivering homilies and encouragement, and listening to their problems. The folk poet wrote the following verse about this period of his life:

In Russia he saw the simple and the rich,
He saw the paupers' sheds and the palaces of emperors,
But nothing led him astray from the path
On which God and God's work is celebrated.[7]

Saint Mardarije never forgot his native land, and when World War I broke out, and Belgrade was under siege, he personally gathered 300 rubles[8] and sent it home for the support of his beloved Montenegro, which was always dear to his heart, and never far from his mind. During his last year of residence in Russia, 1917, he was elected lecturer at the Slavic Gymnasium of Professor Vyacheslav Gribovsky in St. Petersburg, and participated in the meetings of the historic Pan-Russian Sobor, in which St Tikhon was elected patriarch of Moscow and All Russia.

It is difficult to imagine how someone with a schedule so full and busy with study, pastoral work, charity, and preaching could find time to write, but during that period Fr Mardarije authored several works, amongst which were *The Quiet Corner of Christ* (all the proceeds of which he distributed to the poor in Russia), *Collected Sermons*, and *Message to the Russian People*. In this last book, the humble hieromonk called on the people of Russia to defend and fight for the Serbian people, something which resulted in intense reactions in the circles of Germanophile Russians.[9] This, however, was not the first time Fr Mardarije had been faced with such opposition; since his first arrival in Russia, he had tirelessly worked to inform the Russian populace of the plights suffered by their fellow Orthodox Christians in the Balkans. The Slavic people, many of whom shared ethnic and historic roots with their neighbors to the north, had been living under the yoke of the Austro-Hungarian Empire, and the Montenegrin monk made it his mission to sensitize Russians to their cause.

BETWEEN TWO CONTINENTS

The young hieromonk's unusual missionary apostolic zeal could not long be hidden under a bushel, but had to be put upon the lampstand, to give light to all who saw it.[10] His light was destined to shine "amongst all nations," and on July 3, 1917, the Holy Synod of the Church of Russia, under whose jurisdiction he then served, decided to send him to North America to take over the organization of the Serbian Orthodox Mission there. The Serbian Orthodox Mission, which was then a part of the Russian Archdiocese of North America, was established in 1905 by St Tikhon for the purpose of serving the liturgical, spiritual, and pastoral needs of the Serbian Orthodox immigrant community.[11]

In the meantime, however, historical events took over the country, which forcibly expedited his migration. There had been a coup against the emperor, Nicholas II, and after his forced abdication, the Russian Provisional Government under Alexander Kerensky had taken power. The saint was granted a passport from the minister of foreign affairs, but only with the understanding that he would leave Russia immediately. Indeed, after receiving his passport on July 17, he immediately departed for Philadelphia, where he would receive the rank of archimandrite.

In 1918, alongside his duties as head of the Serbian mission, St Mardarije was also appointed dean of the church of the Holy Resurrection in Chicago. He embraced his new position as he embraced all his other duties, with zeal and love for God and his flock. His abilities and gifts were soon obvious to his ecclesiastical superiors, and in the next congress of the Synod the Russian Diocese of America, which took place in Cleveland, Ohio, in 1919, the Russian archbishop of North America, Alexander Nemolovsky, recommended that St Mardarije be elevated to the rank of bishop, to serve over the Serbian populace of the United States and Canada. The archbishop noted that he was the most able man he knew for the task, that he was known in Russia, that he was unquestionably active, and that in the little time that they had known each other, he had found him to be a charismatic person with a thorough knowledge of his people's psychology. The synod approved his proposal, and St Mardarije was officially chosen as bishop of the Serbians in America.

When he had arrived in America in 1917, the Montenegrin archimandrite had received a crash course on the Serbian Orthodox jurisdictional subjugation to the Russian Church. This experience, along with the Serbian Church's inability to send a Serbian bishop to America to shepherd the Serbian flock, had created a deep wound in the souls of American Orthodox Serbs. The continued relations with the Russian Church, under which they had to operate, as they had no diocese of their own on the continent, only widened the rift. Not wishing to make the situation for his compatriots worse by becoming a bishop in the Russian diocese, the saint turned down the position and chose to return to Serbia.

In 1920, he arrived back in his homeland, and the patriarch of Serbia appointed him proistamenos[12] of the Rakovica Monastery in Belgrade, and rector of the monastic school there. His time at the school was a great success, and his efforts proved immensely fruitful in the upbringing and spiritual education of the young students. Despite not receiving any support from the Serbian State, he continued to run both the monastery and the school with great efficacy. His inspired example in both word and deed could not but have a positive effect on the souls of his students. He would say: "Shine in your life as the candles shine in the church and burn as they burn before an icon so that people can see your life and your good deeds and through them glorify our Heavenly Father."[13]

During his three-year tenure at Rakovica Monastery, Archimandrite Mardarije involved in many areas of ecclesiastical and social work. He was invited to lecture on various topics at the Academy of Sciences, the University of Belgrade, the YMCA, and the Belgrade College of Theology, and his powerful oratorical skills were witnessed by many, one of whom wrote the following:

At the podium he looked like a Byzantine fresco, spiritual, ascetic, alive, picturesque, full of successful comparisons and inspired by a sincere feeling; he left a strong and unforgettable impression ... a learned orator .... The Society of Slavic Union prepared at the Hall of the Academy of Sciences an assembly, but the Hall of the Academy of Sciences was too small to receive all who had come—so many were turned away .... The orator was greeted enthusiastically and during his speech was interrupted by the applause of the impressed listeners.[14]

Despite his busy schedule and active ministry in Belgrade, the saint never forgot the Serbian Orthodox flock in America and its pressing needs.

239

He repeatedly requested the Holy Synod of the Church of Serbia appoint a bishop for the United States and Canada, citing the practical difficulties of managing the many problems that arose within the Serbian Orthodox community from such an immense distance and across continents and an ocean. Indeed, after the 1917 coup in Russia, all the officially documented Serbian parishes in America left the ecclesiastical jurisdiction of the Russian Archdiocese of America and asked to join the Church of Serbia.

IN THE NEW WORLD

In 1921, the Church of Serbia established the Serbian Archdiocese of America and Canada, and a year later, in October of 1922, St Nikolai Velimirović, then bishop of Ohrid, was appointed patriarchal representative, reassigned to North America, and sent over to assume the duties of managing the new diocese. Soon after, in the early months of 1923, St Mardarije was also appointed a patriarchal representative and sent to join the former bishop of Ohrid and assist him in the difficult and challenging work of organizing the new diocese. Having two patriarchal representatives (their official title being "Diocesan Administrators") was confusing to the Serbs in America, who thought St Nikolai was their new bishop, and St. Mardarije his assistant bishop, though the latter was still an archimandrite.

Additionally, St Nikolai's overseas appointment, and the prospect of his remaining in America, caused intense reactions from his flock back in Serbia, who refused to accept the possibility of their beloved bishop not returning to them. So, the same year St Mardarije arrived in America, St Nicholai sent a request to the Serbian Patriarchate to relieve him of his duties in the United States and allow him to return home. The appeal was acquiesced to, and so, after a few months of the Serbian Diocese in America having two patriarchal representatives, only St Mardarije remained.

The establishment of the Serbian Diocese in America did not solve all the problems of the flock there, as there was still no bishop in the diocese, meaning there was no Serbian hierarch on the entire continent. With the departure of Bishop Nikolai, who many American Serbians thought was their canonical bishop, and some others thought would soon be assigned as their first bishop, the reactions intensified, and many Serbian parishioners became outright hostile. The Serbian Patriarchate's continued inability to find a bishop for the Serbian diocese in America caused disappointment and anger amongst the immigrant community, and many called for the creation of an autocephalous, independent Serbian Archdiocese of America with, or without connection to or approval from the Serbian Church.

The saint found himself in the middle of the maelstrom, and worked day and night to bring harmony and balance to the opposing factions, and an end to the infighting. In a letter he wrote to Patriarch Dimitrje in April of 1924, he described the tumultuous situation in America during that time of unrest: "For a year and a half in my reports I have urged that this Diocese needs a permanent Bishop as soon as possible, who with his Episcopal authority would gather the lost sheep of Christ's flock within the framework of the church more successfully than a diocesan administrator. No one can do this successfully without full authority. It is sad that this point of view and the repeated urging of this matter by the diocesan administrator have been interpreted by some as a personal matter and even sick ambition. The best proof that this is not true is the fact that not only the Consistory of the Diocese but also official representatives of our state in America have finally found themselves compelled at their own personal initiative to say the same thing that the Diocesan Administrator repeated so many times, adding that it was in the interest of both the church and the nation and state for a permanent Bishop to replace the Diocesan Administrator … Among the many other reasons for urging the earliest possible appointment of a permanent Bishop on whom everything rests and everything depends given the circumstances, a new reason has recently appeared, reflecting a tendency very dangerous for our church. Immediately after the last Holy Assembly of Bishops in the fall of 1923, some of the priests and people here began to campaign in favor of convening a National Church Assembly in America, its competencies including not only the right to resolve purely local internal matters, but also the main one of electing a Bishop for this diocese. This group has been active all this time among our people. I have curbed the harmful activity of these people, their goal being to separate from our Serbian patriarchate … They call my opposition to the convening of a National Church Assembly "despotism" and cause all kinds of troubles for me, especially since in free democratic America they can create difficulties and present me, indeed, as a medieval despot in the eyes of our people in Americans. I do not do this for personal reasons but in the interest of the patriarchate I represent in America."[15]

241

Pointing out the difficulties he faced as patriarchal representative, he also wrote: "To your Holiness's question whether the clergy follow the instructions of the Administrator and Consistory, the correct answer would be: most are indifferent; they obey if the instructions suit them, if not, they consider America a free country and accordingly adjust their conduct toward their superiors. There are priests who upon receiving an act from the consistory exclaim: 'what, priests who are my equals want to give me orders?' There are archimandrites who upon receiving an act from the Administrator say the same thing: 'what, an archimandrite who has less seniority wants to give me orders?' A dissatisfied priest can easily find support among a dissatisfied segment of the population who, in this land of complete religious freedom, despises all authority and despises it even more in the Church where he feels he is entitled to exercise his powerful ego ... It should also be added that here one often has to deal with abnormal circumstances and sick people. It will require a long period of wise, tactful Episcopal administration of this diocese for the clergy and people to become accustomed to the necessary discipline ... To your Holiness's question about the situation of our people and church congregations, the Diocesan Administrator in all conscience, and against his wishes, must give a very somber picture which characterizes most parishes. Churches in most cases are administered by a small group or even just an individual, who generally looks upon the church from the commercial aspect. Most churches are empty for weeks. They are full only at Christmas and Easter. There may be exceptions. If for no other reason, a Bishop should be constantly officiating in the churches, at least two or three times a year in each, which means that he would be traveling around America half the year. In this way he could spiritually awaken the slumbering popular masses and bring them to church."[16]

With deep and heartfelt anguish St. Mardarije wrote: "It is hard for me to hear that Serbian brothers persecute each other and hate each other. My heart hurts and I suffer in my soul, and I am ready to lament this even today when one ought not to cry, when I see that brothers persecute each other and hate each other."[17]

His plight was truly heartbreaking, but the thorny issues surrounding the ordination of a Serbian bishop for America did not limit the saint's multifaceted ecclesiastical and social ministries. While he attempted to answer the many requests to lecture at colleges, universities, and organizations across America, he had his eyes on Illinois.

Before he had departed for the United States, Bishop Nikolai had told Archimandrite Mardarije to find a way, by any means, to purchase land near Chicago, and there to erect a monastery, theological school, printing press, and orphanage. This place would serve as the spiritual center for all the Serbs in America. At the time, there was no way to know the historical and spiritual dimensions or significance of this work, or God's plans for its future, but St Mardarije obediently heeded the wise bishop's words and purchased 33 acres of land in the then rural wilderness of Libertyville, Illinois.

Libertyville, a village about 40 miles north of Chicago, was a beautiful place in which to build the new Serbian monastery. The Des Plaines River ran through it, and the setting reminded St Mardarije of the beautiful monasteries in his home country. On September 3, 1923, an outdoor Divine Liturgy and Blessing of the Waters took place on the spot where the monastery, dedicated to St Savva of Serbia, was to be built. Alongside it would be an Orthodox cemetery, an orphanage, and a care home for the elderly. With deep feelings of holy anticipation, St Mardarije wrote: "No one is ever going to dig over this cemetery and disturb the peace of our departed ones or desecrate either the sanctity of the graves or the due piety that our people have toward their departed ones. At the monastery there will always be a hieromonk who will regularly serve in the church and on certain days will do memorial services at the cemetery."[18]

His great desire for the completion of the monastery began to consume St Mardarije, and reminded one of the psalmist, "For the zeal of thine house hath eaten me up".[19] He spent the last dollar from his minuscule wages for the construction needs of the monastery, to the point where many times he had literally nothing to eat, and would go without food for days. His flock, seeing his touching dedication, would say, "Mardarije is building a monastery, and he himself is starving to death."

The diplomat Dr Božidar Purić,[20] who at that time was serving in the United States as ambassador for the Kingdom of Serbs, Croats, and Slovenes[21], and would later serve as the prime minister of the Yugoslavian government in exile, knew St Mardarije, and held a deep regard and affection for him. His writings preserve priceless memories of that time, as the example below shows:

> Whenever I would object to him not securing a bigger sum for the beginning of the construction, he would say: "Don't worry, Božice (a diminutive, endearing nickname for Božidar). People will give as soon as they see the foundation …."

"Mardarije, you will become Darmarije"[22] I would rebuke him jokingly, to which his usual response would come: "Božice, if we could only get up to the roof, people will give. The Serbian people are good … "

But before the roof was set, there was a meeting in Chicago, which asked of him to present the books to them, barely stopping short of accusing him of theft. Appalled and in disbelief that such a thing was even possible, Mardarije could not even open his mouth.[23]

Due to his political position, Božidar Purić found himself a constant witness to all the infighting and ecclesiastical problems of the American Serbs, and he was also able to carefully observe St Mardarije, and stand in awe at the way he handled the issues, the battles, and the slander that was constantly directed against him. In his biography, which heavily relied on the letters, memos, and documents he had written throughout his life, we see the way in which Purić described the saint: "He was a man ready to be an example through the renouncing of everything, and first of all the renouncing of his very self … He was a monk without hypocrisy, without one grain of envy or hatred, without any vanity. Understanding and forgiveness were not a problem for him because he was goodness without passion … Physically beautiful, lively in his motion, unreal like a dream."[24]

Neither the practical difficulties nor the accusations against him managed to disrupt the saint's work toward the fulfillment of his sacred mission. He knew that a monastery, like a spiritual lung, would ceaselessly revivify the spiritual powers of his Serbian brothers and sisters in America. So despite the worsening tuberculosis, from which he had suffered for years, he gave himself, body and soul, over to the work of construction. He would wake up in the morning, before dawn, and would go to the building site. He would help the workers erect scaffolds around the half-completed church building, and do any other manual labor that was required.

When he was not working on the buildings, he would plant fruit trees, carve out new paths, build small, paved terraces, and dig irrigation trenches. Day by day, as the church reached completion, he could see how beautiful it was going to be, and that gave him new strength to continue, to endure, to pray that he would not fall ill, so that he could see the work completed.

THE GOOD SHEPHERD

On December 7, 1925, the Holy Synod of the Patriarchate of Serbia finally elected St Mardarije to be the first bishop of the Serbian Diocese of America and Canada. His health, however, would not allow him to make the trip to Belgrade for his ordination. His doctors recommended he go to Arizona, where the climate is always warm and dry, to recover before his transatlantic journey. His doctors gave him leave to depart for Serbia in mid-May, but not before then. However, the invitations from Serbia kept coming, one after the next, so the saint decided to leave earlier, in order to fulfill all his responsibilities in Belgrade and return to America as soon as possible to resume care for his flock. "On March 26, 1926, he wrote the following letter to one of his close friends: "I want to return from Serbia to America as soon as possible and to begin as a bishop my hard and holy work, in which, I firmly believe, all those who are honorable and honest in America will help me. Until now, I myself have found it hard to believe how many friends I have among our people in America."[25]

On Palm Sunday, April 25, 1926, his consecration was festively celebrated at the cathedral church in Belgrade. The Serbian diocese in America and Canada, which had existed since 1921, received its own first bishop. He was thirty-six years old. During his ordination sermon, the saint spoke the following words: "I will fulfill the promise that I gave to You, o God, in Your temple, before Your people, because I was there with them. I saw how the fiery sea of forges and factories burns their bodies. Their hands were blackened, but I was afraid to stretch out my hand to them. I was afraid that they would think that I was a gentleman of some kind. So far I was a brother to them and from now on I will be their father and pastor."[26]

Loyal and dedicated to the service of his flock in the New World, the new bishop quickly fulfilled all his duties in Serbia and boarded the steamboat that was to take him back to America. The *New York Times* correspondent in Belgrade reported:

> SERBIAN BISHOP SAILS
> Mardary Is First Appointed for America by the Patriarch.
> Special Cable to The New York Times
> BELGRADE, July 2.
> Bishop Mardary, recently consecrated by the Serbian Patriarch as the first Serbian Bishop to America and Canada, started yesterday to sail

for New York on the 7th on the "France". He has traveled extensively in America in the last four years, organizing Serbian Orthodox dioceses, of which he was then the administrator.

His new work will be to continue this and also establish orphanages and other institutions for his flock of 100,000 Orthodox Serbs, widely scattered throughout the United States. The bishop's seat will be in Chicago.[27]

His July 14, 1926 return to New York, now as Bishop Mardarije, was celebrated with an historic and magnificent welcome. On the shore, a countless multitude of Serbs met him, led by Mihajlo Idvorski Pupin,[28] a faithful Orthodox Christian and renowned Serbian scientist. Dragoslav Dragutinovic, one of his biographers, was present at the momentous occasion, and wrote: "They expected a despot but they saw a Lamb of God. What an evangelical pastor, what a servant of God, what a guardian of the flock that was entrusted to him. The young servant of God was meek and full of humane goodness, ready for sacrifice and to renounce even himself. Overfilled with love, and thirsty for the goodness of people. As such he stretched his hands for an embrace and displayed his open heart to all of the American Serbs. In his gaze and in his countenance one could already see a mark of an earlier martyrdom, an image of life in Russia."[29]

Upon his arrival in New York, Bishop Mardarije telegraphed Patriarch Dimitrije (Pavlovic) that he would soon be leaving for Chicago. Indeed, the saint began his missionary work with the zeal and passion of a new confessor and martyr. Ignoring his physical weakness, he gave all his mental and bodily strength to organizing the newly established diocese in America. As he wrote, "I visited local churches one by one as each one invited me. The people everywhere were exhilarated to welcome their first bishop."[30] From his very first year as bishop, he began ordaining new clerics and consecrating new churches.

Despite his superhuman self-denial, his illness was serious, and at the time, incurable. It was a demanding and cruel adversary, and in a note from his doctor, Mihailo Matanovic, we read: "Bishop Mardarije is here under my supervision. His treatment requires a longtime, perfect rest, and absence of cares. If he stops in the near future with all of his travels and if he has rest and proper nutrition, there is hope for recovery ..." [31]

The saintly bishop, however, had no intention of allowing the disease to stop him from his apostolic work, and the more the disease progressed, trying to limit his activities, the harder he fought against it, and the more he insisted on giving himself up entirely to the ministry of his diocese. On May 24, 1927, his doctor once again wrote: "Against a categorical order of four doctors, Bishop Mardarije suddenly left for Chicago today. He needed to stay in Arizona the entire summer ... I renounce any kind of responsibility for his departure for Chicago ..." [32]

Another biographer recorded the following: "Even before 1927 the bishop was often ill, bur that year the illness became a great threat and it was harder and harder, giving us all an impression that he was not going to live long. For the sake of healing and recovery he went several times to the soothing, blossoming, sunny South, to Arizona, where he would in a short time recover, only then to have the illness come back with more strength and as a greater threat. This would happen especially in those times when he would, due to matters that he had to attend to, leave Arizona for some time and travel to other parts of America in order to fulfill his duties within the diocese or for the monastery. Those matters, travels without rest, and especially discord among the people, prompted by unfounded malicious slander by some priests and a few Serbian academics, contributed to the bishop's illness spreading rapidly and reducing his physical powers, which were already thin, and announcing the end of his life." [33]

In June of 1927 Bishop Mardarije wrote to the Holy Synod about his visit to Los Angeles, where he managed to restore unity and harmony amongst the local Serbs. While in California, he fell seriously ill, and had to be hospitalized in Los Angeles. He was not able to leave for five weeks, after which he returned to Phoenix. A guard at the Libertyville monastery later wrote: "The bishop was sick with tuberculosis. He had one lung removed and in its place they placed an artificial lung made out of cellulose or some such material. For this reason, he needed a lot of oxygen, so he slept out here on this terrace for the last three years, and this is where he received visitors also." [34]

Refusing to allow the illness to stop him from fulfilling his diocesan duties, he once again battled the disease which had nearly cost him his life and began organizing the first ever Serbian Clergy-Laity conference at the monastery of St Savva in Libertyville. Even though the monastery was not yet complete, his fervent desire for the unity of the Serbian diaspora drove him to miraculous lengths, and indeed, 100 clerics, parish council members, Sunday School teachers, and representatives from Serbian parishes, communities, and humanitarian organizations across the United States gathered at this momentous, historic conference. There, St Mardarije presented his drafts for an official charter constitution for the diocese.

The constitution for the Serbian Diocese of America and Canada was a necessary and long overdue administrative concern, due to the circumstances which surrounded it at the time. In the diocese, there had been a constant stream of rumor, infighting, and slander, much of which was directed toward the bishop himself. Upon his ordination to the episcopacy, he had discovered that many of the Serbian priests in the diocese had become used to having a large amount of power and influence, as there had been no canonical head, and that the freedoms which they had enjoyed during that period of chaos proved difficult to give up. That group of clerics proved the saintly bishop's most ardent adversaries, as upon his elevation he began to work on managing and correcting the unhealthy and uncanonical situation in the Serbian diocese. Despite his extreme delicacy and discernment, and the tact and diplomacy which he liberally applied in these situations, the responses from the diocesan priests were often harsh and unyielding.

The necessity of constantly battling those who were supposed to be his dear children and coworkers in Christ took an even greater toll on his weakened health, and the stress he faced on a daily basis while trying to bring health and well-being back to the flock of the church was a constant strain on his frail system.

St Mardarije knew that a charter and constitution would set many wrongs right, and, sooner or later would contribute to the stability and correction of the governing ecclesiastical structure in the new diocese. Indeed, the draft he submitted was immediately accepted by the assembly, which met September 1–5, 1927. In his opening statements, the saint said:

> The Lord gave me the fortune to live and to see today the opening of the Clergy-Laity Assembly, the fruit of my and your work of many years and the guarantee that the life of the Serbian Church in America and Canada will be what it ought to be. It seems to me like everything is a dream. It seems to me like these are still some kind of negotiations and agreements, but actually we are facing reality. This is the Assembly which will solve our most important question in the Diaspora-the question of the Serbian Orthodox Diocese, in which everyone will be put in their place, where they belong according to our moral and spiritual strength[35]

In these words, one can sense the depth of the saint's concern for the future of his diocese, and indeed, he had good reason to be worried during that era of deep-rooted insubordination and chaos. According to the testimony of priests who lived during that time of havoc, there was a very real danger that everything that had been built by so many years of struggle and toil would fall apart and collapse in on itself. And yet, like an expert spiritual horseman, St Mardarije held the reins of the diocese, using all the grace and discernment which he had been given by the Holy Spirit, and all the spiritual gifts which God had bestowed on him, to maintain the delicate balance necessary in order to keep the flock from careening headfirst into the chasm.

Fr Živojin Riscanovic, who was very close to the saint, later wrote: "Things were not in order in the Diocese. Self-will and disobedience were on the rise. Parental and episcopal advice was not helping. There was a real danger of destruction and demolition of that which had been created with heavy toil. Bishop Mardarije avoided to an extreme any kind of drastic measures. In one case he refused to execute the order of the patriarch about the removal of one priest, because he was deeply convinced that that priest knew the way to repentance. That path was always left open to anyone by Bishop Mardarije. But in some cases, in the interest of the Church and peace among the people, there had to be reprimands. In those cases the people unanimously stood behind their bishop and condemned the anarchy and the selfwill of the culprits. But this further shook up and worsened his health and expedited his end."[36]

During this time, St Mardarije made frequent visits back to Serbia, both because he needed to participate in the meetings of the Holy Synod, and to gather funds for the needs of his American diocese. During one of these visits, he was forced to stay in Serbia for fifteen days, waiting for a particularly important donation to the monastery, and in 1928, during another visit, rumors began to circulate in America that he was not returning. Upon hearing this rumor, the saintly hierarch immediately took pen to paper and sent a pastoral letter from Belgrade, informing his flock: "Despite everything, your love has tied me to you, my flock, and I yearn to go back to you as soon as possible. "Do not believe everything you hear", I say to you using the apostolic words (1 John 4:1). Do not believe the rumor that I will receive one of the dioceses here in the Kingdom of Serbs, Croats and Slovenes, of Yugoslavia, and that I will stay here [in Belgrade] … Know that I have no intention to go to any diocese in Europe, because

A ceremony welcoming St Mardarije at one of his parishes.

I have been by God's will tied to the diocese in America and Canada, and know also that I am not thinking of any other position in our Church except the one that I have right now. The peak of my earthly longing is that I serve to my last day the Diocese of America and Canada, my dear Serbian people in the New World, whom I have grown to love so much over the past twelve years of my missionary work in America and with whom I have become spiritually close in both good and trying times ..."[37]

Until the end of his life, Bishop Mardarije had a deep and vivid understanding of his episcopal position and responsibilities. He would say "everything depends on the bishop. The bishop must not be a dictator, but a true servant of the people."[38] The saint did not only extend his fatherly love to his fellow Serbs, but to every Orthodox American immigrant. He worked with other hierarchs in America, from the churches of Russia, Greece, and Syria, and showed exceptional collaborative skills. The saint also had a great love for the sheep "not yet of this flock," the non-Orthodox Americans, for whom he held a deep and fatherly tenderness, and whom he frequently mentions in his letters, which are preserved in the archives of the monastery of St Savva in Libertyville.

St Mardarije's episcopal letters show a depth of love that touches the soul of every reader. During the difficult years of the Great Depression, he wrote to the Serbian people, urging them to take heart during the upcoming feast of the Nativity:

> Let this song of peace also find its way into the hearts and souls of our people that are scattered all over the great America, people who are living through the difficult days of shortages and uncertainties of tomorrow. May the God of peace come into the disturbed soul of my beloved flock, and may today, on the day of the Nativity of the Lord, in the soul of my people also be born faith in a better, happier future. And above all, I wish to everyone that we no longer live, but that Christ may live in us (Gal 2:20). May our good God grant that our people correctly understand this terrible material crisis and that, at a time when the material treasures are being lost, our people do not lose their greatest treasure-their soul. "For what will it profit a man if he gains the whole world, and loses his own soul?" (Mark 3:36).
>
> No matter how harsh and merciless the trials of our lives may be, we always ought to derive a lesson out of them for ourselves and for the

salvation of our souls. Once I watched peasants mercilessly whipping their cattle, so the cattle would exit the burning barn and so that they would save their precious flock from the jaws of a horrific fire. Likewise, the Lord sometimes whips us and beats us with hunger, sickness, and various trials, in order to save us from spiritual death, which is more terrible than any physical death.

Our wise people correctly estimated the value of the body and soul, the value of the earthly and heavenly, and said: "The earthly kingdom is short-lived; the heavenly is forever and ever." When someone commits a transgression and sin, our people do not threaten him with the law and jail, but they say: "Where is your soul going to go?"[39]

During the glorious celebration of Pascha, he wrote:

Our people say that man learns as long as he lives. There is no greater teacher than personal experience. It is the most convincing teacher in life. How can you believe the cries of a hungry man if you yourself have never been hungry? How can you understand the cries and sighs of the sick if you have never been sick yourself?[40]

In 1924, saint Mardarije consecrated the church of the Virgin Mary in Clairton, Pennsylvania. In 1929, he celebrated the service of the blessing of the waters on the parcel of land chosen to be the future site of the church of St Savvas in Merrillville, Indiana, where there was already a significant and constantly growing Serbian population. In 1931 he celebrated the last Divine Liturgy at the chapel of the Resurrection in Chicago, which was to give way to the larger cathedral church of the Resurrection in the same location. Indeed, the holy bishop was there two years later, when, on June 25, 1933, he celebrated the first Divine Liturgy at the new cathedral. During this same time, four more Serbian Orthodox churches were built, in St Louis, Missouri, Lorain and Youngstown, in Ohio, and Joliet, Illinois.

UNTIL THE END

The work to complete the monastery continued, but the saint's illness did not allow him to fundraise at the level which he desired, and construction continued slowly. However, in early 1931 enough of the church and living quarters of the monastery were completed to make it fully habitable and operational. On September 6th of that year, they celebrated the consecration of the church. In its official press release, the diocese of Serbia wrote:

253

The monastery of St Savva of Serbia in Libertyville.

September the 6th, the day of the consecration will be the day of pride for all Serbian people on this side of the Atlantic. On that day all hard work and sacrifices will be crowned. It took too long to build a Monastery. The road was a thorny and difficult one. The economic situation of the country was a difficult one. The Serbs however succeeded building a beautiful place they must be proud of.[41]

There were some who gave little for the creation of the monastery, and some who gave much, but there was one person who gave all, and that was the holy bishop. Knowing his illness required rest, he nevertheless gave, day after day, to reach the desired goal of erecting the first Serbian monastery in North America.

Dr Božidar Purić wrote that during one of his visits to the monastery during its period of construction, he saw the bishop carrying large, heavy, rock slabs on his shoulders. The slabs were to be the path from the entrance of the monastery to the door of the church. When he chided the bishop for lifting such exceedingly heavy things when he knew it would be detrimental to his delicate health, the saint replied that by doing it himself he was saving the monastery money and resources, which were needed elsewhere. Many times, St Mardarije would get on his bicycle and ride miles and miles away to purchase bricks for a price the monastery could afford, then he would load them onto his bicycle and take them all the way back to the construction site. Indeed, there was no one who fought harder for the monastery's creation than the humble bishop, and it is due to his efforts that, despite economic and political obstacles that would have driven a lesser man to despair, the beautiful spiritual haven was not only built, but built so it stands for generations to come.

Shortly after the completion of the monastery, the Greek archbishop of America, Athenagoras, sent a letter to St Mardarije, for whom he harbored a deep love and respect.

> To the Right Reverend Bishop Mardary,
>   Bishop of the Serbian Orthodox Church,
>   Libertyville, IL
>   My dear Brother-in-Christ:
>   I am still moved with the recent imposing ceremony at the consecration
> of the monastery of your Grace. From all my heart I congratulate your

Grace for this wonderful achievement, which is an honor to the brotherly Serbian people in this country and which on the other hand will leave the name of your Grace immortal to the Serbian as well as to the rest of Orthodox Churches of America.

Desiring to have an article appear in the Greek newspaper in connection with this ceremony, I ask your Grace to please send me a few notes regarding the building, etc., and also some photographs. Especially I wish one photograph of Your Grace for my office and one for the newspapers.

Anticipating the pleasure to hear from Your Grace soon,
Archbishop Athenagoras of North and South America[42]

After the monastery of St Savva was completed, and after he had managed to untangle and calm the deep rifts and problems that had troubled the diocese since its inception, the primary missions of the first Serbian bishop of North America and Canada had been seen to a successful completion. As he had brought health back to the governing ecclesiastical structure of his church, his own health had been irreparably damaged, and his earthly life was coming to an end.

His incurable disease began to take a greater and greater toll on his weakened and ascetic body, and there were times that even celebrating the Divine Liturgy was a form of martyrdom, as his heavy mitre and weighty vestments seemed unmanageable for his exhausted frame. When there were ecclesiastical processions or litanies, his knees could barely hold steady. It was clear that he did not have long to live.

Already, from 1927, his Paschal Encyclical letter prepared his flock for the end that he knew was coming. "Today, my dear spiritual children, I rejoice with you as your bishop. I rejoice with you even though I am physically sick, because I believe that there is no death, knowing that I will live even after that hour when I depart this earth … Among all the duties that a man can have, there is no greater duty of which I would like to remind you on this day of Resurrection, than the duty of love. That is a duty above all duties."[43]

He tried his utmost to hide the severity of his illness, but as the years passed, this became more and more difficult. On Pascha, 1934, a year before his repose, he wrote his flock in a heartbreaking torrent of honesty, confessing his soul's anguish: "Over the 17 years of my service to God and people in America, I patiently bore my cross. Sometimes it was easy, sometimes it was heavy, but today that cross is heavier than ever before. At one point in time I was full of ideals, wanting to serve you and leave you with something permanent. But today I am exhausted; my knees are giving way under the weight of that heavy cross. Your bishop now speaks to his flock all over America and from the depth of a soul he cries out: 'People, brothers, is there anyone among you who will help me carry my heavy cross, or are your hearts so hardened that instead of helping you are even adding a burden to my weak back?'"[44]

His illness, and the great and constant difficulties in governing his diocese, did not allow the saint the time required to author numerous books or articles, but throughout his life, and to the time of his death, he maintained a constant and rich stream of correspondence, within which one can find his great talent in speaking and writing. His numerous letters overflow with deep thought, deep friendship, and deep love, and contain words designed to bring instruction, healing, and comfort to the souls of the recipients. The newspaper *Sloboda* (Freedom) published an article by Z. Buncic, which read:

For a little more than three months I have been watching our Bishop, as he writes all day long in his bed, sick and despite the doctors' instructions. A basket of letters comes and goes every day …. Is it honorable to offend this man, who is willing to offer even the last bit of his strength on the altar of our common good? Is it right to make this man suffer when he, serving even in his sickness God and people, burns out as a vigil lamp before an icon?[45]

Bishop Mardarije did not have a chance to enjoy the fruits of his labor for very long. On December 12, 1935, at only 46 years of age, full of grace and sanctity, the sainted bishop's soul left his body, and flew to meet the Saviour he had loved so much, and had served so long. He spent his last hours on earth at the University Hospital in Ann Arbor, Michigan, accompanied by his dear friend and fellow worker in God's field, protopresbyter Živojin Riscanovic, who wrote a detailed account of the saint's passing.

On December 10th of that year I was in Aliquippa, Pennsylvania, where on church business I stayed a few months. Around midnight the phone rang. They called from the hospital in Ann Arbor saying that Bishop Mardarije was on his deathbed and that he wanted to see me. The next day, December 11, at about 5 o'clock in the afternoon, I arrived at the hospital. The nurse led me to his room. Approaching the room, I heard his voice. I stood at the open door. The bishop was lying down on his back and was looking upward without blinking. As if he were talking to someone, he was saying a prayer out loud. I quietly entered the room and stopped. The bishop kept going, praying out loud, without pausing. That prayer was his own, unwritten and never read. He prayed in Serbian language, in order to switch to English, and then to Russian, and then back to Serbian. It is hard to write down that prayer in words just by my memory. I do recall couple of words though:

"Receive, o Heavenly Father, me, Thy servant, forgive me my sins. Have mercy on my people, my spiritual children. Keep them by Thy might, o Lord, bow down Thine ear and hear the cry of the orphans of my brother Stano (the bishop's brother died in a car accident in 1934 and left behind two children) ... Have mercy on all of us unworthy ones ... Save and have mercy on the Serbian Orthodox people, on our Royal House, and all the Orthodox Christians. Forgive me, o God, as I do forgive everybody ... everybody. Amen."

Finally, I decided to speak to him. I thought that he did not see me so I said: "Your Grace, do you see me? I came to visit you." But gazing onward in the same direction the bishop said: "I know you are here. I see you ... I see you always, even when you are not with me ... Thank you." And then he went on to repeat the same prayer. The nurse came and adjusted his pillow. The bishop only then looked around himself. I approached him and took a blessing. He started crying. His lips quivered, he wanted to say something. Tears started streaming down like a river out of his eyes. All of this lasted couple of seconds. And then on the bishop's face appeared an expression of heavy fatigue and exhaustion. His breathing was heavy. He gave a sign with his hand for the nurse to leave the room and then he pointed to the chair by the bed for me. I sat down and waited ...

"Thank you for coming. See, I have made my peace with the Lord. I am ready. Pray for the repose of my soul."

He could not go on ... Suddenly, he fell asleep like a man who just finished a heavy and exhausting trip ... Finally, in the evening of December 12, he asked for some water. The nurse approached with a glass. The bishop looked at me and said quietly: "You, Father Ziko,[46] you give me the water." I took the glass of water from the nurse. She slowly lifted the bishop's head from the pillow. I gave him some water from a little spoon, one spoonful, and another ... Then the bishop suddenly looked upward throwing his head back. Bishop Mardarije was no longer breathing. I looked at my watch. It was exactly 9:45 pm.[47]

St Mardarije's funeral took place on December 18. He was dressed in his episcopal vestments, placed in a wooden coffin, and transferred to the cathedral church of the Resurrection in Chicago, where his body lay in state and could be venerated by the faithful until the evening before the funeral, when it was transferred to the monastery of St Savva in Libertyville. The number of faithful who attended, wishing to see their beloved shepherd one last time, was immense. During the time his body rested in the cathedral, priests stood at a small reader's podium before the casket taking turns reading the gospel aloud.

Three archbishops, numerous priests, and several notable Serbs attended the saint's funeral service in Libertyville. During the Divine Liturgy, after Holy Communion, Fr Živojin Riscanovic read the holy bishop's last will and testament out loud, excerpts of which read:

> This holy monastery, as a place of assembly for Serbs in America, and a common house of prayer, as an eternal house of God, I leave as a heritage to my dear Serbian people so that they can, after my death, keep it and improve it, and so that they can leave it to their offspring in this New World as a beautiful monument of their national and religious conscience, and so that everyone to eternity can know and see, here on the other side of the Atlantic Ocean, that far from their motherland there were Serbs here.
>
> For all those Serbian men and women who helped me during the 18 years of work in America and thus eased my heavy burdens of governing the Serbian Church here, I pray to God to reward them with His mercy, and as for me, I leave to them and their homes my episcopal blessing.
>
> To the new Serbian bishop who will, after my death, be appointed from Yugoslavia, I recommend and urge him that his residence be here at the Saint Sava Serbian Orthodox Monastery in Libertyville, and that he love this monastery as I loved it and improve it as I have improved it by my hand, as I planted every tree on the property by my own hand.
>
> Having premonition of my departure from this world I entrust my dear faithful, my dear Serbian people in America to the protection of the Almighty God. All I ask from my people when in the Monastery, is to light a candle at my graveside and to say a prayer for the repose of my soul. I will pray for all of you even after my death. Goodbye.[48]

Fr Živojin also made sure to fulfill St Mardarije's last instruction, which was that on the day of his funeral, eleven priests be elevated to the rank of protopresbyter, and four others received honorary distinctions. Shockingly, several of these priests were amongst the saint's most bitter foes, ones who had tormented him ceaselessly during his life, slandering him, refusing to subject themselves to his episcopal authority, and causing him nearly constant temptations and sorrow. And yet, despite all this, his last desire was that they be honored and elevated. The Christlike humility, longsuffering, love, and forgiveness of the bishop shocked everyone, and the folk poet who later composed the poetic retelling of the saint's life illustrated this incident in verse:

> *All who hated him publicly and secretly*
> *Were crying by his tomb remorsefully,*
> *And his deeds stayed as a testimony to*
> *How one should fight for the Church and his people.*[49]

At the end of the funeral service, the casket with the saint's body was carried in procession three times around the monastery, and then placed in the crypt of the church, which he himself had made. The Kingdom of Yugoslavia covered the expenses for his funeral, as the first Serbian bishop of America and Canada left this world penniless, and with nothing to his name.

A fellow Serbian immigrant, Petar Perunović, veteran of the Balkan wars and World War I, drew a timeless spiritual portrait of the bishop, describing him as follows:

Bishop Mardarije at first sight appears a humble and meek monk of rather melancholic appearance. But underneath that monastic humility and meekness, like a spark within a rock, is a fiery revolutionary of a burning, sanguine temperament, capable of a great and lengthy battle. What torments were not suffered by that small and physically weak monk? One moment you see him as a fiery reporter, another moment as an apostolic missionary, another moment as a God-given orator and homilist, and in another moment as a very skilled organizer. In all these things Mardarije had nothing but success. Always modest, meek. and considerate, skillful and introspective, he tirelessly fought and marched forward.

People can say whatever they want, but they must admire him, how he lived with his miserable salary, and how he walked around in very poor clothing and a cloak in harsh winters to the consecrations of churches, and to inspire assemblies for the erections of churches. If any bishop of our day and age can be called a martyr, according to his struggles and battles for the Church, then Mardarije can be called a great martyr. If the Serbs in America care about work, order and peace in the Serbian Church in America, I believe that they will find in Mardarije nor only a wise advisor and a good bishop, but also a true Christian, a fiery and progressive Serb, and a brother whose soul is full of love and sacrifice for our people in America.[50]

The translation of the saint's relics took place on Friday, May 5, 2017. It is customary for "Christ Is Risen" and other Paschal hymns to be chanted during the entire service. As soon as his casket was opened, a beautiful, sweet scent poured out. His body was found to be in a state of incorruption, and his hair and beard were still soft, as if he had fallen asleep only moments earlier.

Saint John (Maximovich)
ARCHBISHOP OF SHANGHAI AND SAN FRANCISCO

His memory is commemorated on July 2

CHOSEN FROM YOUTH

Saint John was born on June 4, 1896, in the small town of Adamivka, in the Kharkiv district in modern-day Ukraine. His parents, Boris Ivanovich and Glafyra Michaelovna Maximovich, had descended from nobility. His father's ancestors were of Serbian descent and had migrated to Russia during the Ottoman occupation of Serbia. One of his mother's great grandfathers was a saint of the church, Saint John (Maximovich), Bishop of Tobolsk,[1] who lived at the end of the seventeenth century and had been canonized in 1916.

St John of San Francisco was born Michael Maximovich, his parents choosing his name in honor of the Archangel. In his youth, Michael could not decide whether to follow a military or civil career track, which were two of the more socially acceptable career choices for young men at the time, and ones that promised stability and upward mobility. Finally, he decided on the former, and began his studies in the Military Academy of Poltava, where he was a model student. However, despite his academic success, there were two lessons which he intensely disliked, gymnastics and dance, both required at the time.

It was during those years that he met Archpriest Sergius Chetverikov, later Archbishop Varlaam, who was widely known for his spiritual writings. During the saint's time at the academy, Fr Sergius was serving as professor of religion, and it was through his friendship with him that young Michael began to realize that his decision to pursue a military career may not be what he truly desired. He pressed forward with his studies, but a seed had been planted, and that seed would grow and bear fruit in due course.

St John as a young hieromonk.

On the day of Michael's graduation from the Military Academy, it happened that Archbishop Anthony (Khrapovitsky) was being elevated to the see of Kharkov, the diocese to which the city of Poltava belonged. A noted theologian and illustrious historical figure in his own right, the archbishop would be one of the driving forces behind the reinstitution of the Russian Patriarchate in 1917, and was to be elected one of the three candidates for the position of first patriarch of Moscow, alongside Metropolitan Tikhon, who would be eventually chosen. He was later appointed metropolitan of Kiev, one of the foremost dioceses in the Patriarchate of Russia, but after the continued bloody clerical holocaust of the Communist government, he was to flee his beloved homeland in order to keep the flame of the Faith alive until such time as Orthodoxy could return. He was the primary catalyst behind the creation of the Russian Orthodox Church Outside Russia (ROCOR), and was elected as its first Metropolitan.

It was this Archbishop Anthony who was to become the spiritual guide and lifelong luminary for Michael. The archbishop happened to be informed about the charismatic personality and academic gifts of the new graduate in his diocese, and asked to meet him in person. After this meeting, the young man put himself under the spiritual and fatherly guidance of the bishop, where he remained until the end of the latter's life in 1936.

Michael's soul was blooming with spiritual desire, but he had not yet reached the point of his life-altering decision. Having resolved on a non-military career path, he continued his studies at the law school in Kharkov, from which he graduated in 1918. Following his graduation, he began to work as a lawyer, and though he applied himself, his heart was not in it. He spent all his free time studying spiritual books and reading the lives of the saints.

In 1921, after the Russian Civil War, which followed the Bolshevik Revolution, the Maximovich family was forced to flee their fatherland and settle in Belgrade, at that time the capital of Yugoslavia. The bloody events which upended his homeland were to prove the catalyst for Michael's final turn away from the world. Seeing the glory of Imperial Russia now in ashes, and all he had grown to admire, love, and fight for, destroyed, he realized that the world was a temporal, fleeting, ever-changing thing, on which one could never anchor their life. It was then and there that the young man finally decided to follow a life dedicated to the one and only everlasting kingdom, that of heaven. He enrolled at the Theological School of the University of Saint Savva in Belgrade, from which he graduated in 1925.

During his last year of studies, he was tonsured a reader by his spiritual father, who had also fled to Yugoslavia, and was living in Belgrade. The next year, following a request from the young reader, Metropolitan Anthony tonsured Michael a monk at the Holy Monastery of the Entrance of the Theotokos, giving him the name John, in honor of his ancestor, St John of Tobolsk. Soon after, he was ordained a deacon, and on the feast of the Entrance of the Theotokos, his new monastery's feastday, he was ordained to the Holy priesthood.

A PROFESSOR

After the completion of his theological studies, St John was appointed professor of Religious Studies at the Serbian Theological Seminary of Saint John the Theologian in Bitola. Bitola, located in modern-day Skopje, is located near the northern border of Greece, and was one of the oldest and largest cities in Yugoslavia. It belonged to the Diocese of Ohrid, whose bishop at the time was the renowned Saint Nicholas Velimirovic.

It was precisely during this time, at the beginning of his professorial tenure, that St John's great ascetic endeavors became known. He would liturgize every day, except on rare occasions where he would participate as a layman and receive Holy Communion. His prayer was unceasing, and his fasts were extremely strict. He would eat nothing during the entire first week of Great Lent, and nothing during Holy Week. During the rest of Great Lent, he would survive only on antidoron. Even on normal days, he ate very little, usually only one meal a day, around 11:00 o'clock at night.

It was not long before St John earned the affection and respect of his students, and with genuine fatherly love he imbued their souls with elevated spiritual ideals. The students would look into his face and see all the biblical virtues incarnate in the life of their holy professor. He would pray for them earnestly and with zeal, which they both knew and felt, and they were spiritually drawn to him and his example. Every night the saint would walk through the students' dorm after they were asleep, making sure they were well. He would pick up their blankets from the floor, cover them, and before he left, bless the room and all the students in it individually with the sign of the cross.

The seminarians were the first to discover his ascetic endeavors, and his secret spiritual gifts. During his appointed leisure hours, they would always find him praying. He would never lay down in bed to sleep, even after the

St John after his ordination.

St John with some students in Belgrade.

exhaustion from nightly vigils and prayers set in. He would fall asleep on his knees in front of the icons as he was praying. He kept this practice throughout his life, and even in his later years, when infirmity took over, he would only sleep for a couple hours at a time, sitting on a chair in his cell.

FATHER BISHOP

In 1934, the Synod of bishops of the ROCOR decided to elevate St John to the episcopacy, ordaining him to the see of Shanghai, in China. This development was something that the saint would never have foreseen, as illustrated by the following event.

When he was called to Belgrade to be apprised of his elevation, he met a woman he knew on the bus. Not having seen each other for a long time, they were exchanging news and stories, and when she asked him why he was going to Belgrade, he answered, "there was a serious mailing error. The Synod decided to ordain a Bishop, and it so happens that his name is also hieromonk John, so they accidentally sent the summons to me." He was going to Belgrade to inform them of their error and make sure the letter was forwarded to the correct future bishop. A few days later he was on the bus, returning from Belgrade, and again he saw his acquaintance. When she asked how his journey had been, and if he had accomplished his task, he answered, "the mistake was far greater than I had anticipated, as it was me they decided to ordain."[2]

The saint tried to decline and refuse the synod's decision, citing his speech impediment, and claiming that he could not serve in such an important role with such a handicap. Indeed, he had a speech impediment, and could not articulate clearly, making him difficult to understand for those who were not familiar with his way of speaking. Metropolitan Anthony would not hear of it, however, reminding him that Moses also had the same obstacle, and yet he was used by God in a far greater, though similar, role. Seeing that the elevation was the will of God, St John acceded, and on May 28, 1934, he was ordained a bishop, with his spiritual father presiding. It was the last episcopal ordination that Metropolitan Anthony would ever celebrate, as he fell asleep in the Lord on August 10, 1936, in *Sremski Karlovci* in Serbia.

Before the latter's death, Archbishop Dimitri Voznesensky of Hailar in the Harbin diocese invited Metropolitan Anthony to China, asking him to take over the Diocese of Shanghai. The metropolitan's answer reveals much about his feelings on St John. "My dear brother, I am already exceedingly old and unable to travel, but in my place, I am sending you someone who is like my very self, my very soul, my very heart. I send you bishop John. This small, frail man, who almost looks like a small child, is in reality a wonder of ascetical stability and exactness in this age of complete spiritual deficiency."[3]

IN CHINA

The young bishop, only thirty-nine years old, arrived in Shanghai on November 21, 1935, the anniversary of his presbyteral ordination. Upon arrival, he was immediately greeted by two massive hurdles: completing the Russian cathedral of Shanghai, which was as yet unfinished, and settling a preexisting jurisdictional dispute regarding ecclesiastical administration which had divided the Orthodox of the area into factions.

Soon after arriving, the saint was able to complete both tasks successfully, resolving the dispute and restoring communion and harmony between the Greek, Serbian, and Ukrainian Orthodox communities in the area, and overseeing the completion of not only the cathedral, but also the belltower and a three-floor building for the administrative needs of the church.

Saint John was particularly devoted to the education of the youth in the Faith. He personally taught the older classes at the city's Commercial School, and he was always present for all the oral exams for religious studies at every school in Shanghai. He was the inspiration and trailblazer behind countless charitable and religious institutions in the area. Churches, hospitals, asylums for the mentally ill, orphanages, homes for the elderly, and generally every social charitable organization that the Russian expatriate community in Shanghai started owed their existence, whether directly or indirectly, to him. The saint became one with his flock, and despite his busy pastoral and administrative schedule, actively participated in almost all of the immigrant-led organizations in the city.

He was particularly involved in the creation and operation of the orphanage, which he named "St. Tikhon of Zandonsk." The orphanage did not only take in and care for children who had lost their parents; all poor, indigent children in the city could find a home there. The orphanage, which began with eight children, grew to house hundreds of neglected, abused, and orphaned children during the saint's fifteen-year tenure in Shanghai. Bishop John employed several pious women who assisted with the running of the orphanage, but he always personally retained a close watch and oversight of all aspects of the day-to-day operations. Day and night he would go to the city's poorest and most crime-ridden neighborhoods and rescue orphaned

St John with Grigorii Konstantinovich Bologov, chairman of the Russian Emigrants' Association of Shanghai.

and ill children. There were times where he would exchange bottles of vodka for abused children, trading the abusers alcohol for the child.

His love for children was boundless. After Divine Liturgy he would always stay at the church to play with the children who had assisted him in the altar, lightly tapping them on the head with his bishop's staff. He would play with the young children, giving them as much affection and attention as he could. Even during services at times, though never in the altar, he would kneel down to play with a small child. He met and rescued thousands of children during his life, and he always remembered them all by name; every year he would send them handwritten cards on their birthdays, which he also remembered. As he would always write them the day of, the cards would always arrive late.

The saint would relate that one of the most emotionally difficult times in an orphan's life are the days before the great feasts and celebrations of Christmas and Easter. During those periods they see their fellow Christians come together with their families in love to prepare for the holidays. As this is something absent from their own lives, the orphans feel their loss more deeply and strongly during these times, and so St John took it upon himself to be both mother and father to the children, pouring out his heart into celebratory events, theatrical productions, and presents of musical instruments, all to make them feel the love of the holidays. Despite his strict personal asceticism, he would lavish them with affection and gifts, and fight to assure that they lacked nothing that any other child may have during these annual feasts. The children of the orphanage saw all this and loved the saint even more, many of them later said that they felt neither fatherless nor motherless, as they knew their spiritual father was a powerful protector who would never allow anything bad to happen to them.

The saintly bishop would visit the sick every day, bringing the Holy mysteries with him so they could receive the Holy Eucharist. He didn't have a schedule for these visits, and many times he simply appeared unexpectedly at the houses of those who were shut in. Neither time nor weather stopped him, and many people would observe him walking through Shanghai in the middle of the night, in a rainstorm, holding his staff, his cassock battered by the wind, on his way to these visits.

He did not stop his nightly calls to the sick, even during the period of the Japanese invasion and occupation. He was ready to sacrifice his life for his flock, and indeed, put himself in grave danger every day, as many who were out at night were often shot or killed on the spot. During that period two presidents of the Council of Russian Émigrés were murdered, one right after the other, and in the panic and terror that followed no one would take up the vacant post. The saint then proclaimed himself locum tenens president of the council, despite his flock's pleas to protect himself.

While busy with all these constant and demanding worldly responsibilities, the saint always remained a stranger to the worldly spirit, wholeheartedly devoted to communion with God. He kept his practice of daily liturgizing, along with all the other prescribed services of the Church, no matter where he was. He was very strict about unnecessary conversation and improper behavior in the altar, and personally instructed all the altar servers on the correct conduct and mindset when serving in the Holy of Holies. After the end of the Divine Liturgy, he would often remain in the altar by himself for two or three hours, because, as he explained later, it was impossible to break off communion with God and return to worldly affairs. He wrote with love and care to his flock, advising them:

> God's grace always assists a struggler, but this does not mean that a struggler is always in the position of a victor; sometimes the beasts did not touch the righteous ones, but by no means did they not touch them always. What is important is not victory or the position of a victor, but rather the labor of striving towards God and devotion to Him. Great is the Apostle Paul, but he asks the Lord many times ("thrice" means not once, but many

times) that the messenger of Satan depart from him, for he "buffets" him, making some sort of attacks that are difficult and averse to his spirit. But the Lord leaves him in such a position: "My grace is sufficient for thee," (2 Cor 12:7-9) enough assistance of grace and gifts are provided for him. The Lord wants from the apostle the striving which cleanses his soul.

What is important is the state of the soul, the striving towards God, and not the stature of a victor. "Strength is made perfect in weakness" (2 Cor 12:9). Though a man may be found in a weak state, that does not at all mean that he has been abandoned by God. The Lord Jesus Christ, according to the worldly view, was in trouble, but when the sinful world considered Him to be completely destroyed, in actuality He was victorious over death and hades. The Lord did not promise us positions as victors as a reward for righteousness, but told us, "In the world we shall have tribulation, but be of good cheer, I have overcome the world" (Jn 16:33). The power of God is effective when a person asks for the help of God, acknowledging the weakness and sinfulness of his nature. This is why humility and the striving towards God are the fundamental virtues of a Christian.[4]

TUBABAO

In late 1940, when the Communist regime took over China, the Russian immigrants were forced to once again leave the land where they had made their home and migrate yet again. St John and his flock were torn from their homes with threats and force, leaving behind fifteen years of charitable works, and countless children. In May of 1941, almost 5,000 refugees from Shanghai settled into a refugee camp erected in the nearly deserted island of Tubabao in the Philippines. They lived in squalid conditions, many of them barely surviving, all under the constant threat of the deadly typhoons which plagued the area, and which had made the island nearly uninhabitable and uninhabited. Every night St John would walk around the camp blessing the four corners with the sign of the cross, and, miraculously, not a single typhoon struck during the entirety of their stay.

As their residence permits for the Philippines drew to a close, and no new ones were being issued from any country, the problem of their final destination continued to remain unresolved. That August, the saint decided to travel to America to personally appeal to Congress for US residence permits for his congregation. Indeed, he made the long and arduous journey, and on September 16 he appeared before a subcommittee of the congressional

In front of the tent that served as
the church in Tubabao, Philippines.

judiciary in Washington, to plead his case. "Time is running out for these people. If they are not given an opportunity to begin a new life in America, they are completely lost."

Against all expectations, the laws regarding immigration from China were reviewed, and he was able to secure visas for his entire Chinese fold. Shortly after they all left the Philippines, a deadly typhoon hit the camp at Tubabao, destroying every single building and structure in its path.

Soon after their successful resettlement in America, the flock faced losing their beloved shepherd. In 1951, the Synod of Bishops of ROCOR, under which the saint served, elected him bishop of Western Europe. He was moved to Paris, and later Brussels, to lead his new diocese.

This new post required much travel, and the saint was constantly on the move from one country to another, celebrating the Divine Liturgy and serving all other sacraments for the Orthodox communities throughout the countries of Western Europe. The polyglot bishop celebrated the services in French, Dutch, Greek, Chinese, and English, depending on the needs of the congregation. This new position allowed him to gather information on many ancient, pre-schism saints of the West, who had completely been forgotten in the Eastern Church. Through his efforts, their names and lives were reintroduced to the hagiography of the East, and they were added to the Church calendar.

His linguistic aptitude made him a priceless missionary instrument of the Church, and he brought many Europeans from the darkness of heterodoxy and atheism back to the light of the Church. Even though he served in that post for only a little over ten years, he is rightly considered one of the most important missionary figures of twentieth-century Orthodoxy.

IN THE NEW WORLD

At the end of 1962, the ROCOR archbishop of San Francisco and the West, Tikhon Troitsky, had to resign due to his increasingly ill health. His resignation left a massive vacuum, both spiritually and administratively, in the diocese. The Cathedral church in San Francisco had not yet been built, and its construction had become a divisive issue amongst the congregation. As thousands of the Russians in the area had known St John from his time in Shanghai, they launched a petition to have him take over the vacant position. The ROCOR synod heeded their request, and transferred the saint to San Francisco.

St John with children from the orphanage in San Francisco.

St John arrived in the port city on November 21, 1962. In an odd coincidence, it was the exact same day he had arrived in Shanghai years earlier, the anniversary of his ordination to the priesthood. In an even odder

From the dedication ceremony of the Cathedral of the Virgin Mary, Joy of All who Sorrow, in San Francisco. 1965.

coincidence, the problems he met with in San Francisco were the exact same two issues he had faced in China, namely the construction of a cathedral, and the reconciliation of a divided local community. The saint was once again successful in raising the cathedral, and seeing the entire construction through to completion. His attempts to reconcile the decided community, however, were not as efficacious. Despite his best efforts, there were deep-seated political, economic, cultural, social, and personal hatreds that refused to be conciliated, and individuals who refused to accept his fatherly guidance and spiritual advice.

Undeterred, St John continued to guide his flock, and soon many, though not all, of the issues were resolved. He would suffer the slings and arrows of accusation and slander from disgruntled members of his diocese throughout his life, and in his last years, the ascetic bishop was even dragged through the courts in a civil proceeding. He was indicted, after being unjustly charged with allegedly suppressing evidence of financial misappropriation by his parish council. The saint remained calm and composed throughout the proceedings, refusing to accuse others in order to clear his name. He did not become angry or bitter toward those who had libelously maligned him, but maintained his serenity and tenderness for his flock throughout the temptation, until he was justifiably found innocent of all charges.

The humble saint's spiritual gifts had become evident from the beginning of his ministry in Shanghai, and in the last years of his life in San Francisco, dozens of witnesses wrote down and shared miraculous events that had come about through his intercessions, instances where he had looked into their souls, and revealed things they had never told anyone, and prophetic foresights regarding events that were yet to come.

Beginning in 1966, St John began to speak of his impending death. There was an instance where several parishioners were discussing an upcoming council that was to take place in three years, to which the saint replied "I won't be here then." In May, when speaking to an acquaintance of his, he said "I will die soon, around the end of June, but not in San Francisco, in Seattle." A day before leaving for Seattle in June, he called a local San Francisco newspaper and mentioned that on the feastday of St John the Forerunner (June 24/ July 7) there would be a large service at the cathedral, meaning his funeral. The saint's trip to Seattle, to accompany the miraculous Kursk Root icon of the Mother of God, which usually resided in the San Francisco Cathedral, culminated with a Divine Liturgy at the Cathedral of St Nicholas on June 19/July 2. After the service, as was his habit, Bishop John remained in the altar for three hours, and then carrying the icon, he visited some of his spiritual children who lived near the church. After the visit, the saint retired to the rectory room he had been provided. Some of the people who were accompanying him were downstairs, and they all suddenly heard a loud crash. They rushed up the stairs to the saint's room, from where the sound had come, to find him on the ground. They immediately lifted him up and placed him on his chair, which faced the icon of the Virgin of Kursk, and it was then that the holy bishop finally gave his soul to the God he had so faithfully served.

279

After his repose, they took his body and laid it on the bed. It was the first time the saint had lain on a bed in forty years. Everyone was moved. This most basic of human comforts was something he had ascetically denied himself, and seeing him in that position for the first time since meeting him years earlier, his dear friend and fellow bishop Averky (Taushev) of Syracuse and Holy Trinity whispered, his voice breaking from emotion, "Rest now, in peace."

The holy hierarch's funeral took place on June 24/July 7 at the Cathedral of the Holy Protection of the Mother of God in San Francisco. Five archbishops and scores of other clergy concelebrated, and the cathedral was filled to capacity. His body was buried in the church's underground chapel, where it lay until the translation of his relics on October 12, 1993. His body was found to be incorrupt, and after his official canonization in 1994, his relics were placed in the main church, where they remain to this day, to be venerated by the faithful.

PART III

Historical Vignettes

Father Theoklitos (Triantafyllidis) of Galveston

The Forgotten Greek Saint of America

When looking at Father Theoklitos, few at the time could know that they were gazing upon the face of the first Greek saint in America. Though he has not yet been officially canonized, he is one of the most notable spiritual figures to mark the history of Orthodoxy in the United States.

Fr Theoklitos, born Theodore Triantafyllidis, came into the world in Athens, Greece, in November of 1833. His parents named him after the famous hero and general of the Greek War of Independence, Theodore Kolokotronis, who, after helping free his country from the 400-year grip of the Ottoman Empire, had died just four years earlier. Young Theodore's name was not simply a tribute to an unknown or vague national figure. His own father, a fisherman by trade, had left his home in Athens when the war broke out, and travelled to the Peloponnese to join the forces of "The Old Man of Morea," a nickname by which Kolokotronis was known. When independence was finally achieved and the war ended, the elder Triantafyllidis settled in Egio, a village on the shores of northern Peloponnese. His young son, known as "Theos," celebrated his namesday on the feast of St Hierotheos, the first bishop of Athens and disciple of the Apostle Paul. Theos grew up helping his father with fishing, and spent the first years of his childhood at the waterfront of Egio.

The young boy's first formal education, like that of many of his peers, was at the local church. The Ottoman Turks, who had ruled the country for the last four centuries, had closed most of the country's schools, and many young Greek children were forced to choose between going abroad, an option only the wealthy could afford, and the secret church schools, run by clergy and monastics, often at night, in churches and monasteries throughout Greece. For the first years after independence, these church schools were still the only option available in many areas, as the economically nascent country attempted to rebuild itself after four centuries of oppression and servitude.

Education was not the only problem the newly liberated country faced. Armenian merchants and Bulgarian bankers quickly filled the power vacuum left by the retreating Ottomans, and though these new masters were destructive to the country, they were personally beneficial to the young Theos, who became exposed to new cultures and languages, and was able to immerse himself in new, foreign acquaintanceships, something which would become a big part of his future calling.

His mother, a pious woman, and native Peloponnesian, hoped to see her son follow a career in the church and dedicate his life to God. Her wish was fulfilled when the young man decided to become a monk, taking the name Theoklitos (literally "called by God").

In his younger days, he frequented the majestic historical monastery of Great Lavra, which had been the official place of inception for the Greek War of Independence. The Turks, knowing this, had burned down the monastery during the war, but during the postwar years it was rebuilt, and many foreign Orthodox nations contributed money and sacred treasures to its restoration. Empress Catherine the Great of Russia sent a gilded Gospel book which bore her inscription, and the Russian Athonite monastery of St Panteleimon sent many icons, some which remain there to this day.

Theos's contact with this Russian spiritual, liturgical, and aesthetic tradition may be one of the reasons he soon traveled to Mount Athos and settled at the monastery of St Panteleimon, where he picked up both Russian and Slavonic, becoming fluent in both. The polyglot monk was also a frequent visitor to the Serbian monastery of Hilandar, where he also learned Serbian. He spent much time devoted to the study of languages, and his linguistic talent would prove immensely valuable in his future missionary calling.

A few years later, Fr Theoklitos was called to complete his education and take up a professorial post at the Theological Academy of Moscow, run by the Holy Lavra of the Trinity, known today as the Monastery of St Sergius of Radonezh. Indeed, he completed his theological education, and for several years worked as a professor, but being one of the foremost theological and academic figures of his native land, he was called back to Greece by the then king, George I, to take over the education of his young son, George II.

He had only just completed the education of the young Greek prince when Alexander III, Tsar of Russia and brother-in-law of George I, invited him back to Russia to tutor his own six children in Religion and the Greek Language. Fr Theoklitos accepted the post, and through it became the personal tutor of the future Tsar and passion-bearer, Nicholas II. Years later, when the young Tsar married Alexandra Feodorovna, he was one of the thirty priests who were invited to preside at the wedding. It was due to these connections that his later parishioners in Galveston took to calling him "the priest of the three kings."

GALVESTON

Galveston is an island city on Galveston Island, on the gulf coast of Texas. Being a port town from its earliest days, it was thoroughly familiar with the culture and mores of the Mediterranean and Eastern Europe, as many Orthodox tradesmen and immigrants passed through its docks. At the beginning of the American Civil War in 1861, a group of Orthodox Christians living and working in the city began to set up prayer meetings, and as they became more organized, they named their community "The Parish of Sts. Constantine and Helen."

During the late 1880s and early 1890s these Serbian, Russian, Greek, Bulgarian, and Arab immigrants to Galveston had come together and started gathering funds to construct a church. Aside from their common Orthodox community, they each started their own ethnic organizations to serve the needs of their countrymen. Each of these groups had separately sent numerous petitions to their homelands, asking for a parish priest to serve their bourgeoning city. Sadly, they had received only refusals; citing the distance and the cost, many of these responses suggested that they petition the Russian Orthodox Mission Diocese in North America, as it would be more likely to have an available priest.

The Galveston community did just that, writing three separate telegrams, one for the Holy Synod of the Church of Russia, one to the head of the Russian diocese in America, Bishop Nicholas (Ziorov), and the third to the Tsar himself, Nicholas II. Upon receiving their telegram, the Tsar began collecting funds, as well as printing a Gospel Book, commissioning vestments, liturgical and sacred instruments, an iconostasis, complete with all the icons, and an antimension, which bore his signature. He then sent a telegram to the community, informing them that he had received their request and was taking care of all that they had asked. The Tsar invited his former tutor, Fr Theoklitos, to come and see him, and when they met, the emperor of Russia personally asked him to take over the new parish, joyously encouraging him with "let there be an Orthodox church in Galveston!"

Fr Theoklitos was then already an elderly man, sixty-one years old, at a time where life expectancy was in the fifties, but he accepted the task, and began preparing for the long and treacherous voyage. He had traveled much in his life, and in the process had picked up an astounding number of languages. Other than his mother tongue, Greek, he also spoke fluent Russian, Slavonic, Serbian, Latin, Bulgarian, Arabic, Hebrew, and Dutch. He also knew a good deal of Spanish, English, French, German, and Romanian. Upon learning that this famous cleric was coming to America, the Russian ambassador in the United States acquired full American citizenship for him, and all this before he had even left Russia.

A few weeks before the elderly priest's departure, Tsar Nicholas elevated him to the rank of archimandrite, and gave him a large pectoral cross, a gift which Fr Theoklitos wore until the end of his life.

His journey to far off Texas began with several companions, amongst whom were Bishop Nicholas (Ziorov), Romanian Deacon Pavel Grepashewsky, who would serve with him in Galveston, and St Raphael (Hawaweeny), then only a hieromonk, and beginning his own journey in the New World, which would lead to his later glorification. They stopped in several countries along the way, including Austria, Hungary, Switzerland, France, and England, and in each of these destinations they would celebrate the Divine Liturgy and visit the famous churches and museums of the city. Finally, on October 25, 1895, they left London for New York, arriving on November 2. A few days after their arrival, Fr Theoklitos joined Bishop Nicholas in the service of the Blessing of the Waters for the Syrian chapel in New York, which St Raphael had managed to organize in those very few days following his landing.

A few days after that, Fr Theoklitos and his deacon left for Galveston, stopping in the Native American region of Hartshorne, Oklahoma, to celebrate the Divine Liturgy for a group of Russian miners who lived there. When he arrived in Galveston, in January of 1896, the community was shocked to see that they had not simply been sent a priest, but a highly educated and multilingual archimandrite, accompanied by a deacon. Only a few days earlier they had purchased a plot of land, and the parish council had begun construction on a new wooden church, in accordance with Orthodox ecclesiastical architecture. Fr Theoklitos saw the task to completion, never asking for any financial assistance from his parishioners, preferring that all the money go to the enlarging and sustenance of the Orthodox community. His salary came directly from Tsar Nicholas, who sent him 2,000 rubles a month[1] for the remainder of his life.

In Galveston, the saintly archimandrite lived as a simple monk. He didn't only fulfill pastoral duties, but took it upon himself to educate his flock, becoming a teacher. The services were in Slavonic, Greek, and Arabic, and the piety with which he liturgized quickly made his flock realize they were in the presence of a holy man.

On June 3, 1896, by the old calendar, Bishop Nicholas came to Galveston to celebrate the consecration of the newly completed church, dedicated to the royal saints, Constantine and Helen. The saints, who had been chosen by the very first migrants in Galveston, were celebrated on that day in the New Calendar (May 21), and their feastday coincided with the opening of the new church.

A few months later, in early 1897, Bishop Nicholas invited Fr Theoklitos to San Francisco, to speak to the Greek community about the horrible losses sustained by the Cretans in their revolt against the Ottoman Empire (1895–1898). Fr Theoklitos accepted the invitation, and began the journey, stopping once again in Oklahoma, as well as Denver, Colorado, to celebrate Divine Liturgy. Following his Greek-language homily to the San Francisco community, he was asked to accompany Fr Sebastian (later St Sebastian of Jackson) to Portland, Oregon, and Seattle, Washington, to speak there as well. He once again acquiesced, celebrating the Divine Liturgy in Greek, Slavonic, and Arabic for all the local communities.

The next year, 1898, he was invited back to San Francisco to concelebrate at the ordination of the new bishop of the Aleutian Islands and Alaska, Tikhon, later Patriarch of Moscow and All Russia, who succeeded Bishop Nicholas. Saint Tikhon visited the Galveston parish twice during his American tenure, once in 1899, and once in 1902.

Fr Theoklitos did not limit his missionary activity to Galveston. He traveled all throughout Texas, across the length of the Gulf Coast, East, all the way to Mobile, Alabama, South, to Corpus Christi, and North, to Fort Worth, San Antonio, San Angelo, and Austin. Everywhere he went he would perform weddings, baptisms, and all other sacraments, and, of course, celebrate the Divine Liturgy for the residents.

On September 8, 1900, Galveston Island was hit with the greatest natural disaster in its entire history. The Great Galveston Hurricane killed more people than any other natural disaster in the history of the United States, claiming the lives of 12,000 of the 30,000 residents, and destroying almost every structure in its path. During that unprecedented time, Fr Theoklitos remained in the church for thirty consecutive hours, praying ceaselessly, and providing shelter to parishioners and neighbors who fled to the church for safety and succor.

When the storm finally subsided, the church had remained intact, though it had suffered a significant amount of damage, and the entire structure had been blown three meters west. Everyone in the church credited Fr Theoklitos's intercessions and presence for saving their lives. The community members immediately came together and moved the structure back to its original position, fixing all the damage which it had suffered during the hurricane.

Two years later, Bishop Tikhon once again visited Galveston, this time under orders from the Tsar himself, to honor Fr Theoklitos with the Crosses of the Order of St. Vladimir and the Order of St. Anne.[2] During his visit, the archbishop visited the Orthodox cemetery in Galveston, which, after the hurricane, had been filled almost to capacity. Realizing that more room would soon be needed, St Tikhon donated the funds to purchase the twenty-seven parcels of land adjoining the cemetery for future expansion.

Fr Theoklitos had become a fixture in the Galveston community, not just amongst the Orthodox, but amongst all residents of the city, who admired his simplicity, his Orthodox monastic way of life, and his pure character. When he would return from his many pastoral and business trips, neighborhood children of all ages, ethnicities, and faiths would gather on the steps of the church and wait for him. He would always bring back a large bag full of fruit and the newest sweets and candy, specifically for them, and it was a huge event in many of their young lives.

He would regularly visit the local hospitals, Catholic St. Mary's, and John Sealy, in the Medical Center of the University of Texas. There he met and began friendships with many of the patients, as well as their families. Seeing how much his presence soothed and comforted those in illness and pain, many of the patients' friends and loved ones were converted to Orthodoxy. In this way, Fr Theoklitos became one of the first priests in America to bring Americans, with no ethnic Orthodox background, to the true Faith.

He was featured in the *Galveston Daily News* on January 8, 1914, where portions from his Christmas sermon from the day before[3] were published verbatim, accompanied by glowing commentary.

He began by recounting the story of the star, the wise men, their gifts, and King Herod. Then, "Father Theoklitos took off his spectacles and used them to gesticulate with, as he preached a fatherly sermon on charity and its relation to happiness.

My children: Before Jesus came into our world the earth lacked the attributes of sympathetic understanding, which we find necessary to our happiness in this era. The Lord gave us his son, Jesus, to soften us, to give us understanding of human wants, to give us a sense of forgiveness, to teach us that to forgive is our duty, and to teach us charity.

My children, be charitable, open your hearts, for only in charity is there happiness. Make life brighter for your brother and your sister and the candle you light for them will make your light brighter.

God gave us Jesus, and Jesus gave us his all, even his life. We can do no more than emulate Him, and in doing that we do all.

Think today of the poor whom he loved, lighten their burdens, even as he did. Open your hearts, oh, my children, even as did Jesus of Bethlehem.

My children, when he came among us he did not ask, 'Of what nationality art thou? What is thy belief?' No! He came down among us and was one of us and he ministered to us. Open thy hearts, likewise, my children, and go among the poor and succor them; all the poor, for they are thy brothers and sisters, my children, and they are his people.

My children, many of you are not native to this land and it is well to treasure memories of thine own country, but think that this is a good land, and its people are good to thy people, and you all are His people. Learn to love, be honest, tolerant, forgiving, and charitable.

I pray you Merry Christmas, my children, and many, many years of happiness."

After the sermon, Fr Theoklitos passed a plate to collect alms for the poor. "The plate was heaped high with bills and coins, the merry chink-clink-chink of the contributions accenting like tiny cymbals the smooth melody of a beautiful hymn."[4]

In every Divine Liturgy, Fr Theoklitos would commemorate his former student, the Tsar of Russia, and his family. His prayers only increased in frequency and ardor upon finding out that the future passion-bearer's only son and heir, Alexis, suffered from the then-incurable disease of hemophilia, which daily put his life in danger. When rumors of planned and attempted coups reached the holy archimandrite during the tumultuous years of World War I, he redoubled his prayers for the benefactor of the Galveston parish. The rumors would prove to be true, but the faithful servant of God would be spared the horrors and anguish of his beloved Tsar's murder, as the Lord would call him into His bosom soon before his adopted country's involvement in the War, and before the bloody events of the October Revolution in Russia.

In August of 1915, another catastrophic hurricane hit Galveston. Fr Theoklitos once again opened the doors of the church to anyone who wished to seek shelter, and remained in the temple with his flock, praying unceasingly, until the storm subsided. God once again protected all those who were in the church, and though the wooden structure of the building was lifted and moved 15 meters north, and the entire front wall split into two pieces, not a single person inside was hurt.

After the hurricane, a parishioner found the Gospel Book, which had been the gift of Tsar Nicholas, about 60 meters away in the cemetery. Though the entire area had been flooded, the book remained almost completely untouched by water.

The parishioners once again came together, and using mules, they once again moved the church back to its original position. The eighty-one-year-old priest once again oversaw the repairs of the church, which was restored back to its pre-hurricane condition.

After twenty-one years of service in the New World, the pious archimandrite's earthly life came to a close. After a serious bout of illness, which lasted six weeks, he contacted the diocesan authorities and informed them of his condition. He asked his parish council to find a way to bury him under the altar of the church he had so loved, and had so loyally served. He was certain that if his body were to be buried in the church, the church would continue to operate, and would not be allowed to fall into disrepair, no matter what the future had in store.

He fell asleep in the Lord at St. Mary's hospital, at 8:15 p.m. on November 22, 1916. Six days later, on October 28 (by the Old Calendar), his body was buried in a solemn funeral service.

Elder Ephraim of Arizona
THE FOUNDER OF MONASTERIES IN THE NEW WORLD

THE EARLY YEARS

The righteous Elder Ephraim was born in the Greek city of Volos on June 24, 1928, the feastday of the birth of St John the Baptist. His parents were deeply pious, and saw the date of his birth as a special blessing, deciding to name their newborn John, after the Forerunner.

From a young age, John showed a great inclination toward the spiritual life, and his early guide on this godly path was his devout mother, who was a sainted soul. When he was still an infant, his mother received a revelation from above regarding the future calling and destiny of her child. Elder Ephraim described the event in his own words.

> My mother lived ascetically with fasting, vigil, and prayer. She was an exceptionally virtuous person who loved monasticism. She kept me by her side, because when I was an infant, God informed her that I would become a monk. One day as she was sitting beside me and praying, she had a vision of a star leaving our house and going towards the Holy Mountain. She heard a voice saying: "Of your three children, only this one will live", meaning that only this one would live close to God.[2]

In his hometown there lived a hieromonk who had come from Mount Athos. That hieromonk, whose name was Ephraim, had lived near the holy Elder Joseph the Hesychast on the Holy Mountain, and would tell his flock in Volos wondrous stories about the superhuman ascetic feats of the famous hesychast. Fr Ephraim became the spiritual father of both John and his mother, and soon realized that the young boy was zealous for the monastic life, and deeply desired to go learn asceticism at the feet of Elder Joseph. Knowing, however, the difficulty of that life, Fr Ephraim refused to give his blessing and

Elder Ephraim
at a young age.

Elder Ephraim
as a young monk.

allow the boy to go until he was more mature, so despite all his pleas, and his soul being aflame with holy desire, John obeyed and waited.

Waiting for the fullness of time, John decided to help his family make ends meet, as they were poor, and the German occupation of Greece during World War II had destroyed the livelihoods of the vast majority of the Greeks. Hunger was a daily reality for many families, including John's, and though he worked at his father's woodworking shop, he soon had to drop out of high school to find more work, as every day more and more people lost their lives to mass starvation. He took whatever jobs he could get, selling koulouria,[3] quinine,[4] buttons, matches, and other miscellaneous items at the Volos open air markets and on the street. Some days his entire family could barely stand from lack of food, and it was no surprise that like many Greek children of the era, young John grew up weak and sickly. There were instances where his very life was despaired of, such as the time when he got a fever that refused to subside, and no doctors in his area could diagnose the cause or find a cure. His great faith in God, however, gave him the strength to keep fighting, recover, and endure every later hardship with determination and fortitude.

When he was nineteen, after many years of difficulties and struggle, he was finally able to receive the blessing of his spiritual father and fulfill his dream. The Elder would later say, "I bless the day and the moment that my God and Lord directed my steps, with the help of my spiritual father and my holy mother, to Elder Joseph." Truly, this was to be one of the most important events of his life, and that blessed day would seal the saintly elder's journey toward the completion of his holiness.

AT MOUNT ATHOS

It was September 26, 1947, the feastday of the conception of St John the Forerunner, when the young boy first set eyes on the holy peninsula of Mount Athos. As he disembarked at the small port of the Skete of St. Anne,[5] he was greatly surprised to find an old monk waiting for him. The monk was none other than the blessed Elder Arsenios, the fellow ascetic of Elder Joseph the Hesychast, who asked him,

"Aren't you Yiannakis[6] from Volos?"

"Yes, but how do you know me?"

"Oh, the Honorable Forerunner appeared to Elder Joseph last night and told him: 'I am sending you a little lamb. Put it in your sheepfold.'"

Elder Joseph the Hesychast was then living at the cell[7] of the Forerunner at the Skete of Little St Anne[8] with his small entourage, which was made up of Brothers Arsenios, Joseph (later abbot of Vatopedi), and Athanasios, the biological brother of Elder Joseph.

With young John's arrival at that remote place, watered with the sweat and tears of so many ascetics and saints, he began a new life, full of difficulty and struggles, but also of blessings and experiences of grace. The thing, however, which most deeply marked his life and determined his future was the relationship he was to develop with his Elder Joseph.

After nearly a year of living on Mount Athos, Elder Joseph tonsured young John a monk, naming him Ephraim. Years later, Elder Ephraim would nostalgically remember those days, and life near Elder Joseph, who disciplined him with thoroughness, exactness, and persistence. He later told the stories of his early life to his own spiritual children, and they reveal both the great spiritual experience of the Hesychast, and the complete and total obedience for which Elder Ephraim always struggled from the moment he set foot on Mount Athos.

In general, Geronda[9] was very strict. In all the years I was beside him, only twice did I hear him mention me by name—and even then, it was when he was talking with someone else about me. He usually showered me with every epithet imaginable, or called me "zave", "vavouli", or "koutsiko".[10] The truth is that it really hurt when he scolded me like that, but now my soul is deeply grateful for the surgical incisions of his sharp tongue.

He constantly censured, scolded, and humbled me. He knew that only reproaches and insults would benefit me spiritually, because by being patient with such treatment, a person's ego and vainglory are quelled, and he wins spiritual crowns. He hammered away in every way possible in order to remove the rust I had within me.

Scoldings day and night—not every other day but every day. My, my! What Geronda did to me was something else! Not even for a moment did the scolding subside to let me catch my breath.

Geronda was on the lookout for opportunities to chop down my ego. Not long after I had arrived, he asked me: "Tell me something, koutsiko. You're so weak you can barely stand on your feet. If some day one of the brothers loses his patience and yells at you or even slaps you, what would you do?"

"I will say, Evlogison."[11]

"But will you really say, 'Evlogison'?"

"What else could I say?"

"Fine. We'll see."

After a few days had passed, Geronda thought, "He must have forgotten about my question by now." It was Friday, and the following morning Papa-Ephraim of Katounakia was coming to serve Liturgy. So Geronda told me: "Listen, you are going to chant tomorrow. Make sure you practice first!"

"Evlogison" I answered.

I had no clue about chanting, as I had just come from "the world", but I had heard others chant in my parish, so I knew a few things by ear, though I had no theoretical knowledge or experience with chanting.

The next morning, Papa-Ephraim came and began the liturgy. The chapel inside the cave was very tiny. Geronda was on one side, elder Arsenios was on the other side, I was in the middle, and Fr Athanasios and Fr Joseph were in the back. Since it was Saturday, after the Small Entrance we had to chant "With the Saints grant rest."

So Geronda told me, "Chant 'With the Saints grant rest.'" Since this kontakion is also chanted in memorial services, I had heard it before and knew how it went. What I didn't know, however, was that there are two versions of it: the long, elaborate melody for memorial services, and the short, simple melody for the Liturgy. So I began chanting "wiiiiiiiiiith theeeeeeeeee" slowly and elaborately.

All of sudden, before I got any further, Geronda slapped me so hard right there in the chapel that I saw stars, telling me sharply: "What are you doing? What kind of chanting is that? Idiot! Is that how people chant?"

Papa-Ephraim, who was inside the altar, was so surprised he froze.

I said "Forgive me, Geronda."

"What do you think we're doing? A memorial service?"

"Forgive me, Geronda."

"You are deluded! As soon as the Liturgy is over, you are going to kneel by the door and bow to everyone as they leave, asking their forgiveness for being deluded."

After Liturgy was over, I knelt by the door and said, "Forgive me, fathers, I am deluded."

"Yes, you are deluded."

"I am deluded. Forgive me."

That is how strict Geronda was with me. Nevertheless, in reality he was an exceedingly blessed person whose heart was overflowing with love. He didn't discipline me out of anger or passion, but he did so to heal me from the great pride I had brought with me from the world. Not a single day passed without Geronda reprimanding me.

Much later, though, I found out from the others that even though he would constantly scold me in my presence, as soon as I left he would secretly bless me. Papa-Ephraim from Katounakia remembers that one day when I was still a novice, he came and Geronda shouted at me, "Hey Vavouli, make us some coffee!"

"May it be blessed," I answered immediately.

As I was leaving to go make the coffee, instead of saying "thank you," Geronda showered me with insults as usual and sent me away. But as soon as I was out of sight, Geronda quietly said to Papa-Ephraim, "God is so pleased—and so is an elder—when a disciple says, 'May it be blessed' and is obedient." Then he made the sign of the cross in my direction and said, "May you always be blessed, my child!" He frequently blessed me with many prayers behind my back! But at the time, I didn't realize this, of course. They only told me much later, after Geronda's repose.[12]

Elder Joseph put all his disciples through these rigorous exercises of humility and obedience, but he foresaw, through the grace of God, that the young Ephraim would have a significant and unusual life, and would become a jewel for the Church and a spiritual rock for thousands of faithful from every corner of the world, and so he took the time to cultivate him with particular care. In his way, he wanted to prepare him for the humility which would be necessary for the great apostolic work for which God was preparing him.

The following event clearly shows that the Hesychast had been given the gift of foreknowledge, and knew the journey which the young Fr Ephraim would take in his life.

One day my former spiritual father, Fr. Ephraim from Volos, visited us. An older monk from our brotherhood had a conversation with him, but I didn't dare, since I was just a youngster. Even though he was my spiritual father in the world and had significantly helped me to follow the monastic life, he was like a stranger to me in the sense that I would not say a word to him. How could I leave my Geronda and speak with him? So I didn't speak with him at all.

Geronda took me aside and said,

"Koutsiko, do you see that Brother speaking with your spiritual father?"

"Yes, but I'm not speaking with him."

"I know you're not speaking with him."

Geronda kept an eye on all of us, and nothing escaped his notice.

I was thinking: "The other monk is older, and I'm just a nobody. Who am I to talk?"

"As much as you are silent now," Geronda continued, "you will speak later in the Church. You will see this some day!"

These prophetic words of Elder Joseph, spoken through the Holy Spirit, referred to the role that Elder Ephraim would later play on an international stage. However, living in the rocks and caves of the most difficult areas of Mount Athos, forgotten by the world, the young monk could not even imagine what his elder could have possibly meant when he said that. A few years later, Fr Ephraim was ordained a deacon, and shortly after, a priest. Life in the brotherhood of Elder Joseph was strict, and extremely ascetic, but it always ran at the same steady pace, and with faithful adherence to the same daily schedule. The nightly vigil was a central part of their day-to-day lives, as Elder Ephraim later described:

The focus of our day was our vigil. Everything was done with the aim of being able to pray at night with ease. We went to bed very early so that we would have all night to say the prayer. Our schedule in the wilderness of the Small Skete of St. Anne was as follows:

We woke up at sunset for our vigil and immediately had some coffee for the sole purpose of helping us in our vigil. Geronda insisted that everyone drink coffee before vigil, unless someone was unable to. He allowed the weaker brethren to have a little snack, too, for more energy.

After having coffee, we would take Geronda's blessing and quietly leave. We went to our cells without saying a word. Geronda attached great importance to this point. He emphasized that after waking up we must be very careful with our senses so that we can dedicate the "cream" of our mind to God through prayer. No talking, no daydreaming, no nothing. After our vigil we can discuss whatever is necessary.

301

As soon as we entered our cells, we would begin our nightly prayers following Geronda's method: We would recite the Trisagion, the Creed, and Psalm 50, and then we would sit on our stools and cultivate mourning, recall death, hell, and paradise, and we would meditate on the crucifixion of Christ and the lives of the saints. (There wasn't anything else to think about, anyway.) In this manner we would be moved to compunction, contrition, and repentance. We would not pass a lot of time with those thoughts, however, but immediately after feeling contrition and humility of heart, we would begin saying the prayer.

The Jesus prayer was the center of these monks' lives. St Joseph the Hesychast would tell them:

As soon as you wake up and open your eyes, immediately begin saying the prayer. Don't let your mind wander here and there, wasting the time that is precious for saying the prayer. When you force yourself like this, God will also help you acquire the habit of saying the prayer as soon as you wake up. Then you begin your day and work while saying the prayer. In this way, everything is sanctified: the work, the area, the time, the mouth, the tongue, the heart, and the entire person who is saying the name of Jesus Christ.

Truly, every moment of every day was filled with the divine name of Christ, and so the days and years passed in the peace of God, and the endless ascetic toils for the attainment of the heavenly kingdom, which was the only goal for the small group of monks in Elder Joseph's company. With martyric self-denial the younger monks followed the path that their elder had forged, and on which he walked himself.

The area in which the small brotherhood lived was not only difficult to get to, but the climate was particularly harsh, causing the health of both the Elder and the monks to suffer. After praying about the issue, the Elder's prayers were answered, and he received Divine information that he was to move to New Skete, to the cell of the Annunciation of the Theotokos. So, in 1953, the small group moved there. Six years later, in 1959, the body of the hesychast Elder, which had for so long been subject to the mandates of his holy soul, finally succumbed, and the Elder fell seriously ill. It was clear that the time he had so deeply desired was at hand, and soon he would depart for his beloved Lord.

Understanding that his elder's time was at hand, Fr Ephraim wanted to know if he had given his elder's soul joy, peace, and rest.

> When I first became a disciple of Elder Joseph, he told me the patristic saying: "Have you pleased your elder? You have pleased God." As I mentioned earlier, my goal in life was to accomplish this, otherwise I would be an utter failure. So I would pray: "My dear God, count me worthy to have his blessing."
>
> I served Geronda until his final breath, and I did everything I could to make his life more pleasant. Even though my conscience was at rest that I had succeeded, when his end was approaching, I still wanted to hear it from his own mouth, to be certain. Yet I hesitated to approach him on my own and ask him this big question. But since I was agonizing over it, I finally mustered up the courage to ask him: "Geronda, all these years I lived night and day with the concern to succeed in pleasing you. Everything I did, I did it for your sake. By the grace of God, was I successful?"
>
> "In the same way you have pleased me and given me rest, my child, may God also give you rest."
>
> That was it! Hearing that meant the world to me.
>
> One day, shortly before his repose, I asked him, "Geronda, can you say a prayer for me now?"
>
> "Come here, my child."
>
> He gave me a hug, took my head on his chest, and then kept blessing me with his dear hands while saying his own improvised prayers. This was the reward for all my labors. That was all I wanted.

On August 15, 1959, the feast of the Dormition of the Mother of God, the holy elder also gave his soul to God, after a life filled with ascetic struggles, difficulties, and great experiences of Divine Grace.

After his repose, his disciples, including Fr Ephraim, heeded their blessed elder's words and split up, accepting disciples of their own and creating new monastic brotherhoods. Many monks were drawn to Fr Ephraim, and it wasn't long before he became their spiritual guide. In 1968, they settled at the cell of St Artemios, at the Skete of Provatas,[13] and four years later, in 1973, the Fathers of the holy monastery of Philotheou asked the Elder to come and live with them, with his brotherhood, and be their abbot. Initially Elder Ephraim hesitated; he did not want to take over as abbot of a monastery, with all the

Elder Ephraim reads aloud for his fellow fathers.

worldly cares that entailed. He preferred the quiet environment of the skete. However, God had other plans for him, and informed him accordingly in his prayers, so the Elder accepted the position, and on October 1, 1973, he was enthroned as abbot of the historic tenth-century monastery.

Elder Ephraim's reputation as an experienced and wise spiritual father and guide soon grew, and he was one of the primary reasons that the community of monks at the Philotheou monastery grew at a rapid and unexpected pace. In 1981, the monastery numbered eighty-one fathers, and soon The Holy Synod of Mount Athos asked him to send some monks to repopulate other monasteries, which suffered from a lack of monks. In this way, the monasteries of Xiropotamou, Kostamonitou, and Karakallou were soon strengthened, and the three monasteries put themselves under the spiritual guidance of Elder Ephraim.

The stories of Elder Ephraim's miraculous spiritual journey could not be confined within the bounds of Mount Athos, and were soon spread through the length and breadth of Greece. Visitors came flooding in from every corner of the country, hoping to meet the elder and receive his blessing. Additionally, monasteries throughout Greece wrote to him, seeking a spiritual guide under

Elder Arsenios, with cane, is sitting in the center,
and Elder Ephraim is seated to his right.

whom they could operate, and whose direction they could follow, and their requests were not denied. Many monasteries, both male and female, including the monastery of the Forerunner in Serres, the monastery of the Virgin Mary the Directress in Portaria, near his hometown of Volos, and the monastery of the Archangel Michael in Thasos, found a loving and experienced guide in the ways of the monastic life in Elder Ephraim.

IN THE NEW WORLD

In 1979, some health issues required Elder Ephraim to fly to Canada for some medical procedures. Initially it appeared this would be a short trip, but soon Divine Providence began to slowly reveal its plan. It would be a mission of vast importance, unfathomable in scope, and rare in our modern times. Soon, Elder Joseph's prophetic words would be fulfilled, and Elder Ephraim would ascend the noetic ambo of the Catholic Church to call the sheep of the North American flock back to the fold of Orthodoxy.

During his stay in Canada, many Greeks living in the area flocked to the Athonite ascetic who had found himself among them from the other side of the world. Taking advantage of this providential opportunity, they asked the elder to hear their confessions, and to teach them how to live spiritually.

After receiving the blessing of the local bishop, Elder Ephraim indeed began to confess, advise, and teach the Canadian Orthodox Greeks, moved by their deep thirst for spiritual nourishment.

After a three-month stay in Canada, during which he completed all the necessary medical procedures, the holy elder returned to Mount Athos. However, it was not long before waves of new invitations and pleas began arriving from the faithful whom he had met in North America, begging him to make another visit and spiritually encourage and guide them. His fame soon spread, by word of mouth, from the Greeks in Canada to the Greeks in the United States, and new invitations began to arrive at Mount Athos. Bishops and clergy as well as laymen and women across the continent began sending him letters, asking him to visit their cities or parishes, and teach them the ways of grace and salvation.

The sheer number of invitations caused Elder Ephraim to hesitate, considering whether it was his place as a monk to be traveling abroad and preaching. His duty as abbot was to his monks and the monasteries under his spiritual direction, and as a monastic, his spiritual task was to leave the world in order to dedicate himself wholly to praying for the world. Pastoral duties belonged to the clergy in the world.

However, as the invitations kept coming, the elder decided to pray about the issue. The answer finally came in 1980, at the first celebration of the feast of St Kosmas of Aetolia, on the year in which he was canonized as a saint in the Orthodox Church. During the all-night vigil at the monastery of Philotheou, the holy elder received a response to his prayers from Saint Kosmas, who informed him that he was to follow in his steps, as a monastic missionary. It is truly wondrous that the saint, who had also been a hieromonk at Mt. Athos, at the very same monastery of which Elder Ephraim was now abbot, revealed the divine mission to the holy elder.

Elder Ephraim had always been a shining example of perfect obedience, and so despite his own desires and reservations, he did not refuse the call of Divine providence and the Church. He decided to accept the work of striving for the spiritual nourishment and salvation of the faithful in the New World. From that point on, his visits to both Canada and the United States increased in frequency, and his pastoral work in North America kept growing.

Once, one of the elder's spiritual children asked him to come to Hawaii and hear the confessions of the local Orthodox Christians there. Considering the distance and the difficulty of opening up another front away from the

American mainland, Elder Ephraim once again gave the issue up to God, and that same night, his elder, Joseph the Hesychast, appeared to him in a dream, placing a large amount of oranges in front of his disciple, and saying: "We will plant oranges, koutsiko. You will see how much fruit we will grow!" With that, the elder understood that America was now to be his primary field of mission.

Elder Ephraim recognized that during the long periods of time between his visits, the American and Canadian Orthodox lost their zeal and spiritual vigor. Without any monasteries, which have always been centers of deep spiritual restoration and rejuvenation for and from the world, they were not always able to retain the spiritual flame which nourished them. He decided that it was necessary to establish monasteries, so even when he was not there, the faithful would have a place in which they could leave behind all worldly cares, and refocus their lives toward God.

Despite this realization, the elder did not wish to take on the massive responsibility which the task entailed. He did not speak English fluently, and he did not know the laws and customs in America; he was a simple monk from Greece, who had not even completed high school. He was certain that the Lord desired someone else, someone more experienced, to take on the task. He once again turned to God in prayer, pouring out his soul, humbly citing his inability, in all the ways of man's logic, to take on this challenge. Yet, at one point Christ made his will firmly and irrevocably known, dashing any doubts that the elder harbored.

"No." He received a response in his prayers. "No. You will be obedient and you will take on the responsibility."

Seeing that God's answer was now clear, the elder humbly bowed his head and accepted. "As you wish, Lord, but please give me enough love so that it may be sufficient for all that may come to me for guidance."

Convinced, now, that the Lord's will was for these monasteries to be established, and for his primary mission to be in North America, he began the work, and soon two monasteries were built, one in Montreal, and one in Pittsburgh, Pennsylvania.

At the same time as he was building monasteries across the Atlantic, Elder Ephraim continued to serve as abbot of Philotheou, and spiritual head of three monasteries on Mount Athos and eight female monasteries across Greece, which put him in a serious dilemma. The spiritual field of America, which he had been called by divine providence to till, required more and more of his time and attention, and his physical presence was more and more often necessary. His constant trips between Greece and North America did not allow him to fully dedicate himself to either place, and the division of his physical and spiritual energies threatened to be detrimental to both. Once again, he turned to the ultimate source of guidance, and prayed on his knees for God to show him how he wanted him to proceed. Should he continue serving both flocks, the monastic one in Greece and the lay one in America? Or should he dedicate himself wholly to one of the two?

The answer finally came. America was the place where he would dedicate his life. He would be a new missionary, equal-to-the-apostles, on a new continent.

In 1990, he resigned as abbot of Philotheou, desiring that a new brother, more able to fully and solely dedicate himself to the needs of the monastery, take over the mantle. He boarded a plane, leaving behind his homeland, and all he had known and loved, to dedicate himself wholly to the difficult task for which God had prepared him from the beginning of time.

His decision to resign and leave Mount Athos permanently confused many. Father George Metallinos of blessed memory described the public reaction as follows:

> I remember that there were many, even amongst his fellow monastics, who expressed their doubts about their elder's "daring" and "inexplicable" decision. However, as it turned out he had the enlightenment and guidance of the Holy Spirit, and proved a new Father Kosmas[14] in our troubled times. St. Kosmas Aitolos, a great Philothean monk himself, departed from the Holy Mountain after seventeen years of strict asceticism, but he did not leave in spirit. Instead he brought the essence of the Holy Mountain, with its noetic prayer, its nepsis,[15] and its ascesis, to the world, proving that the true goal of Mt Athos is to serve as a spiritual lighthouse and source of strength to those battling in the world.
>
> This is what Elder Ephraim did, bringing the Athonite light to the center of the modern world, using the word "world" in the New Testament sense, to the metropolis of the worldly West. He went much further than the great Orthodox theologians of the 20th century, and the Russians in diaspora, led by that blessed protopresbyter, Georges Florovsky. They moved in the circles of academia and academic theology, and were greatly fruitful in the areas of theological studies and scientific composition, but Fr Ephraim widened the gate of the monastic and ascetic life, which constitutes the

immovable root and basis of the prophetic, apostolic, and patristic, in other words the Orthodox, theology.

The "exodus" of Fr Ephraim from Mt Athos into the world can be seen as the modern equivalent of the exodus of St Anthony the Great from the desert to Alexandria in the 4th century to strengthen the Orthodox faithful and combat the delusion of Arianism and the Arian heresy. By his move to North America, and with the monasteries he established in the US and Canada, Fr Ephraim built hearths of hesychastic experience and baptismal fonts of regeneration. This is constantly attested to by Greeks and Americans from the furthest reaches of the West, and by my humble self, every time I visit his place of ascesis in Arizona. There is overflowing gratitude for F Ephraim, not only by the American monks and nuns now residing in his Athonite monasteries, but from the many visitors who visit, seeking the light of Orthodoxy. He has been recognized by the Americans, both those who are Orthodox and those who love Orthodoxy, as the ultimate in Orthodox spiritual authenticity, and someone who belongs in the choir of the great fathers and shepherds of our Holy Tradition.[16]

After his departure from Mount Athos, Elder Ephraim moved to the monastery of St Anthony the Great in the Arizona desert, a monastery he himself had founded. Working tirelessly, he hand-picked six monks from Mount Athos, inviting them to help him build the monastery. The work began in 1995, after the land was purchased. The location of the monastery was decided by miraculous means. While out looking for the appropriate plot, bells were heard, identical to the bells of the Philotheou monastery in Athos. Hearing them, the elder knew that this was the place where God desired the monastery be built.

The first living quarters of the monastery were four mobile homes, about 260 square feet in diameter. After these arrived, Elder Ephraim and the six monks began the process of building the main church, the monks' cells, and the trapeza.[17] They planted a small vegetable garden, a small vineyard, a few acres of citrus trees, and an orchard with olive trees, which were the first horticultural endeavors of the monastery.

Shortly after, they were able to purchase 1,200 acres surrounding the initial plot, in which they planted different fruit-bearing trees. The area, which had previously been a dry, waterless, bleak desert, was transformed into a verdant, blooming oasis, thanks to the water which flowed plentifully and freely, after a miraculous revelation to Elder Ephraim, which indicated where precisely they should drill their wells.

Every monastery the elder founded had similarly miraculous stories as to how they were established, how the decisions were made regarding which land to purchase, and how and where to build. The elder also had to decide which monks and nuns to bring from Greece or other places in America, and how to ensure financial assistance from prominent and wealthy local Orthodox families for the establishment of the monasteries.

Before the monks and nuns would arrive in each one of his new monasteries, elder Ephraim would go and carefully and lovingly prepare their monastic quarters. He personally went in and decorated them, wanting to make them comfortable and beautiful. He would be on his hands and knees, planting flowers in the gardens, he would place small, lovely statues of animals in the flowerbeds, and he would fill the refrigerators with fresh produce and groceries on the days before their arrival. He did not simply oversee the building and establishment of the monasteries, he cared about every individual monk and nun, and took pains to make sure their transition would be as easy as possible, and that their monastic life would be interrupted as little as is humanly feasible. After they came, and he made them comfortable, he would have to leave, and the monks and nuns would be left on their own, taking over the mission which he had begun. So he would return to Arizona, with the new responsibility for the spiritual, practical, and pastoral care of another monastery.

The monks and nuns in every monastery Elder Ephraim founded in North America follow the tradition, holy services, and general typikon[18] of Mount Athos. The majority of the monastics in these monasteries are now made up of American Orthodox converts, coming from different ethnic, social, cultural, and religious backgrounds, and yet every one of them is fluent in the Greek language, which is the primary tongue of the monastic services. It is wondrous to see men and women, born and raised in America and Canada, chanting the beautiful, historic Byzantine melodies across the North American continent.

The monasteries are centers of charity, and the poor can always find a warm meal, served with love and prayer. St Anthony's leads the way in this tradition, serving hundreds of thousands of visitors, pilgrims, and poor every year.

While having his primary residence at St Antony's, Elder Ephraim traveled the length and breadth of the continent, visiting the monasteries which he founded and the Orthodox communities surrounding them. He guided monastics and laypeople alike on the path to salvation through his divinely inspired words and the holiness of his life. There are numerous accounts of the miracles which took place through his prayers, not only in spiritual matters, but in worldly matters and health issues. The miracles which came about through his prayers touched the lives not only of those who knew him, but many times also those of complete strangers. This became the cause for multitudes of heterodox to come and experience the light of Orthodoxy, and join the true Church, becoming witnesses to Elder Ephraim's sanctity and spiritual power.

From the time he began to the time of his passing, Elder Ephraim established seventeen monasteries, all under the jurisdiction of the Greek Orthodox Archdiocese of America and Canada:

1) The Holy Monastery of the Nativity of the Theotokos, Pittsburgh, Pennsylvania.
2) The Holy Monastery of St Kosmas the Aetolian, Bolton, Ontario.
3) The Holy Monastery of the Virgin Mary of Consolation, Brownsburg, Quebec.
4) The Holy Monastery of the Protection of the Theotokos, Weatherly, Pennsylvania.
5) The Holy Monastery of St John Chrysostom, Kenosha, Wisconsin.
6) The Holy Monastery of the Life-Giving Spring, Dunlap, California.
7) The Holy Monastery of St John the Baptist, Goldendale, Washington.
8) The Holy Monastery of St Anthony the Great, Florence, Arizona.
9) The Holy Monastery of the Archangels, Kendalia, Texas.
10) The Holy Monastery of the Virgin Mary of Blachernae, Williston, Florida.
11) The Holy Monastery of the Annunciation of the Theotokos, Reddick, Florida.
12) The Holy Monastery of the Trinity, Smith Creek, Michigan.
13) The Holy Monastery of the Virgin Mary, Proussiotissa, Troy, North Carolina.
14) The Holy Monastery of Panagia Pammakaristos, Lawsonville, North Carolina.
15) The Holy Monastery of the Transfiguration, Harvard, Illinois.
16) The Holy Monastery of St Nektarios, Roscoe, New York.
17) The Holy Monastery of St Paraskevi, Washington, Texas.

Elder Ephraim lived at St. Anthony's in Arizona until the end of his life, offering spiritual guidance to both the monasteries he established and the thousands of faithful who came to see him every day from every corner of the globe. For sixty years, he poured his heart and soul, using his monastic experience to transform Orthodoxy in the Western Hemisphere. His eminence the Archbishop of America, Elpidophoros, was quoted as saying: "I bow to the holy venerable Geronda Ephraim with reverence and gratitude, for he established Orthodox monasticism in America and cultivated our country's barren spiritual desert."[19]

Full of Grace and full of days, the holy elder gave his soul to God on December 8, 2019, at the age of ninety-one.

In his touching and poignant eulogy, his eminence the archbishop of America said the following:

> An entire continent, all of America, owes the emergence of Orthodox monasticism from the East to Geronda Ephraim, whom we have in front of us today to offer our last embrace. It was not easy for Geronda. It was a difficult mission to come to a very secular land, devoid of the savor of asceticism and noetic prayer, the savor of Orthodox monasticism. And of course, in his efforts to plant the Orthodox monastic life, he faced many difficulties. He was judged, he was slandered, he felt pain, he wept, but he never gave up …. And the difficulties and the accusations whitened his soul and lifted him up to Heaven …. He is a saint. He lived as a saint, and he leaves us as a saint. Memory eternal to you, Geronda, and where you are on high at the Throne of the Lord, do not forget us, because you were delivered from the battle with evil and sin, but we here still struggle and we will need your prayers and blessing. Eternal and unforgettable be your memory![20]

Sixty years earlier, shortly before he fell asleep in the Lord, St Joseph the Hesychast had told his young disciple, "If I find favor with God, I will come and take you when it is your time to leave the world. I will be there with you." St Joseph undoubtedly kept his promise, and with the death of his last disciple, the entire company of the Hesychast has been reunited in heaven, and intercedes ceaselessly for the salvation of the world.

May we have their blessing.

Amen.

Acknowledgments

The original edition of this book was published in the Greek language by the Brotherhood of the Holy Monastery of the Holy Forerunner, Mesa Potamos in Cyprus. Their inspiration was the work of the historian and researcher Matthew Namee who founded the Society for Orthodox Christian History in the Americas (SOCHA). He is the editor of and writes extensively for the website Orthodox History : The Orthodox Church in the Modern World (*OrthodoxHistory.org.*) Matthew shared archival material from countless sources as well as advising the brotherhood during the writing and preparation of the book. Holy Trinity Publications also express their gratitude to Matthew Namee for his valuable contribution to the English edition.

The Brotherhood of the Holy Monastery of the Holy Forerunner, Mesa Potamos has provided the digital images used throughout the work. They in turn credit Charalambos Yakovou for the technical editing of the photographic material, and Olga Sirnina for the colorization, and Yiangos Jiapouras for the sketches which were digitized by Haralambos Iakovou of A&C Photokinisi Ltd in Cyprus.

Notes

PART I: HISTORICAL CONTEXT

THE ORIGINS OF ORTHODOXY IN AMERICA

1 *St. Innocent: Apostle to America*, Paul D. Garrett (Crestwood, NY: SVS Press, 1979).

2 In 1900, the diocese was renamed "Diocese of the Aleutian Islands and North America."

3 https://www.oca.org/holy-synod/past-primates/vladimir-sokolovsky-avtonomov

4 The church in New Orleans, established in 1864 and consecrated the next year, it was dedicated to the Holy Trinity, and was the first canonical Greek Orthodox parish in the United States.

5 https://www.oca.org/holy-synod/past-primates/nicholas-ziorov

6 George Papaioannou, "The Diamond Jubilee of the Greek Orthodox Archdiocese of America, 1922-1997," *The Greek Orthodox Theological Review* 45:1–4 (Spring 2000), 223. This article was written in 1997 and published posthumously.

7 John Erickson, "Organization, Community, Church: Reflections on Orthodox Parish Polity in America," *Greek Orthodox Theological Review* 48:1 (Spring 2003), 72.

8 These records were published in 1906, 1911, and 1918.

9 Eleftherios Kyriakou Venizelos (August 23, 1864–March 18, 1936) was a Greek statesman and a prominent leader of the Greek national liberation movement. He was elected prime minister of Greece eight times, and had such profound influence on the internal and external affairs of Greece that he is credited with being "The Maker of Modern Greece," and the "Ethnarch." He and the Greek king (Constantine I) began parting ways during World War I, when Venizelos desired Greece join the Allied powers, while the king, whose wife was German, preferred Greece remain neutral. Venizelos submitted his resignation in 1915, but the same year his party won the elections and he formed a new government. Even though Venizelos promised to remain neutral, after the elections of 1915, he abandoned that policy. The dispute between Venizelos and the king reached its height shortly after that and the king invoked a constitutional provision giving the monarch the right to dismiss a government unilaterally. The dispute continued between the two men, and in December 1915 Constantine forced Venizelos to resign for a second time and dissolved parliament, calling for new elections. In 1916, Venizelos publicly announced

his disagreement with the Crown's policies, which further polarized the population between the royalists who supported the Crown, and Venizelists, who supported Venizelos. In 1916, Venizelist army officers organized a military coup in Thessaloniki, and proclaimed the "Provisional Government of National Defense." Venizelos agreed to form a provisional government, and they founded a separate "provisional state" including Northern Greece, Crete, and the Aegean Islands, with the support of the Entente.

PART II: LIVES OF THE SAINTS

SAINT ALEXIS TOTH OF WILKES-BARRE

1 These series of "unions" is why they have long been known to the Orthodox as Uniates.

2 Genesis 12:.1

3 Jorgenson, "Fr. Alexis Toth and the Transition … " SVTQ 32:2, pp. 127–128.

4 Soldatow, The Writings of St. Alexis Toth. p. 53.

5 Ibid., 57.

6 Ibid., 58.

7 Jorgenson, "Fr. Alexis Toth and the Transition … ", SVTQ, 32:2, p. 131.

8 Ibid., 132–133.

9 Soldatow, The Writings of St. Alexis Toth. p. 58.

10 Very Rev. Edward Pehanich, "St. Alexis Toth—Confessor of the Orthodox Faith in America." Retrieved on June 15, 2020, from the official website of the American Carpatho-Russian Orthodox Diocese of the U.S.A. https://www.acrod.org/readingroom/saints/stalexistoth

11 Jorgenson, "Fr. Alexis Toth and the Transition … ", SVTQ, 32:2, pp. 133–134.

12 Ibid., 132–133.

13 Old Czech work for "church."

14 The Polish word for priest. Fr Alexis often used the term to describe the Roman Catholic clergy.

15 Soldatow, The Writings of St. Alexis Toth, p. 58.

16 Jorgenson, "Fr. Alexis Toth and the Transition … ", SVTQ, 32:2, p. 133.

17 New Calendar.

18 Over $3,000 today.

19 [The term "Liakh" is a pejorative for "Poles."]

20 [*Hochverrat* means "High treason" in German.]

21 Soldatow, Archpriest Alexis Toth, Letters, Articles, Papers and Sermons, Vol. 1, pp. 79–82.

22 Soldatow, Vol. 3, p. 49.

23 The Imperial Order of Saint Anna was a Russian order of chivalry. Membership of the Order was awarded for a distinguished career in civil service or for valor and distinguished service in the military. The Order of Saint Anna entitled recipients to nobility.

24 The Imperial Order of Saint Prince Vladimir was an Imperial Russian order established on October 3, 1782, by Empress Catherine II in memory of the deeds of Saint Vladimir, the Grand Prince and the Baptizer of the Kievan Rus'. The order had four degrees and was awarded for continuous civil and military service.

SAINT TIKHON

1 Pskov is one of the oldest cities in Russia. It is located in the northwestern part of the country, about twelve miles east of the present-day Estonian border, on the Velikaya River.

2 Today the city of Chelm, in Poland.

3 The Imperial Order of Saint Anna was a Russian order of chivalry. Membership of the Order was awarded for a distinguished career in civil service or for valor and distinguished service in the military. The Order of Saint Anna entitled recipients of the first class to hereditary nobility, and recipients of lower classes to personal nobility.

4 1 Corinthians 13:11.

5 The omophorion (something borne on the shoulders) is the distinguishing vestment of a bishop and the symbol of his spiritual and ecclesiastical authority. By symbolizing the lost sheep that is found and carried on the Good Shepherd's shoulders, it signifies the bishop's pastoral role as the icon of Christ. Clergy and ecclesiastical institutions, including seminaries, subject to a bishop's authority are said to be "under his omophorion."

6 "Russian Bishops of America," *The Kansas City Star*, December 13, 1898, p. 5.

7 Canadian Orthodox History Project, Saint Tikhon (Bellavin).

8 Hebrews 13:17.

9 Kishkovsky, "Archbishop Tikhon in America," SVTQ, 19:1, p. 10.

10 Canadian Orthodox History Project, Saint Tikhon (Bellavin).

11 "Head of Russian Church Here," *Democratic Herald*, November 14, 1898.

12 Kishkovsky, "Archbishop Tikhon in America," SVTQ, 19:1, p. 17.

13 His life is included in part III of this book.

14 Saint Savva † 14 January 1236, known as the Enlightener, was a Serbian prince and Orthodox monk, the first archbishop of the autocephalous Serbian Church, the founder of Serbian law, and a diplomat. Born Rastko Nemanjić, he was the youngest son of Serbian Grand Prince Stefan Nemanja (founder of the Nemanjić dynasty).

319

He left his worldly honors and departed for Mount Athos, where he became a monk with the name Savvas. At Athos he established the monastery of Hilandar, which became one of the most important Serbian religious centers in the world. In 1219 the Patriarchate exiled in Nicaea recognized him as the first Serbian archbishop, and in the same year he authored the oldest known constitution of Serbia, the *Zakonopravilo* nomocanon.

15 https://orthodoxcanada.ca/Saint_Tikhon_(Bellavin).

16 Ibid.

17 Kostadis, 200.

18 Ibid., pp. 201–202.

19 Ibid.

20 The Imperial Order of Saint Prince Vladimir was a Russian order established by Empress Catherine II in memory of the deeds of Saint Vladimir, the Grand Prince and the Baptizer of the Kievan Rus'. The order had four degrees and was awarded for continuous civil and military service.

21 $80,000–$85,000 today.

22 Kostadis, Pictures of Missionary Life, p. 201.

23 "The New Russian Church," *New York Times*, May 23, 1901, p. 5.

24 Canadian Orthodox History Project, Saint Tikhon (Belavin).

25 "New Russian Orthodox Church Consecrated," *New York Times*, November 24, 1902, p. 9.

26 America purchased the territory of Alaska from Russian Tsar Alexander II in 1867 for 7.2 million (approximately 136 million dollars today). By the time of St Tikhon's tenure in America, it had been an American territory (though not a state) for over thirty years.

27 https://orthodoxcanada.ca/Saint_Tikhon_(Belavin).

28 The life of this fascinating and holy man can be found at https://orthodoxcanada.ca/Metropolitan_Innocent_(Pustynsky).

29 "Alaska Given a Coadjutor," *The San Francisco Call*, January 25, 1904, p. 3.

30 Canadian Orthodox History Project, Saint Tikhon (Belavin).

31 "Views of Questions to Be Examined by the Local Council of the Russian Church," *Russian Orthodox American Messenger*, March Supplement. New York, 1906.

32 Canadian Orthodox History Project, Saint Tikhon (Belavin).

33 Kostadis, 207–208.

34 Ibid.

35 Ibid., p. 209.

36 Ibid., p. 218.

37 Ibid., p. 226.

38 Ibid.

39 Canadian Orthodox History Project, Saint Arseny (Chahovtsov).

40 Kostadis, 220–230.

41 Ibid.

42 Ibid.

43 Ibid.

44 Ibid.

45 Ibid., p. 209.

46 A little over $30,000 today.

47 Philippians 2:7.

48 https://orthodoxcanada.ca/Saint_Tikhon_(Belavin).

49 Ibid.

50 https://orthodoxcanada.ca/Saint_Tikhon_(Belavin).

51 John 17:6–26.

52 Luke 22:31–32.

53 Ephesians 2:8.

54 2 Peter 1:15.

55 Canadian Orthodox History Project, Saint Tikhon (Belavin).

56 Matthew 5:15.

57 Matthew 28:19; Mark 16:15.

58 Jeremiah 29:7 (Masoretic).

59 Canadian Orthodox History Project, Saint Tikhon (Belavin).

60 The Imperial Order of Saint Alexander Nevsky was established by Empress Catherine I of Russia, in memory of the deeds of Saint Alexander Nevsky, patron Saint of the Russian capital of Saint Petersburg, for defending Russia against foreign invaders. The order was originally awarded to distinguished Russian citizens who had served their country with honor, mostly through political or military service.

61 An ecclesiastical synod, sobor, or assembly of the Eastern Orthodox Church.

62 In his efforts to bring the church under the authority of the state, Tsar Peter I had abolished the patriarchate. When Patriarch Adrian of Moscow and all Russia died in October 1700, Peter prevented the election of a new patriarch, and instead appointed a patriarchal "exarch" locum tenens, (custodian) of the patriarchal throne. The church under Peter was ruled by an episcopal council, and the Russian state under subsequent monarchs continued to create and enforce laws placing governmental oversight over ecclesiastical functions. The Patriarchal throne remained empty for 217 years, until the restoration of the patriarchate in 1917.

63 In Russian ecclesiastical practice, a metropolitan is higher than an archbishop, and has several bishops operating "under" him.

64 The coup actually took place on November 7, by the new calendar, but as the old calendar was still in wide use at the time, it is known as the October Revolution, as it took place on October 25, by the old calendar.

65 The synod met until September 20, 1918, but as the Bolshevik persecution of the church intensified, it was no longer feasible for it to continue.

66 https://blog.obitel-minsk.com/2021/10/and-unto-the-angel-of-the-church-of-russia-write.html.

67 3 Kingdoms 19:12.

68 3 Kingdoms 19:10.

69 Paul Smirnov, "And unto the Angel of the Church of Russia write." Retrieved from Orthodox Christianity, https://orthochristian.com/106978.html.

70 Galatians 1:4.

71 I Timothy 5:20.

72 1 Corinthians 5:13.

73 Romans 8: 35.

74 Matthew 16:18.

75 Bunyan and Fisher, Bolshevik Revolution, pp. 587–589.

76 The Treaty of Brest-Litovsk was a peace treaty signed on March 3, 1918, between the new Bolshevik government of Russia and the Central Powers (German Empire, Austria-Hungary, Bulgaria, and the Ottoman Empire), which ended Russia's participation in World War I. The treaty was signed at German-controlled Brest-Litovsk after two months of negotiations. The treaty was agreed upon by the Russians to stop further invasion and as a result of the treaty, Soviet Russia defaulted on all of Imperial Russia's commitments to the Allies. However, the terms of the treaty were shockingly punitive to the Russians, and the Treaty was universally criticized. The German General Staff had formulated extraordinarily harsh terms that shocked even the German negotiator. When Germans later complained that the 1919 Treaty of Versailles was too harsh on them, the Allied Powers responded that it was far more benign than the terms imposed by the Brest-Litovsk treaty.

77 Matthew 26:52.

78 Matthew 7:9–10.

79 John 15:13.

80 A kulak was a name given to a peasant in Russia wealthy enough to own a farm and hire labor. Emerging after the emancipation of serfs in the nineteenth century, the kulaks resisted Stalin's forced collectivization, but millions were arrested, exiled, or killed.

81 Hebrews 11:32.

82 Isaiah 59:7.

83 Romans 13:3.

84 Luke 11:50.

85 Matthew 26:52.

86 Patriarch Tikhon (Bellavin), "Epistle to the Soviet of People's Commissars." http://orthochristian.com/108201.html.

87 Canadian Orthodox History Project, Saint Tikhon (Belavin).

88 St Hermogenes of Moscow was patriarch of Russia from 1606 to 1612. His fierce opposition to the false authorities which had seized power and his martyric death by their hand made him a national symbol of opposition to tyranny.

89 A politburo, or political bureau, is the executive committee for communist parties.

90 https://orthodoxcanada.ca/Saint_Tikhon_(Belavin).

91 A samovar (self-brewer) is a metal container traditionally used to heat and boil water, most commonly for tea.

92 https://pravoslavie.ru/86631.html.

93 "The Light of Russia" by Donald A. Lowrie.

94 The timing of the repeated assassination attempts, as well as the patriarch's documented state of health prior to his deterioration, gives some credence to the stories that St Tikhon did not die a natural death, but was poisoned by the Bolsheviks.

95 Swan, Chosen for his people, p. 103.

Saint John Kochurov of Chicago

1 At the time, the church was dedicated to St Vladimir.

2 *American Orthodox Messenger*, 1898, N24, pp. 681–682.

3 The church is located at 1121 N. Leavitt St. Chicago, IL. 60622, and is open to this day.

4 Meaning that $25,000 had been collected in America.

5 This is St Anatole Kamensky, who would later become a hieromartyr during the Communist rule in Russia.

6 7410 since the beginning of time.

7 "Russians begin a church," *Chicago Daily*, April 14, 1902, p. 7.

8 Over 1.6 million in today's money.

9 "Church Aided by Czar Opened by the Bishop," *Chicago Daily Tribune*, March 30, 1903, p. 11.

10 AOM, 1905, N17, pp. 340–341.

11 Ibid., pp. 340–342.

12 A molében is a service of intercession, or service of supplication.

13 Vserosiysky Tserkovno-Obschestvenniy Vestnik (VTOV), November 5, 1917.

14 Ibid.

15 Ibid.

16 AOM, 1905, N17, pp. 340–342.

17 Tserkovniye Vedomosty, 1917, N48-50, pp. 2–3.

18 VTOV, December 15, 1917.

SAINT ALEXANDER HOTOVITZKY OF NEW YORK

1 An "Oblast" is a region, an administrative division.

2 Volhynia, is a historic region in Eastern Europe, between southeastern Poland, southwestern Belarus, and western Ukraine. Originally inhabited by nomadic Scythian tribes, it was later settled by proto-Slavic peoples. In the Middle Ages it was ruled by Lithuanian and Polish rulers, and in the sixteenth century it came into the Polish Lithuanian Commonwealth. The borders of the region are not clearly defined, but the territory that still carries the name is Volyn Oblast, in western Ukraine. Volhynia has changed hands numerous times throughout history. At one time all of Volhynia was part of the Pale of Settlement designated by Imperial Russia on its southwestern border. In 1795, at the third partition of Poland, it came under the rule of the Russian Empire, where it remained until 1921, when it was united to the newly formed country of Poland. In 1939 it came under Nazi Germany, but shortly thereafter was annexed to the USSR, where it came to be part of the Ukrainian Soviet Socialist Republic.

3 Canadian Orthodox History Project. Saint Alexander Hotovitsky.

4 The magazine continued to be published monthly or bimonthly until 1973.

5 Approximately $83,000 today.

6 Canadian Orthodox History Project. Saint Alexander Hotovitsky.

7 Ibid.

8 "New Russian Orthodox Church Consecrated," *New York Times,* November 24, 1902, p. 9.

9 *Russian American Orthodox Messenger,* January Supplement 1904, pp. 2–3.

10 In 1906, President Theodore Roosevelt won the Nobel Peace Prize for the role he played in the negotiations that ended the conflict, becoming the first US president to be awarded this honor.

11 Canadian Orthodox History Project. Saint Alexander Hotovitsky.

12 Ibid.

13 Ibid.

14 Ibid.

15 Ibid.

16 Ibid.

17 Ibid.

18 A Bolshevik term of derision, describing those who remained loyal to Patriarch Tikhon, rather than joining the new "Living Church" which the Soviet authorities had established.

19 Canadian Orthodox History Project. Saint Alexander Hotovitsky.

20 Ibid.

21 One of the first Russian settlements in Siberia, Turukhansk was founded in 1607 as a winter camp for Cossacks and merchants. In the Soviet Union it was often used as a destination for political exile. Among the people exiled there was St Luke of Simferopol.

22 Canadian Orthodox History Project. Saint Alexander Hotovitsky.

23 Also known as the Great Terror, it was a series of political assassinations, exiles, etc. ordered by Joseph Stalin to eliminate all threats to his authority. Beginning in 1936 and ending in 1938, it is estimated that over 700,000 people were killed. After Stalin reversed his Purge policy in 1938, many of the documentation was destroyed, which is one of the reasons there is so little extant information about the death of St Alexander.

SAINT RAPHAEL OF BROOKLYN

1 Under dhimmi status, Jews and Christians were defined as second-class citizens. They were subjected to a series of humiliating laws, amongst which were that they could not carry weapons, could not make converts, were not allowed to live in houses higher than those of Muslims, could not make a public display of their rituals, could only ride donkeys and not horses, could not build new churches or synagogues, and had to pay a yearly poll tax. In addition, they had to wear distinctive clothing to differentiate them from Muslims.

2 Lutsky, "Lebanon, Syria and Palestine in the Period of Tanzimats (1840–70)," *Modern History of the Arab Countries* (Moscow: Progress Publishers, 1969), pp. 135–136.

3 The Patriarch's reluctance is also interpreted by some to be the result of the wide-ranging policy of the Greek Patriarchate of Antioch in the 1800s, which discouraged the higher education of its Arab clerics.

4 Issa, *The Life of Raphael Hawaweeny*, p. 4.

5 Proistamenos ("the one who presides") is the title of a cleric or monastic who is in an administrative leadership position in an ecclesiastical or monastic institution. Biblical in origin, it comes from Romans 12:8.

6 A metochion or metochi is an ecclesiastical embassy church, or a dependency of a monastery or patriarchate.

7 From approximately $10,000,000 down to $8,000,000 in today's money.

8 Ibid., p. 11.

9 Approximately $1,600–$1,800 today.

10 In the Eastern Orthodox liturgical tradition, the omophorion (meaning "something borne on the shoulders") is the distinguishing vestment of a bishop and the symbol of his spiritual and ecclesiastical authority. By symbolizing the lost sheep that is found and carried on the Good Shepherd's shoulders, it signifies the bishop's pastoral role as the icon of Christ. Clergy and ecclesiastical institutions subject to a bishop's authority are said to be "under his omophorion."

11 Approximately $900 today.

12 The Druze are an Arabic-speaking esoteric ethnoreligious group originating in the Middle East. Druzism is a monotheistic, syncretic, and ethnic religion based on the teachings of Hamza ibn Ali ibn Ahmad, and-Hakim bi-Amr Allah, as well as ancient Greek philosophers like Plato, Aristotle, and Pythagoras. Founded in the eleventh century, it incorporates elements of Isma'ilism, Christianity, Gnosticism, Neoplatonism, Zoroastrianism, Buddhism, Hinduism, and other philosophies and beliefs.

13 "Minister for Syrians," *New York Times*, September 15, 1895, p. 16.

14 The Epitaphios is a large, embroidered cloth, bearing an image of the body of Christ after he was taken down from the cross, often accompanied by his mother and other figures, following the Gospel account. It is used during the liturgical services of Holy Friday and Holy Saturday in the Orthodox Church.

15 "Syrians Greet Easter's Advent," *New York Herald*, April 5, 1896, p. 10.

16 The Imperial Order of Saint Anna was a Holstein ducal and then Russian imperial order of chivalry. It was established by Karl Friedrich, Duke of Holstein-Gottorp, in honor of his wife Anna Petrovna, daughter of Peter the Great of Russia. Membership of the Order was awarded for a distinguished career in civil service or for valor and distinguished service in the military. The Order of Saint Anna has four classes, and entitled recipients of the first class to hereditary nobility, and recipients of lower classes to personal nobility. The motto of the Order is "Amantibus Justitiam, Pietatem, Fidem" ("To those who love justice, piety, and fidelity").

17 Issa, *The Life of Raphael Hawaweeny*, p. 23.

18 The Typika is a service on the days when either there is no liturgy at all, or there is only a Vesperal Liturgy. The Typika follows the Ninth Hour and contains the Typical Psalms (Psalms 102 and 145) and the Beatitudes.

19 Issa, *The Life of Raphael Hawaweeny*, p. 30.

20 The canonization of this holy man is considered by most to be only a matter of time.

21 Approximately $160,000–$180,000 today.

22 Issa, *The Life of Raphael Hawaweeny*, p. 36.

23 The Order of Saint Prince Vladimir was an Imperial Russian order established by Empress Catherine II in memory of the deeds of Saint Vladimir, the Grand Prince and the Baptizer of the Kievan Rus'. The order had degrees and was awarded for

continuous civil and military service. It has no relation to the later 1957 "Order of Saint Vladimir of the Russian Orthodox Church."

24 Around $650,000 today.

25 Issa, *The Life of Raphael Hawaweeny*, p. 40.

26 "Syrian Church Dedicated," *The Sun*, November 10, 1902, p. 24.

27 Issa, *The Life of Raphael Hawaweeny*, p. 40.

28 Psalm 115:1.

29 I Corinthians 3:6,7.

30 Issa, *The Life of Raphael Hawaweeny*, p. 42.

31 Issa, *The Life of Raphael Hawaweeny*, p. 45.

32 February 29 or March 13, depending on the ecclesiastical calendar.

33 "New Greek Bishop Ordained," *The Evening Post*, March 14, 1904, p. 12.

34 "New Bishop Consecrated," *The Sun*, March 14, 1904, p. 10.

35 "New Bishop of Greek Consecrated," *New York Times*, March 14, 1904, p. 9.

36 "Ordain Raphael Bishop," *New York Daily Tribune*, March 14, 1904, p. 3.

37 "Czar Appoints New Bishop," *The San Francisco Call*, March 14, 1904, p. 3.

38 Issa, *The Life of Raphael Hawaweeny*, p. 52.

39 Bishop Basil (Essey), "Raphael Hawaweeny, Bishop of Brooklyn," *The Word*, May 2000, pp. 5–8.

40 Axion Estin (It Is Truly Meet), is a magnification Hymn to Mary used in the Divine Services of the Orthodox Church. Dating partly from AD773, it reads "It is truly right to bless thee, O Theotokos, the ever blessed, and most pure, and the Mother of our God. More honorable than the cherubim, and beyond compare more glorious than the seraphim, you who without corruption gave birth to God the Word, the true Theotokos, we magnify thee."

41 Issa, *The Life of Raphael Hawaweeny*, p. 54.

42 "Despite Threats Syrian Bishop Holds Service," *The Daily Standard Union*, September 25, 1905.

43 Philippians 3:14.

44 Approximately $500,000 today.

45 Luke 18:1–5.

46 Mark 7:26.

47 Matthew 15:21–28.

48 Sermon delivered on February 4, 1907. Archive of the Antiochian Archdiocese, Englewood, NJ. Translated from the Arabic by Samuel Noble.

49 Over $60,000 today.

50 Depending on the ecclesiastical calendar.

51 Bishop Alexander succeeded Bishop Innocent as bishop of Alaska and auxiliary bishop of the Diocese of the Aleutians and North America. Prior to that he had been an archimandrite at the parish of Sts Peter and Paul in Jersey City, New Jersey. His ordination took place in St. Petersburg on November 15, 1909. He returned to America to assume his episcopal duties on March 3, 1910.

52 Twenty-three of the priests were Syrian, eighteen were Russian, and three were Greek.

53 The Antiochian Village is a center for Orthodox Christian gatherings in Bolivar, Pennsylvania (5 miles north of historic Ligonier). Founded in 1978, it is under the jurisdiction of the Antiochian Orthodox Christian Archdiocese of North America and consists of a Camp and Retreat and Conference Center.

SAINT SEBASTIAN OF JACKSON

1 Herceg Novi is a coastal town in Montenegro, located at the entrance to the Bay of Kotor and at the foot of Mount Orjen.

2 There had been some native-born Alaskans who had been ordained prior to this time, but this was at the time when Alaska was still a province of the Russian Empire.

3 Fr Sebastian Dabovich, "Pravoslavnaya Tserkov v Kaliforniye" (The Orthodox Church in California), *Amerikanskii Pravoslavnii Vestnik* (American Orthodox Herald), nos. 15–16 (April 1898). Written by Fr Sebastian in San Francisco, February 12, 1897. Translated from Russian by Robert A. Parent.

4 Ibid.

5 The informal name given to a Bishop in Russian.

6 During that period there was no permanent bishop at the American diocese, as Bishop John had been transferred back to Russia in 1876, and his successor, Bishop Nestor, had tragically died at sea in 1882.

7 The Tlingit are an indigenous people from the Pacific Northwest. Their name means "People of the Tides," though the Russians call them "Koloshi" (for the labret worn by the women). The Tlingit occupied an area from the Portland Canal along the border between Alaska and British Columbia, north to the coast of the Copper River delta, as well as almost all of the Alexander Archipelago.

8 Bishop Sava, *History of the Serbian Orthodox Church in America and Canada 1891–1941*, p. 256.

9 Bishop Vladimir served in America from 1887–1891.

10 "The Pulpit," *San Francisco Daily Evening Bulletin*, December 31, 1888.

11 As the whole church was under the Old Calendar at the time, the ordination took place on January 6, 1889.

12 "Brief Mention," *San Francisco Daily Evening Bulletin*, January 7, 1889. [Many biographies of the saint place his tonsure and ordination in Russia, during his studies there, but these biographies are mistaken, as contemporary sources place both events in San Francisco.]

13 Fr Sebastian Dabovich, "The Orthodox Church in California."

14 In modern-day Ukraine.

15 The article was clearly written by someone with little to no knowledge of the Orthodox Faith, and therefore some names and events are expressed in the language of an outside observer. However, the journalist did preserve priceless glimpses and details of this historic event.

16 "An Ordination Service," *The San Francisco Morning Call*, August 29, 1892, p. 2.

17 St. Nicholai, "Father Sebastian Dabovich," The Path of Orthodoxy, Vol. 42, p. 5.

18 Alaskan-Russian Church Archives, Records of the Russian Orthodox Greek Catholic Church of North America—Diocese of Alaska (Library of Congress, Manuscript Division, 1984), container D511/13, reel 520.

19 Tarasar and Erickson, *Orthodox America 1794-1976*, p. 96.

20 The World's Columbian Exposition (World's Fair: Columbian Exposition), also known as the Chicago World's Fair, was held in Chicago in 1893 to celebrate the 400th anniversary of Christopher Columbus's arrival in the New World in 1492. It was an influential social and cultural event and had a profound effect on architecture, sanitation, and the arts. The exposition covered 690 acres, featuring nearly 200 new buildings of predominantly neoclassical architecture, canals and lagoons, and people and cultures from forty-six countries. More than 27 million people attended the exposition.

21 The Mother Lode is a long alignment of hard-rock gold deposits stretching northwest-southeast in the Sierra Nevada of California. It was discovered in the early 1850s, during the California gold rush, and stretches from 0.93 to 3.73 miles wide and 120 miles long, between Georgetown on the north and Mormon Bar on the south.

22 *Cf.* Galatians 3:29, I Corinthians 13:5, Philippians. 2:21.

23 William H. Seward, the twenty-fourth United States Secretary of State, purchased Alaska from the Russians in 1867 for $7.2 million. Initially, Alaska was loosely governed by the military. Starting in 1884 it was administered as a district, with a governor appointed by the US president. In the 1890s, gold rushes in Alaska and the nearby Yukon Territory brought thousands of miners and settlers to Alaska. Alaska was officially incorporated as an organized US territory in 1912.

24 The Imperial Order of Saint Anna was a Russian order of chivalry, awarded for a distinguished career in civil service or for valor and distinguished service in the military. The Order of Saint Anna entitled recipients of the first class to hereditary nobility, and recipients of lower classes to personal nobility.

25 The Order of Prince Danilo I was an order of the Kingdom of Montenegro. It is awarded to prominent champions of the preservation of Montenegrin independence and for other humanitarian, scientific, artistic, and pro-social achievements.

26 "Order of St. Anne Conferred Upon Him—Rev. Sebastian Dabovich, Who Has Been Honored by the Czar of Russia," *The San Francisco Call*, June 7, 1899, p. 4.

329

27 The Metropolitanate of Belgrade was a metropolis of the Serbian Orthodox Church between 1831 and 1920. It had ecclesiastical jurisdiction over the territory of Principality and Kingdom of Serbia. It was formed in 1831, when the Ecumenical Patriarchate of Constantinople granted church autonomy to the Principality of Serbia. Territorial enlargement and full canonical autocephaly were gained in 1879. Metropolitan Mihailo Jovanović (August 19, 1826–February 5, 1898) was the metropolitan of Belgrade from 1859 to 1881 and again from 1889 until his death in 1898. His time in office was marked with modernization in church management and in the education of priests. During his tenure, the Metropolitanate of Belgrade was awarded autocephaly from the Ecumenical Patriarchate of Constantinople, following the Serbian–Turkish Wars of 1876 to 1878. He was a convinced Russophile and so came into conflict with the Austrophile Prince Milan Obrenović, who already disliked him, as the hierarch refused to grant him a divorce from his wife, sparking the so-called Church Question. Metropolitan Mihailo was deposed in 1881, living in exile in Bulgaria and Russia from 1883 to 1889, only returning after Milan Obrenović had abdicated. The metropolitan also laid the foundations of the discipline of theology in Serbia. Within the church, he separated administration from the judiciary, improved the training of clergy, and promoted the monasteries.

28 Bishop Sava, *History of the Serbian Orthodox Church in America and Canada 1891-1941*, pp. 23–24.

29 "Order of St. Anne Conferred Upon Him—Rev. Sebastian Dabovich, Who Has Been Honored by the Czar of Russia," *The San Francisco Call*, June 7, 1899, p. 4.

30 Dabovich, Preaching in the Russian Church, p. 128–32.

31 Ibid., pp. 160–4.

32 Ibid., pp. 9–63.

33 Dabovich, *The Lives of the Saints*, pp. 164–166.

34 Tarasar and Erickson, Orthodox America 1794–1976, p. 33.

35 Ephesians 4:15.

36 Dabovich, *The Lives of the Saints*, p. 181.

37 Ibid.

38 "Rev. Sebastian Dabovich Talks to Catholic Club. Russian Priest Gives Lecture on 'The Holy Mount Athos and Oriental Monasticism,'" *The San Francisco Call*, March 3, 1905, p. 16.

39 In the Greek Church, an abbot is simply the head of a monastic community, but in the order of Russian Church hierarchy, it is a clerical position, ranking between hieromonk and archimandrite.

40 In 1936–1937, the name of the street was changed, and so the new address became 1950 West Schiller Street.

41 Hieromonk Damascene, "Archimandrite Sebastian Dabovich, Serbian Orthodox Apostle to America," *The Orthodox Word*, 43:1–2, p. 45–46.

42 Slovo Pravoslaviya v Amerike: Propovedi i poucheniya Svyatitelya Tikhona (The Word of Orthodoxy in America: Sermons and Teachings of Holy Hierarch Tikhon) (Moscow: Sretensky Monastery, 2001), pp. 143–144.

43 Matthew 24:8.

44 The Patriarchate of Serbia had been abolished by the Ottoman Turks in 1766, and was not reestablished until 1920.

45 $15,000-$20,000 today.

46 St Nicholai, "Father Sebastian Dabovich," The Path of Orthodoxy, Vol. 42, p. 5.

47 Chyhyryn is a historic city located in modern-day central Ukraine.

48 Archives of the American Orthodox Church, no. 1129, July 23, 1908. Bishop Sava, *History of the Serbian Orthodox Church in America and Canada 1891–1941*, p. 216.

49 Bishop Sava, *History of the Serbian Orthodox Church in America and Canada 1891–1941*, p. 278.

50 The April 18, 1906, San Francisco earthquake was one of the worst and deadliest earthquakes in the history of the United States. Devastating fires soon broke out in the city and lasted for several days. More than 3,000 people died, and over 80 percent of the city of San Francisco was destroyed. The death toll remains the greatest loss of life from a natural disaster in California history.

51 Bishop Sava, *History of the Serbian Orthodox Church in America and Canada 1891–1941*, pp. 34–36.

52 Ibid.

53 Ibid.

54 Ibid.

55 Saint Basil of Ostrog (December 28, 1610–April 29, 1671) was a Serbian Orthodox bishop of Zahumlje.

56 This is a mistake on his ecclesiastical rank on the newspaper's part.

57 Approximately $3,000 today.

58 The author of the article was misinformed, as the Order of Danilo was given by Crown Prince Nikola I Petrović-Njegoš, who did not become king until 1910.

59 "Patriotic Sacrifice," *Los Angeles Times*, January 25, 1912.

60 Acts 20:35.

61 St Nicholai, "Father Sebastian Dabovich," The Path of Orthodoxy, Vol. 42, p. 5.

62 Vasilevic p. 58.

63 Bishop Sava, History of the Serbian Orthodox Church in America and Canada 1891–1941, p. 60.

64 Ibid., p. 184.

65 St. Nicholai, "Father Sebastian Dabovich," The Path of Orthodoxy, Vol. 42, p. 5.

66 Genesis 22:8.

67 St. Nicholai, "Father Sebastian Dabovich," The Path of Orthodoxy, Vol. 42, p. 5.

68 Bishop Sava, *History of the Serbian Orthodox Church in America and Canada 1891–1941*, p. 86.

69 Later this letter is said to be from 1924.

70 Bishop Sava, *History of the Serbian Orthodox Church in America and Canada 1891–1941*, pp. 109–110.

71 The life of this great saint will be included in the second volume of the present work.

72 Out of humility, St Nicholai did not quote the sentence that follows, in which Fr Sebastian writes: "I am thankful to His Grace Bishop Nicholai, who is doing all he can to restore my health."

73 St Nicholai, "Father Sebastian Dabovich," *The Path of Orthodoxy*, Vol. 42, p. 5.

SAINT MARDARIJE OF LIBERTYVILLE

1 Petar I Petrović-Njegoš (Serbian Cyrillic: Петар I Петровић Његош; 1748–October 31, 1830) was the ruler of the Prince-Bishopric of Montenegro as the Metropolitan (*vladika*) of Cetinje, and Exarch (legate) of the Serbian Orthodox Church in Montenegro. He was the most popular spiritual and military leader from the Petrović dynasty. During his long rule, Petar strengthened the state by uniting the often-quarreling tribes, consolidating his control over Montenegrin lands, introducing the first laws in Montenegro (*Zakonik Petra I*). His rule prepared Montenegro for the subsequent introduction of modern institutions of the state: taxes, schools, and larger commercial enterprises. He was canonized by the Serbian Orthodox Church as Saint Peter of Cetinje (*Sveti Petar Cetinjski*).

2 The Nemanjić (Serbian Cyrillic: Немањић) was the most prominent dynasty of Serbia in the Middle Ages. The princely, royal, and imperial house produced twelve Serbian monarchs, who ruled between 1166 and 1371. Its progenitor was Stefan Nemanja, scion of a cadet branch of the Vukanović dynasty (1101–1166). Stefan was from the Zeta region of Montenegro, and in 1196, after three decades of wars and negotiations which established Serbia, separating her from both the Western and Eastern Byzantine spheres of influence, Stefan stepped down from the throne, giving it to his middle son, who held the same name, and became the first King of Serbia. Stefan Nemanja followed his youngest son to Mt. Athos, where he became a monk with the name Symeon. His son, Savvas, had already been ordained first archbishop of the Serbian Church. The father and son became great saints, and funded the building of the Serbian monastery of Hilandar on Mt. Athos in 1198–1199. Saints Symeon and Savvas are greatly honored amongst the ascetics for their monastic endeavors and ceaseless prayer. After his death, St Symeon was given the title Myrrhstreamer, as his relics poured fourth myrrh. He is also known for being the founder of what came to be known as the Serbian Empire, and establishing the Church of Serbia, which later became a patriarchate. He was a great figure of Serbian civilization and history, and

a great patron of the church, the arts, and literature, being a noted author himself. The Serbian Academy of Arts and Sciences named him one of History's most notable Serbs for his contribution to literature.

3   Dragutinovic, Zivotopis Vladike Mardarija (New Gracanica, 1992), p. 157.

4   Canadian Orthodox History Project, Saint Mardarije (Uskoković).

5   *Synkellos* (Greek: σύγκελλος, latinized *syncellus*) is an ecclesiastical office in the Orthodox Church. In the Byzantine Empire, the *synkellos* of the ecumenical patriarch of Constantinople was a position of major importance in the state, and often was regarded as the successor-designate to the reigning patriarch. The term is Greek and means "one who lives in the same cell" in a monastery. It is attested from the fifth century onward for the closest advisor of a bishop or archbishop, who then lived in the same residence or cell.

6   Dragutinovic, Zivotopis Vladike Mardarija (New Gracanica, 1992), p. 157.

7   Vasilevic, p. 20.

8   Over $4000 in today's money.

9   At the time, pro-German feelings ran high in the elite social circles of Russia, and even during the bloody years of WWI, nobility throughout the capital cities of Russia openly and passionately advocated for Germany. The treasonous affair of the Russian elite with the enemy was one of the primary catalysts for the brutal propaganda against Tsar Nicholas II and his German-born wife, Alexandra, who was a German national. The obvious hypocrisy and double standards of those who would slander an ethnic German, who yet showed complete loyalty to her adopted country, while ignoring the bombastic Germanophilia and open treason of the aristocratic and other social circles within the country is despicable.

10 Matthew 5:15.

11 This Mission is described in more detail in the lives of St Tikhon and St Sebastian.

12 Proistamenos ("the one who presides") is the title of a cleric or monastic who is in an administrative leadership position in an ecclesiastical or monastic institution. Biblical in origin, it comes from Romans 12:8.

13 Dragutinovic, p. 91.

14 Vasilevic, pp. 25–26.

15 Vasilevic, "The Serbian Christian Heritage of America," pp. 344–345.

16 Ibid.

17 Dragutinovic, p. 56.

18 Vasilevic, p. 31.

19 Psalm 69:9.

20 Božidar Purić is a fascinating figure, and was at the forefront of most of Serbian political life in the early twentieth century. In 1919 was appointed as chargé d'affaires of the Kingdom of Serbs, Croats, and Slovenes in Washington, D.C. In 1920 he

became the consul in San Francisco, and in 1922, he was appointed as the consul in Chicago, a position in which he served until 1926. In February 1926, he was promoted to secretary of the Ministry of Foreign Affairs. In 1935 Purić was appointed as an envoy to Paris and the permanent Yugoslav delegate to the League of Nations in Geneva. He was appointed prime minister of the Yugoslav government-in-exile on August 10, 1943. He died in Chicago in 1977.

21 The name "Yugoslavia" was adopted in 1929.

22 Serbian for "troublemaker." A play on words.

23 Vasilevic, p. 33.

24 Ibid., p. 32.

25 Vasilevic, p. 34.

26 Zivojin Ristanović, "Bishop Mardarije" in the *Memorial Book*, p. 53.

27 *New York Times*, July 4, 1926 p. E2.

28 Mihajlo Idvorski Pupin, also known as Michael Pupin, was born on October 4, 1858, and died on March 12, 1935. He was a Serbian physicist, physical chemist, and philanthropist based in the United States, who was best known for his thirty-four patents, including a means of greatly extending the range of long-distance telephone communication (known as "pupinization"). Pupin was a founding member of NASA, and he participated in the founding of American Mathematical Society and American Physical Society. In 1924, he won a Pulitzer Prize for his autobiography. Pupin was elected president or vice-president of the highest scientific and technical institutions, such as the American Institute of Electrical Engineers, the New York Academy of Sciences, the Radio Institute of America, and the American Association for the Advancement of Science. He was also an honorary consul of Serbia in the United States from 1912 to 1920. He taught at the University of Columbia in New York, and two of his students went on to receive Nobel prizes. He was well known as a patron of the arts and a pious Orthodox Christian.

29 Dragutinovic, p. 63.

30 Bishop Sava, *History of the Orthodox Church in America and Canada*, p. 208.

31 Vasilevic, p. 37.

32 Ibid., p. 38.

33 Dragutinovic, p. 59.

34 Ibid.

35 Vasilevic, pp. 40–41.

36 Ibid., pp. 43–44.

37 Ibid., p. 44.

38 Bishop Sava, *History of the Serbian Orthodox Church in America and Canada 1891–1941*, p. 156.

39 Vasilevic, "To the Glory of God the Father," p. 171.

40 Ibid., p. 173.

41 www.stsavamonastery.org/monastery-history

42 Vasilvic, "To the Glory of God the Father," p. 47, footnote: 78.

43 Vasilevic, p. 43.

44 Ibid.

45 Ibid., p. 53.

46 An affectionate diminutive for Živojin.

47 Vasilevic, pp. 54–56.

48 Ibid., p. 51.

49 Draguunovic, p. 157.

50 Ibid., pp. 89–90.

Part III: Historical Vignettes

Father Theoklitos (Triantafyllidis) of Galveston

1 Approximately $120 at the time, or $4,000 today.

2 Of which class is unknown.

3 Christmas in the Old Calendar being on January 7.

4 https://orthodoxhistory.org/2012/02/08/fr-theoclitos-of-galveston-on-charity

Elder Ephraim of Arizona

1 Elder Ephraim is often referred to as the *Cenobiarch* of the New World. *Cenobiarch* in Greek is κοινοβιάρχης, comes from cenobium (monastery) and arche (leader/ beginning of), and is used to denote a founder of monasteries.

2 My Elder Joseph the Hesychast, SAGOM Press, 2009.

3 A sesame bread ring, crunchy on the outside, soft on the inside, sold throughout Greece by street vendors. Some historians trace its roots to antiquity, but it was popularized during the Byzantine Empire and remains a popular street snack in Greece to this day.

4 Quinine was a common and daily medicine for many Greeks of the period, as it protected them from many of the diseases than ran rampant during the harsh years of the Nazi occupation.

5 A skete is a form of monasticism that combines a lifestyle of relative isolation, but also allows for communal services and shared resources. Small groups of monks, usually with one elder and a few disciples, live in sketes. It is one of four types of early monastic orders, along with eremitic (one monk living completely on his own), lavritic (a group of hermits who live on their own, but gather together at the lavra on Saturdays and Sundays for services and a common meal), and coenobitic (a

335

community of monastics living together in a monastery under the same rule). Skete communities usually consist of a number of small cells or caves in which monks live, with a central church or chapel that they share for services and sacraments. Sketes are a sort of bridge between eremitic monasticism and coenobitic monasticism.

6 "Johnny." Yiannakis is the diminutive of Yiannis, the Greek name for John.

7 A monastic cell is a small hut, cave, or building on which a monk or a small group of monks live.

8 The skete of Little St. Anne was established in the sixteenth century by Sts Dionysios and Mitrofanis, and is located in the area known as the "desert of the Holy Mountain." It is a rocky area with very little green, perched on the side of a hill. It is under the spiritual jurisdiction of the skete of St. Anne, and it contains seven cells in which monks can live.

9 Greek for "elder."

10 These words do not translate exactly, as they are a Greek "village" dialect. They are mild insults, which a parent may direct toward a child who does something foolish. The rough equivalents would be "simpleton," "little dunce," and "little lame one."

11 "May it be blessed." A common response in monasteries, which can and is used in a multitude of situations.

12 My Elder Joseph the Hesychast, SAGOM Press, 2009., 340–342.

13 Provatas-Shepherd.

14 St Kosmas Aitolos.

15 Wakefulness or watchfullness

16 Η Τέχνη της Σωτήριας, Vol. 2. Introduction. Translated into English by Katherine Psaropoulou-Brits.

17 Monastic dining hall.

18 A "Typicon" is a book that gives the rubrics for the order of the divine services throughout the Orthodox Christian Church year.

19 Precious in the Sight of the Lord, p. 8.

20 Ibid.

Bibliography

ENGLISH SOURCES

- Bunyan, James, and H.H. Fisher, (eds.), Bolshevik Revolution, 1917–1918: Documents and Materials. Stanford: Stanford University Press; H. Milford: Oxford University Press, 1934.

- Constantinou, Stavros T., and Milton E. Harvey, "The Persistence of Greek American Ethnicity among Age Cohorts under Changing Conditions," in John W. Frazier and Eugene L. Tettey-Fio, (eds.), *Race, Ethnicity, and Place in a Changing America.* Binghamton, NY: Global Academic Publishing, 2006.

- Dabovich, St. Sebastian, *Lives of the Saints,* and Several Lectures and Sermons. San Francisco, CA, 1898.

- Dabovich, St. Sebastian, *Preaching in the Russian Church: Lectures and Sermons by a Priest of the Holy Orthodox Church.* San Francisco, CA, 1899.

- Dabovich, St. Sebastian, *The Holy Orthodox Church: The Rituals, Services, and Sacraments of the Eastern Apostolic (Greek-Russian) Church.* San Francisco, CA, 1898.

- Dragutinovic, Dragoslav, Zivotopis Vladike Mardarija. [Third Lake, Ill.]: Izd. Fonda "Milosrda" Mitropolije Novogracanicke, 1992.

- Erickson, John H., *Orthodox Christians in America.* New York: Oxford University Press, 1999.

- Garrett, Paul D., *St. Innocent: Apostle to America.* New York: St. Vladimir's Seminary Press, 1979.

- Issa, Andre G., *The Life of Raphael Hawaweeny Bishop of Brooklyn 1860–1915.* Crestwood, NY: St. Vladimir's Orthodox Theological Seminary, 1991.

- Kostadis, Hieromonk Andrew, *Pictures of Missionary Life.* Crestwood, NY: St. Vladimir's Orthodox Theological Seminary, 1999.

- Lutsky, Vladimir Borisovich, "Lebanon, Syria and Palestine in the period of Tanzimats (1840–70)," in *Modern History of the Arab Countries.* USSR Academy of Sciences, Institute of the Peoples of Asia, Progress Publishers: Moscow, 1969.

- Maximov, Alex, and Dr David C. Ford, (trans. and eds.), *St. Tikhon of Moscow: Instructions and Teachings for the American Orthodox Faithful (1898–1907).* South Canaan, PA: St Tikhon's Monastery Press, 2016.

- Oleksa, Michael, Orthodox Alaska: *A Theology of Mission*. Crestwood, NY: St. Vladimir's Orthodox Theological Seminary, 1992.
- Perekrestov, Archpriest Peter, *Man of God, Saint John of Shanghai & San Francisco*. New York: Nikodemos Orthodox Publications Society, 2005.
- Rose, Hieromonk Seraphim, *Blessed John the Miracle Worker*. Platina, CA: St Herman Press, 1987.
- Saint Anthony's Greek Orthodox Monastery, *Precious in the Sight of the Lord Is the Death of His Saints*. Arizona, USA, 2020.
- Sava, Bishop of Shumadija, *History of the Serbian Orthodox Church in America and Canada 1891–1941*. Kragujevac, Serbia: Kalenich, 1998.
- Soldatow, George, (ed.), Archpriest Alexis Toth, Letters, Articles, Papers and Sermons. Volumes 1–4. Canada: Synaxis Press, 1978–1988.
- Soldatow, George, (ed.), The Writings of St. Alexis Toth, Confessor and Defender of Orthodoxy in America. Minneapolis, MN: AARDM Press, 1994.
- Swan, Jane, *Chosen for His People: A Biography of Patriarch Tikhon*. Jordanville, NY: Holy Trinity Seminary Press, 2015.
- Tarasar and Erickson, (eds.), *Orthodox America 1794–1976: Development of the Orthodox Church in America*. Syosset, NY: Orthodox Church in America, Dept. of History and Archives, 1975.
- Vasiljevic, Maxim L., Bishop of Los Angeles and Serbian Orthodox Diocese of Western America, (ed.), *To The Glory of God the Father: The Lives of Saint Mardarije of Libertyville and Chicago and Saint Sebastian of San Francisco and Jackson*. Los Angeles, CA: Sebastian Press, 2015.
- Vasiljevic, Maxim L., Bishop of Los Angeles and Serbian Orthodox Diocese of Western America, (ed.), *The Serbian Christian Heritage of America: The Historical, Spiritual, and Cultural Presence of the Orthodox Diaspora in North America 1815–2019*. Los Angeles, CA: Sebastian Press, 2019.

Greek Sources

- Γεροντος Εφραιμ Φιλοθειτου, Ο Γεροντας μου Ιωσήφ ο Ησηχαστης και Σπηλαιωτης (1897–1959). Αριζονα, ΗΠΑ: Ιερά Μονή Αγίου Αντωνιου, 2008.
- Η Τέχνη της Σωτηρίας, Αγιον Ορος: Ιερά Μονή Φιλοθεου, 2015.

Russian Sources

- Александръ (Хотовицкій), Святой, Документы, письма и стихи, Т. 1-3, Minneapolis, Minnesota: AARDM Press, 1998.
- Дабовичъ С., «Православная церковь въ Калифорніи», Американскій православный вѣстникъ, 1898. № 15, С. 455-460, № 16. С. 479-482.

- Слово православія въ Америкѣ. Проповѣди и полученія святителя Тихона, патріарха Московскаго и всея Руси, просвѣтителя Сѣверной Америки. М.: Срѣтенскій монастырь, 2001, с. 143-44.

ARTICLES

- Basil (Essey), Bishop of Wichita, "Raphael Hawaweeny Bishop of Brooklyn," *The Word.*, Englewood, NJ: Antiochian Archdiocese, May 2000.

- Canadian Orthodox History Project, "Saints," Retrieved on October 08, 2018 from http://orthodoxcanada.ca

- Dabovich, Sebastian, "The Orthodox Church in California," Russian Orthodox American Messenger 15 (April 1–13, 1898), 455–60 and 16 (April 15–27, 1898).

- Damascene, Hieromonk, "Archimandrite Sebastian Dabovich, Serbian Orthodox Apostle to America," *The Orthodox Word*, #43: 1–2., Platina, CA: Saint Herman Press, January-April 2007.

- Dobrijevic, Mirko (later Irinej, Bishop of Australia and New Zealand), "The First American Serbian Apostle: Archimandrite Sebastian Dabovich," Again 16: 4 (December 1993).

- Garrett, Paul D., "The Life and Legacy of Bishop Raphael Hawaweeny," in George S. Corey, et al., (eds.), The First One Hundred Years. A Centennial Anthology Celebrating Antiochian Orthodoxy in North America. Englewood, NJ: Antakya Press, 1995.

- Gray, Christopher, "Streetscapes/The 1902 Cathedral of St. Nicholas, at 15 East 97th Street; Old Czarist-Soviet Battleground Enters a New Age," New York City, NY: *New York Times*, November 26, 2000.

- Jorgenson, James, "Fr. Alexis Toth and the Transition of the Greek-Catholic Community of Minneapolis to the Russian Orthodox Church," St. Vladimir's Theological Quarterly 32: 2 (1988), pp. 119–38.

- Kishkovsky, Leonid, "Archbishop Tikhon in America," St. Vladimir's Theological Quarterly 19: 1 (1975), pp. 9–31.

- Ledkovsky, Marina, A Linguistic Bridge to Orthodoxy In Memoriam Isabel Florence Hapgood, A lecture delivered at the Twelfth Annual Russian Orthodox Musicians Conference, October 7–11, 1998, Washington, D.C. Retrieved on December 17, 2018 from http://anglicanhistory.org/women/hapgood/ledkovsky.pdf

- Milosevich, Mimo, "The Forgotten Saint of the Forgotten Church on the Forgotten Island," Retrieved on May 6, 2020 from https://orthodoxhistory.org/2010/01/20/the-forgotten-saint

- Nicholai (Velimirovich) of Zicha, St., "Father Sebastian Dabovich," The Path of Orthodoxy, The Official Publication of the Serbian Orthodox Church in the United States of America and Canada 42, (October 2007), p. 5. First published in: Serb National Federation Commemorative Book, 1951.

- Namee, Matthew, "The First Orthodox Liturgy in the American South," Orthodox History (August 12, 2009), Retrieved on May 6, 2020 from https://orthodoxhistory.org/2009/08/12/thefirst-orthodox-liturgy-in-the-american-south

- Papaioannou, George, "The Diamond Jubilee of the Greek Orthodox Archdiocese of America, 1922–1997," The Greek Orthodox Theological Review 45: 1–4 (Spring 2000).

- Ristanovic, Protopresbyter-Stavrophor Zivojin, "Bishop Mardarije," in *Memorial Book: 30 Years of Saint Sava Monastery and 60 Years of the Serbian Orthodox Church in America*, Libertyville, IL, 1953.

- Russin, Keith S., "Father Alexis G. Toth and the Wilkes-Barre Litigations," St. Vladimir's Theological Quarterly 16: 3 (1972), pp. 140–9.

- Smirnov, Paul, "And unto the Angel of the Church of Russia write," Retrieved on March 20, 2020, from Orthodox Christianity, https://orthochristian.com/106978.html.

- Tikhon (Bellavin), Patriarch of Moscow, "Epistle to the Soviet of People's Commissars," Retrieved on March 19, 2020, from Orthodox Christianity, http://orthochristian.com/108201.html

Multimedia Sources

- The Life of Saint John Maximovich, Archbishop of Shanghai and San Francisco, Directed by Greg Redmond & Aaron Freese, Western American Diocese, Forever Studios and Sabre Films.

HOLY TRINITY
PUBLICATIONS
JORDANVILLE, NEW YORK

PSJP PRINTSHOP OF
SAINT JOB OF POCHAEV

HTSP HOLY TRINITY
SEMINARY PRESS

Herman, A Wilderness Saint
From Sarov, Russia to Kodiak, Alaska

By Sergei Korsun with Lydia Black

The memory of St Herman, defender of the native peoples, has spread well beyond Alaska. In a speech to the 91st United States Congress it was said that "his canonization will serve to yield new benevolence and understanding to provide the Aleut and other native people of Alaska the rewards of their faith in their Church, and the rewards of their faith in America."

This comprehensive work brings to light primary sources that illuminate the story of St Herman in a wider historical context.

ISBN: 9781942699415

Chosen For His People
A Biography of Patriarch Tikhon

By Jane Swan

Preface and Notes by Scott M. Kenworthy

St Tikhon, Patriarch of Moscow (1865-1925), is one of the most important figures in Orthodox Church history in the twentieth century. Yet ninety years after his death this remains the only complete biography published in the English language. This edition is updated and revised with a preface and bibliography, together with revised and additional endnotes, by Scott M. Kenworthy. All together these reveal a humble man who accepted the call of God and the people to guide the Church during the most turbulent of times as it faced both internal upheavals and external persecution.

ISBN: 9781942699026